Research Methods in Library

Series Editors: Ronald R. Powell and Lynn Westbrook

DISCARD

Stimulated Recall and Mental Models

Tools for Teaching and Learning Computer Information Literacy

Lyn Henderson
Julie Tallman

Research Methods in Library and Information Studies, No. 2

The Scarecrow Press, Inc.
Lanham, Maryland • Toronto • Oxford
2006

SCARECROW PRESS, INC.

Published in the United States of America
by Scarecrow Press, Inc.
A wholly owned subsidiary of
The Rowman & Littlefield Publishing Group, Inc.
4501 Forbes Boulevard, Suite 200, Lanham, Maryland 20706
www.scarecrowpress.com

PO Box 317
Oxford
OX2 9RU, UK

British Library Cataloguing in Publication Information Available

Library of Congress Cataloging-in-Publication Data

Henderson, Lyn, 1945-
  Stimulated recall and mental models : tools for teaching and learning
computer information literacy / Lyn Henderson, Julie Tallman.
     p.   cm.— (Research methods in library and information studies ; 2)
  Includes bibliographical references and index.
  ISBN 0–8108–5222–5 (pbk. : alk. paper)
  1. Electronic information resource literacy—Study and teaching—Evaluation.
2. Teacher-librarians—Psychology.   I. Tallman, Julie I., 1944-   II. Title.   III.
Series.
  ZA4065.H46   2006
  025.04'072—dc22
                                                          2005022055

∞ ™ The paper used in this publication meets the minimum requirements of
American National Standard for Information Sciences—Permanence of Paper for
Printed Library Materials, ANSI/NISO Z39.48–1992. Manufactured in the United
States of America.

To our family and friends with love and thanks
for their unwavering support over the years.

To the teacher-librarians and students in this study—
they have taught us so much.

The authors express appreciation to the
Spencer Foundation for the research grant
that enabled the study leading to this book.

Contents

Foreword

Research Methods in Library and Information Studies, the monographic series of which this book is a part, addresses research in all areas of library and information studies by presenting, delineating, explaining, and exemplifying a full range of research methodologies. Works in this series are intended to serve the needs of scholars, graduate students, library managers, information professionals, interdisciplinary faculty, teacher-librarians, library media specialists, and teachers.

Both applied and theoretical works are appropriate for this series, as it ranges from action research (e.g., cost–benefit analysis techniques) to analytic approaches (e.g., bibliometrics). Works on both macro (e.g., historical analysis) and local (e.g., performance/output evaluation) levels are germane, as are works representing qualitative, quantitative, and mixed approaches.

In addition to the topics already treated by this series, others may include historical analysis of information provision, design, and resources; biographical treatment of leaders, change-agents, and key figures; bibliometric analysis of the web, e-journals, and other digital resources; applied techniques for community information needs analysis and library evaluation; quantitative analysis of library collections, resources, and delivery mechanisms; theoretical analysis of relevance criteria in various settings; feminist analysis of document representation in classification and subject access systems; content analysis of library and information studies literature; and explanations and examples of key statistical techniques used by library managers in action research projects.

This book by Lyn Henderson and Julie Tallman is ideal for this series in both subject and approach. The authors provide an excellent description of, rationale for, and methodological explication of their approach to studying mental models in the instructional context. To exemplify and expand on their explanations, they carefully incorporate the results of their timely research in this significant area. Mental model research incorporates work in cognitive psychology, sociocognitive analysis, and learning theory—a rich framework that makes this volume's explanatory approach particularly useful.

Indeed, their research on teaching through the perspective of teachers' mental models has important implications for understanding the elements that govern choice of teaching strategies. That understanding is the essential first step toward changing teaching beliefs and methods. Finding the underlying thinking that exposes their mental models in action, which affect their actual use of teaching strategies, is the most difficult aspect of studying mental models. The problem is identifying the most effective method for discovering teachers' thinking in action without undue distortion from the researcher or the participant. The stimulated recall method was selected as the most reliable and valid method for identifying and exploring mental models through the teachers' thinking while they were actually teaching. Clearly detailed are various surprises that would not have been revealed by using interviews, discourse analysis, and/or observation rather than stimulated recall.

An exemplar of how researchers proceed through the various stages of research is provided through the authors' meticulous paper trail of how their theoretical constructs inform and are informed by their research instruments, data categorization, findings, analyses, and conclusions. The authors clearly demonstrate the worth of careful adherence to strict protocols while administering their data collection tools—a pre-interview to establish espoused mental models, a videotape of the information literacy lesson, a stimulated recall interview using the video as a prompt to ascertain in-action stimulated recall mental models, and an enhanced post-interview to explore reasons for, and critical reflection on, particular strategies and actions that occurred during the lesson. Through within-case and across-case examination, the authors demonstrate the viability of mental models as either a liberating change-agent or stultifying status-quo manager of their pedagogy, even when teachers voice accurate critical self-reflection, a strong commitment to change certain mental models that were problematic and ineffective for their students, and identified how they would accomplish their commitment to change.

A new analogy of mental models as interwoven threads is argued. This analogy is demonstrated by delineating how the teachers' mental models operated together to either manage the teacher or be managed by the teacher. By ascertaining certain mental models and how they combined through "if ... then ...." scenarios, the authors conclude that mental models have predictive power, particularly with respect to pedagogic strategies, even if the opposite were espoused.

Ronald R. Powell
Lynn Westbrook
Series Editors

1

The Research Study

"I'm not really a natural teacher," a teacher-librarian[1] divulged in her pre-interview. Furthermore, she added that she had thankfully left the classroom to take on the more enjoyable responsibilities of planning, administrating, and integrating computerized technologies in the school library program. A few minutes later, she told us that she was an innovator with information technologies in the wider school system, and had worked with them and practiced enough that she instinctively knew how to teach the use of computer information literacy and technologies. It was this type of contradiction that had prompted our research. Undeniably intrigued, we utilized a Spencer Foundation grant to discover the what, how, and why of teacher-librarians' thinking, beliefs, and images; that is, their mental models, as delineated through their verbalizations and actions before, during, and after each of two lessons. The grant funded a study of six United States and four Australian teacher-librarians' espoused (before), in-action (during), and reflective (after) mental models while they were teaching two students individually how to use a computer information database resource.

The first task of the book is to detail our research study and the second task is to contextualize the book within the wider research study. As we elaborate further in this chapter, the purpose for this book is to demonstrate the ways and extent to which stimulated recall methods can inform our understandings of teaching with electronic computer databases and thereby prove a useful tool, not just for researchers, but also for teachers who want to discover more about their teaching and what their students were thinking. This would allow them to individualize further their teaching strategies and to troubleshoot problems with student misunderstandings. Our study occurred before we conceptualized this book.

The rationale for our research study was prudent on three major counts.

One substantial motive was the opportunity to weld our teaching and research strengths (see About the Authors) in order to examine the role mental models played in teacher-librarians' pedagogy, practice, and self-reflections when teaching computer database information literacy skills.

A second rationale was an analysis of the teaching of critical thinking skills for identifying information needs, locating information, and accessing, evaluating, synthesizing, and applying information to a problem that is a primary responsibility of the teacher-librarian in today's education environment. It has become an even more important role with the explosion of electronic computer resource tools as well as the incalculable quantity and dubious quality of much electronically accessed information. This responsibility is only beginning to receive the emphasis that it needs in teacher-librarian preparation programs in the United States because of previous dependency on the requirement in many states that teacher-librarians already had classroom teacher certification. Most programs assumed that teacher-librarians had acquired the skills to teach through their pre-service teacher education and classroom experiences. However, the elimination of the classroom teaching certification requirement in some states in the United States and an increasing diversity and availability of electronic information tools prompted the question of how prepared United States teacher-librarians were to teach students these skills. In Australia, to become a teacher-librarian involves a minimum of one year's further study beyond the baccalaureate[2] with an entry requirement of some years as a classroom teacher. Most are then employed for half their week as teacher-librarian and half as classroom teacher. Nevertheless, the same question of information literacy preparedness applied to Australian teacher-librarians.

Teacher-librarians benefit from the creation and maintenance of appropriate procedural and conceptual mental models for a range of information resources. Because mental models form as a result of the teachers' own learning and teaching experiences, they cannot simply transplant or transfer these to their students. Teacher-librarians ideally share their mental models to help students form their own conceptual mental models about the information tool, how it works, what information it contains, and how to apply their knowledge to troubleshoot technical problems. With a print resource, students could reasonably understand what it contained by visual inspection. With computer information resources, students depend on abstracts, help menus, and preliminary information plus their experiences with the resources to inform them about the content and how to search the tool. They cannot physically see the resource as a whole. Thus, it is much harder for them to grasp a conceptual understanding about the nature of the computer information tools and what skills they need to use it effectively.

Teacher-librarians often teach the process of using these information tools without helping students gain a conceptual understanding of the tool. Because of their press for time and the students' impatient "find the resource for me now" stance, teacher-librarians concentrate on providing the steps to retrieve a specific information product without explaining how or what is happening that enables the tool to retrieve that information (Rogers, 1992). Frequently, teacher-librarians do not think about the need to prepare the students conceptually (Dimitroff, 1992; Pitts, 1995). Some teacher-librarians assume that students will automatically learn how to search for information by watching their teachers demonstrate the steps to take in a once-off exercise. Although this strategy is sometimes appropriate, without accompanying and ongoing explanations about what is happening and why the steps are necessary, students will find they are not able to replicate or transfer their new skills to other searches (Duff, 1992; Seel, 1995). Knowing when, how, and why to provide conceptual understandings to help students gain independence in using the tool is critical for their troubleshooting abilities and future success. If the teacher-librarian stays satisfied with the procedural approach, the student's ability to transfer that brief learning to all but expressly similar situations is reasonably negated.

The third rationale or motivation for the research continues to be a steadfast commitment to our theoretical construct. Mental models are "representations of part of a real or imaginary world," created and utilized in short term memory and stored and retrieved from long-term memory (Garnham, 1987, p. 150; Garnham, 1992). From our literature review (see chapter 2), we understand that when we teach, we activate mental models of planning, teaching, and evaluating a lesson. Mental models therefore allow us to plan, conduct, critique, and troubleshoot past, current, and future situations. We use our mental models of the students' needs and skills as we prepare our lessons and choose the teaching strategies and activities. Our teaching methods are a combination of how we have been taught, what we have learned about teaching, and our actual teaching experiences. Thus, they are those that are most comfortable for us. Our mental models of our teaching methods would more likely define our pedagogy as a combination of those events rather than following a particular teaching pedagogy described in the curriculum texts.

The literature emphasizes the complexity of mental models and their many uses in various disciplines to identify how people think and respond to the situations presented to them. Mental models serve as belief systems that guide the actions of teachers and learners. In a sense, a mental model has its own philosophy and rules that describe its features. The holder of the mental model chooses either to let the mental model control the situation or to manipulate the mental model to respond to the situation (Jih and Reeves, 1992; Senge, 1992; van der Henst, 1999). If the mental model is based on procedural understandings, its holder will not easily transfer it to new situations. If the mental model is based on conceptual understandings, the mental model is more difficult to manipulate but has more transferability to new and complex situations as conceptual understandings change and develop. If the mental model is based on both conceptual and procedural understandings, the holder has the opportunity to control, manipulate, and transfer the mental model to fit new and potentially unpredictable situations, making it a powerful tool for teachers and learners.

Unfortunately, mental models are frequently difficult to ascertain, especially during the actual teaching. To ask teacher-librarians to remember what they were thinking during a lesson will usually result in an explanation of what they intended to do or were trying to do, not what they were actually thinking. Explanations of an intention do not allow researchers to discern or understand the actual mental models underlying the intentions. Without that understanding, the teacher-librarian and researchers would have difficulty identifying the mental models with a high degree of accuracy and analyzing the role the mental models play in governing the teacher-librarians' responses to the teaching situation. That identification and analysis contribute to critical reflective evaluation about teaching. The benefits hopefully extend to a real change in the practice of teachers who typically revert to the ways they themselves were taught and behavior-managed. If teacher-librarians understand the role that their identified mental models play in why and how they teach the way they do, their ability to alter or adapt their strategies to various teaching situations should improve.

We had four major research objectives.

1. To identify and categorize the teacher-librarians' espoused (pre-lesson), in-action (lesson), and reflective (post-lesson) mental models from their interviews and lesson transcripts.
2. To analyze how the in-action mental models matched their espoused mental models and influenced their teaching methods and critical self-reflective mental models during and after each lesson.
3. To identify and analyze either if and how the teacher-librarians controlled and managed their mental models by letting their mental models evolve to fit the needs of the lesson or if and how their mental models controlled the way the lesson proceeded.
4. To ascertain if the teacher-librarians' voiced a commitment to change

strategies based on their critical self-reflection mental models and examine whether this did, or did not, occur in the next lesson and, if so, in what ways.

Based on these research objectives and our literature review, we theorized that our research would confirm mental model theory and some of its various functions and characteristics. We additionally theorized that our research would reveal more clearly than other published studies the multitude of mental models or fragments of mental models being utilized in parallel or in hypermedia mode during segments in the lessons. Another conjecture was that our research would reveal a new twist from examining the teacher-librarians over two lessons, in terms of the compatibility between (a) their espoused mental models and their in-action mental models and, particularly, (b) their critical self-reflection mental models and their in-action mental models in the second lesson.

Because critical self-reflection is lauded as a key for changing teacher practices (cf. Brookfield, 1995; Mezirow, 1990; Valli, 1992; Wear and Harris, 1994; Zeichner and Liston, 1996), we thought that the teacher-librarians' reflective mental models would have an impact on their espoused and in-action mental models in terms of their actions and practices before and during the second lesson. Conversely, the research that highlighted the difficulty people can have in changing their mental models led us to speculate as to whether the teacher-librarian's critical self-reflection about their lesson's performance and beliefs would be adequate to change self-identified inadequate mental models for the second lesson. We therefore hypothesized that our findings would offer important insights pertinent to the critical self-reflective research.

Our case studies (chapters 4 and 5) of two different teacher-librarians provide answers and explanations for these conjectures, as this was where mental model theory and application, theoretical methodological paradigms and tools, and data analysis interacted. Each chapter is a within-case study. Chapters 6 and 7 contain across-case analyses of the two teacher-librarians. Chapter 6 compares the role of stimulated recall across both cases for identifying the mental models and their changes from espoused to in-action and post-reflective mental models. Chapter 7 contains a cross-case comparison of the mental models themselves, resulting in an explanation of the mental model influences and how they affected the outcomes of the teaching-learning episodes.

METHODOLOGY

We chose to use an empirical qualitative methodology to implement the research objectives of our study. We used a case study approach for ten teacher-librarians, each with two students. The major theoretical construct is that of mental models (chapter 2), which we ascertained through utilizing information processing theory, the mediating processes paradigm, and introspective processing tools (chapter 3). Within this construct, our major research instrument was that of the stimulated recall interview, which provided the most useful and reliable tool to identify the teacher-librarians' and students' mental models at the time of the lesson. Chapter 3 clarifies how the study utilizes triangulation of data, interrater reliability checks, and other methods to strengthen the validity and reliability of the findings.

The ten teacher-librarians ranged in age from thirty to sixty. Their range of experience as classroom teachers and teacher-librarians was equally diverse. Some had years of experience in the classroom prior to taking up the responsibilities of the teacher-librarian. One had no experience or training as a classroom teacher, but was in her second year as a teacher-librarian. Others had several decades of experience as teacher-librarians. Some participants in Australia were half-time librarians with the other half of their school day spent teaching a content area subject, acting as lead teacher in their subject, or acting in a public relations role for the school. All were female and volunteers for the study. (Although one male teacher-librarian would have enjoyed participating, he was unavailable during the research period as he alternated his appointment between two rural schools, one of which he accessed via airplane.)

In the United States, there were seven male and five female students. In Australia, three male and five female students participated. The students ranged from Grade 4 to Grade 12. We ensured that we had a boy and girl in Grade 4 both in the United States and Australia. Except for one Grade 7 student in the United States, the other students were from Grade 8 through Grade 12. We obtained ethics clearance from both universities and from the schools, teachers, parents/guardians, and students. Appointments were made with each teacher-librarian to interview her and each of the two students prior to the teaching-learning sessions, at times convenient to them.

We chose the data collection tools carefully to accommodate our research objectives. For each participant, the data collection tools consisted of an audiotaped ten- to fifteen-minute pre-lesson open-ended structured interview, followed in sequence by (i) a videotaped fifteen- to thirty-minute lesson conducted in the library, (ii) an audiotaped twenty- to sixty-minute stimulated recall interview individually with the student and then the teacher-librarian, and (iii) an audiotaped ten- to forty-five-minute enhanced semi-structured open-ended post-interview (see chapter 3, particularly table 3.2). The longer times were with the teacher-librarians. At the end of the second lesson's sequence of interviews, the teacher-librarians had the chance to report any final reflective comments about teaching computerized electronic database resources. This was an informal audiotaped interview of approximately ten minutes. The audiotapes and videotapes were transcribed as were our debriefing discussions after each day's data collection. The data collection tools and questionnaires were grounded in a pilot study with a teacher-librarian prior to the commencement of this study. The tools and questionnaires were also drawn from literature in the following areas: teacher-librarian professional literature, learning and teaching with computer databases and the cognitive science literature, as well as the information processing, mediating processes, stimulated recall literature, and mental model literature.

A major tenet for our research was the avoidance of the words or concept "mental model," during our research with the participants. In the consent forms and letters, our study referred to ascertaining what the participants were thinking or feeling before, during, and after the lessons. Cogently argued in the ethics applications, our rationale was influenced by two factors. The first rationale was the multitude of popular and academic definitions of a mental model (see chapter 2). Even if we had provided an example, the probability was high that the participants' conceptualization would have varied (see chapter 2) or not been the same as all other participants given the variance in age and experiences. The second rationale was commitment to minimize researcher bias and to maximize reliability of our data, particularly as stimulated recall is premised on these protocols. As demonstrated in the case study chapters, we accomplished this goal.

In response to the pre-lesson question probes, the teacher-librarians explained their role as teacher-librarians, their preferred ways of teaching and learning with electronic computer technologies, their in-service and conference participation, and their conceptual understanding of, and experience with, the computer database resources. The teacher-librarians were not asked for information about their knowledge of the two students they would be teaching and their students' information needs. The students were invited to tell us about their experiences with computers and databases, their understanding of a database, their computer skill level, and the availability of a computer in their home. Students were also asked if they liked learning computer skills by themselves, with the teacher, a friend, or a peer who knew more than they did.

Immediately following each of the open-ended, structured pre-lesson interviews, the teacher-librarian taught a lesson with one of the students individually. The researchers videotaped the session using two cameras feeding into a recording deck that combined the two signals into a split screen format. One camera aimed at the computer screen and hands on the keyboard while the other camera focused on the participants' faces.

The deck also recorded sound synchronized with the video. The researchers used additional audiotape recorders as backup.

All participants, although teaching and learning in their normal library environment and with their normal technologies, had cameras focused on their actions and conversation in addition to what was happening on the computer screen. The researchers also stayed behind them in the room as observers in order to monitor the equipment's operation but did not otherwise participate in the sessions. Three teacher-librarians professed nervousness about the research. The others, plus two of the previous three, claimed that they quickly focused on the student and the database and ignored the research paraphernalia and extra people. Interestingly, the students did not seem fazed by the equipment, possibly because we allowed them to play with the cameras beforehand.

The videotaped lessons differed in five ways from the normal one-on-one teaching-learning episodes that teacher-librarians experience in their daily teaching responsibilities.

1. For our study, the teacher-librarians asked teachers to suggest students who might want to participate in this research and learn about a technology information resource that would help with a current assignment. We wanted the research to have an authentic purpose. As it happened, one of the teacher-librarians whose case study is described in chapter 5 chose one student and asked the class teacher to choose another to participate in different authentic activities that the teacher-librarian identified as beneficial to each of them.

2. The teacher-librarians also had a better-than-usual opportunity to get to know the students in the time preceding the lessons and what the students thought their information needs were. A few took advantage of this opportunity. Others used the beginning of the interview to ask the student about his or her information needs and prior technology skills. In their jobs, most one-on-one lessons for teacher-librarians occurred spontaneously when a student asked for help in finding information.

3. The teacher-librarians also had a better-than-usual opportunity to refresh themselves with the electronic information tool(s) that they chose to teach. Because some of the teacher-librarians were novice users of the electronic resources they selected, some of them spent considerable time preparing for their teaching. Others allowed only a small amount of time, regardless of their experience with the resource.

4. Some of the teacher-librarians did not take advantage of the opportunity to talk with the classroom teachers about the students' authentic assignments. In the course of everyday events, teacher-

librarians, if they were not part of the classroom teachers' curriculum team, would not necessarily know about assignments that required students to search for information using computer resources.

5. Most of the teacher-librarians did not question the students to find out the students' information-seeking skills or technology strengths, or their interpretation of their information needs. Most of the time, it would be normal for teacher-librarians to find out about the student's skills at the start of lessons, if that were part of their teaching strategies.

Other unusual factors influencing each lesson included interviews with the researchers and students before the lessons, longer-than-normal periods of time allotted for each lesson, and, although some did occur (see chapter 3), fewer interruptions from other students or teachers who wanted help with immediate information needs. Additionally, there was the presence of the camera and recording equipment with the researchers observing out of direct sight of the participants, except for occasionally checking equipment operation.

So that the students could return to their normal class, the students were interviewed immediately after each lesson, followed by the teacher-librarian. Prompted by the replay of the video and the researcher's questions, the stimulated recall interview followed strict protocols (see chapter 3). The researchers' prompts invited the participants to tell us what they had actually been thinking during the course of the lesson. Through nondirective questions, such as "Can you tell us what you were thinking then?," we sought to have the teacher-librarian and student remember and relate their actual thoughts during the session, rather provide us with a justification or a rationale for their actions and comments.

This book is part of a series that examines how particular research methods and methodologies can inform our understandings. Therefore, chapter 3 details stimulated recall methodology's theoretical underpinnings, its strengths and weaknesses, its characteristics and protocols, and its particular usefulness for our study in comparison with other research methods of data collection, such as think-alouds and observations. We also outline in more depth the enhanced post-stimulated recall interview, which we define briefly in the following paragraph.

We attached the "enhanced" label to this interview because we included the repetition of most of the pre-lesson interview questions (in order to assess any change) in addition to the standard post-interview, and we asked participants about their recalled thoughts prompted by the previous stimulated recall questions and video replay. The enhanced post-stimulated recall interview was the time and place for the interviewers to ask about anything that struck them during the observation of the lesson or during the stimulated recall answers, allowing the teacher-librarian and student an opportunity to reflect on the events of the lesson. Question examples included why the teacher-librarian had asked a particular question or responded in the way she had; why the teacher-librarian had taught the way she did; what thoughts the students had about the way the teacher-librarian taught them; what each thought about the session, the electronic tool, and what they had learned; what the teacher-librarian thought her student had learned; and if there was anything that she would change. The entire process, minus the pre-lesson interview with the teacher-librarian, was repeated with the second student. Generally, the second lesson occurred between one to seven days later, except for four teacher librarians for whom it occurred on the same day, with two hours intervening between the first and second lesson.

The objective of the second lesson was to gauge whether and how the teacher-librarian might have changed mental models after reflecting on them during (a) the enhanced post-stimulated recall interview at the end of the first lesson and (b) the intervening period before the second lesson. We hoped to ascertain how the teacher-librarian responded to different students through planning, student learning needs, and tool use. Because the teacher-librarian had control over what computer database resource was to be used, the tool could be changed for the second student if she wished. Further, it was crucial to ascertain whether teacher-librarian reflections had prompted changes in mental models of the databases, students, assignments, and teaching strategies that would motivate her to modify plans for the second lesson, and whether an evaluation suggested improvements for the student for a certain item.

The computer tools used ranged from encyclopedia CD-ROM databases to automated university or public library catalog databases online to searching the Internet for particular resources. Five teacher-librarians used the same electronic database for both lessons, but two of these did not do anything different with that database, regardless of the students' prior experiences, use of the electronic resource, or the student's perceived need for the particular resource. In addition, three of these teacher-librarians did not inquire before, at the beginning of, or during the lesson if the student had previously used the resource. Another five teacher-librarians inquired of one student but not the other. Only two teacher-librarians inquired of both students. If they did and they discovered that the student already knew how to use the resource, three teacher-librarians still did not adjust their planned teaching agenda. For four teacher-librarians, the constraints of the videotaping equipment and the type of technology setups available constrained their ability to change to another resource because they had not pre-planned for such a possibility.

Two teacher-librarians were very inexperienced using electronic resources, much less teaching their use to students, although their libraries had computerized access points to electronic computer resources for student use. These two teacher-librarians practiced extensively with the resources for this research project. They voluntarily used the research project as a stimulus for learning a new computer resource and bravely taught one of their first lessons with the resource. Seven teacher-librarians knew their electronic resources quite well and the tenth teacher-librarian was considered an expert by her peers. With respect to the twenty student participants, seventeen students had not used the resource chosen by the teachers, although seven were knowledgeable computer users. Three students had used the resources before, with the teacher-librarian successfully extending the skills of one of the students. Unfortunately, the teacher-librarians did not expand the skills of two of these students, according to the students, nor did these students either have or take the opportunity to suggest the teacher-librarian change to a more useful resource.

There were a total of 140 transcripts involving the participants; eight for each teacher-librarian and three for each student (the video transcript played a dual role for teacher-librarian and student). Each set of teacher-librarian data files produced an average of 100 typed pages of transcripts. The transcripts included the participants' non-verbal and relevant computer sounds to align with each participant's voiced comments. The transcriber also noted pauses. This helped our memories and our decision-making about the significance of certain statements. When in doubt, we re-ran the video.

We began with the teacher-librarians' transcripts, specifically the eight files for each teacher-librarian. We coded one teacher-librarian's set of eight files together, identifying the mental models based on the literature and what emerged from the data. We discussed any differences of opinion until we reached a compromise. If a compromise proved impossible, we excluded that data. This was particularly important in the stimulated recall interview coding. We also excluded any recalled thoughts where we believed we had led the participant. For instance, instead of the neutral, "Can you remember what you had been thinking then, at that point in the lesson?" we asked, "What were you thinking? Was it to do with the student's comment?" We could not designate the teacher-librarian's answer to that type of question as an "in-action stimulated recall mental model" because we had inadvertently skewed the participant to think about the student's comment, which may not have been in their mind at that time. After coding the first set together, we coded and categorized the next ones individually, meeting regularly to compare results with the time span between meetings increasing as our inter-rater reliability increased. We kept a percentage count of our discrepancies. By the end, we were consistently obtaining 95.4 percent or more compatibility.

Another strategy was the regular re-checking of previous categorizations of mental models to maximize reliability. The categorization of mental models was grounded in the literature (chapter 2); however, as clarified in chapters 4 and 5, we allowed the data for each transcript to establish the categorization for that transcript. Although we re-checked our categories among participants, it was never our intention that any new category or possible category would be made to fit previous categories.

The purpose of the pre-interview was to discover the participant's mental models that existed up to entry into the first lesson. The mental models identified from the pre-lesson interview transcripts we therefore categorized as the "espoused mental models" (cf. Strauss, 1993). They provided a comparative benchmark for the subsequent identification of mental models.

The videotaped lesson allowed identification of two types of in-action mental models. First, from the lesson's discourse we identified in-action (videoed) lesson mental models. We based these mental models on our interpretation of what participants said and did during the lesson. Second, the video replay and our question prompts were the triggers to stimulate the participants to recall what they had been actually thinking during a particular point in the lesson. Either the researcher or participant would stop the video to prompt or recall a thought, respectively. We also queried if the teacher-librarian or student had the thought during the lesson or only in hindsight, during the interview. We identified and categorized recalled introspective thoughts as particular "in-action stimulated recall mental models"; for instance, "self-concept" mental models (see chapter 5).

The purpose of the in-action (videoed) lesson mental models was to determine whether the espoused mental models were implemented in practice. The purpose of the in-action stimulated recall mental models was to ascertain if either or both the espoused and in-action (videoed) lesson mental models were those that the participants actually had in their heads as they progressed through the lesson or if there were a divergence. Indeed, we often found a discrepancy between the espoused and in-action (videoed) lesson mental models, and between both of these and the teacher-librarian's and student's actual thoughts at that point in the lesson; that is, their "real" or more accurate in-action mental models.

The purpose of the enhanced post-stimulated recall interview was to identify self-reflective mental models and to determine whether they referred to any other identified mental models or, instead, were new types. It allowed the participants the chance to reflect and, particularly for the teacher-librarians, to self-evaluate their lesson and their thoughts. It provided the opportunity for the participants to ask questions and allowed the students and teacher-librarians to justify, elaborate, explain, and extend the thoughts they had recalled in the stimulated recall interview. A further and essential function was to establish, first, if the teacher-librarians committed themselves to changing their strategies or pedagogy that they had evaluated as needing to be changed and, second, if they actually made the changes in the second lesson. This last interview would help answer the question, "Did their mental models dominate their behavior or did they dominate their mental models to allow change to occur?" The enhanced post-interview allowed us to address our third and fourth research objectives.

The very last interview at the end of both lessons for the teacher-librarians permitted them the occasion to comment on the whole experience. We noted the areas and identified any mental models that they indicated as significant. Another function was to act as a culminating activity to provide a sense of closure to the research experience.

RAISON D'ÊTRE AND STRUCTURE

A particular focus of this book is the identification of the teacher-librarians' mental models to help inform our understanding of the teaching role and espoused, in-action, and self-critical reflective practices of teacher-librarians (and other teachers). We acknowledge that the cause-effect combination of the teacher-student interactions would also offer insights to this goal. We, however, leave that to another book or articles. This book emphasizes the use of stimulated recall methodology to help researchers identify in-head mental models rather than resorting to the process-product paradigm that would have us using observable actions to conclude the participants' mental models. As we note in the case study chapters, in-head thoughts and observable actions conflicted often enough to throw doubt on the accuracy of the process-product paradigm as a useable research tool, particularly for the professional world of teaching.

In chapter 2, mental models provide the theoretical construct by which we developed questions to examine our data. There is a synergy between the use of stimulated recall as an introspection tool, which accesses and uncovers participants' mediating processes that occur in short-term memory (see figure 3.1), and mental models, which are created and manipulated in short-term memory and stored in long-term memory. We define mediating processes as the participants' thoughts about such things as their pedagogy, roles, beliefs, and attitudes—that is, their mental models.

An in-depth exploration of the worth of stimulated recall interviews to the act of teaching demanded that it be given center stage or, more accurately, joint center stage with mental models. Chapter 3 therefore examines this research tool's theoretical and methodological underpinnings, its implementation, and its strengths and weaknesses.

In chapters 4 and 5, two teacher-librarians' within-case studies rather than the whole ten or an amalgam of the ten teacher-librarians individual cases are presented to provide a comprehensive examination allowing teachers and other researchers to obtain a holistic view. For convenience, we refer to the two teacher librarians as Anne and Marie. We used examples from the other eight cases where applicable in all chapters, but particularly in the two case study chapters. We chose these particular case studies for their representation of two teaching styles and lesson goals, and how these impacted the teacher-librarian's mental models. Within each case study chapter, we presented an extensive analysis of the teacher-librarian's mediating processes, how this translated into observable performance in a lesson, and how she critically self-evaluated her thoughts and actions.

We have organized the within-case study chapters in sequence to emphasize the relevance of order; that is, when during our phases of data collection the participants constructed their mental models. Thus the major sections are espoused mental models, in-action (videoed) lesson mental models, in-action stimulated recall mental models, and enhanced post-reflective (stimulated recall) mental models. We maintained a fairly complex protocol, discussing our analysis of mental models in each of the major sections as if we had no prior knowledge of the mental models in the forthcoming sections for the first lesson. The exception was the discussion of various mental models and the causality and impact of those mental models for the second student's lesson. We then allowed comparison with the first lesson's data and analysis. (This is re-clarified at the beginning of each case study.) Also, in the second case study, chapter 5, we compared and contrasted with the previous teacher-librarian's mental models and actions where relevant.

Chapter 6 provides a discussion of the role of stimulated recall in disclosing unobservable thoughts that impacted mental models in the two case studies. We employed an across-case study methodology to compare the teacher-librarians' mental models for patterns that emerged from the data, allowing insights into the mental models that were common or conflicting across all our instruments. The stimulated recall interviews confirmed various consistencies and highlighted surprising discrepancies between Anne's and Marie's individual espoused and in-action mental models. One of the roles of across-case studies is to present data in various ways to substantiate interpretations. We did so in this chapter and found that the accepted analogies of running mental models or fragments of mental models in parallel or in hypermedia mode are perhaps incorrect. A more appropriate and powerful analogy is that we weave distinguishable fragments and complete mental models when running our mental models and that this has implications for working memory overload.

Chapter 7 highlights the comparison of mental models between the two teacher-librarians with flowcharts of how each participant's mental models interact to contribute to the overall teaching–learning lesson outcomes. A major emphasis in the chapter is the teacher-librarian's ability to control and to change or maintain mental models, and the consequences of these actions. Additionally, we summarize the value of stimulated recall methodology for identifying mental models in-action and offer implications from our work for pre-service teacher and teacher-librarian preparation programs as well as for in-service teacher development.

CONCLUSION

This Spencer Foundation–funded research study was undertaken to explore the mental models influencing and contributing to a teacher-librarian's teaching when using electronic databases. Because so little attention has been paid to the importance of the teaching role for the teacher-librarian, individual teacher-librarians can decide how much or how little teaching they want to emphasize as part of their responsibility. Originally, we desired to explore the mental models that were the most influential in how, why, and what the teacher-librarians taught their students about using electronic computer databases. The study focused on these tools mindful of the increasingly vital importance such resources play in students' information literacy.

What the study also uncovered was the importance of using stimulated recall methodology in revealing in-action thoughts that at times contradicted what the researchers observed and the video cameras, recorded as the teaching took place. Preliminary insights and understandings about a teacher-librarian's mental models that were running during the teaching episode were changed based on the new information about their actual thinking. We were therefore enabled to identify more accurate mental models that the teacher-librarian was running, resulting in a deeper understanding of how the teacher-librarian taught and why she focused on what she did.

NOTES

1. The term "teacher-librarian" is inclusive of library media specialists and school, college, university, and public or government librarians. It also can encom-

pass classroom teachers because they, too, are involved in teaching procedural and conceptual information literacy skills. Sometimes we use "teachers" to encompass teacher-librarians, lecturers, and instructors.

2. In Australia this is referred to as an undergraduate degree; e.g., Bachelor of Education.

2

Mental Models

Discussion of this book with a friend, who was an advisory teacher supporting classroom teachers in small, remote Aboriginal communities in Northern Australia, yielded the following story from his experience:

> I was invited by some Aboriginal men to go fishing with them. We fished using the traditional long spear in clear, still, calf-high water. They were catching fish; I missed every time. I began to watch closely what they were doing and how they were standing and throwing, but I still didn't get what they were doing right nor what I was doing wrong! After another frustrating miss, I thought about what I could do to work out a different way to solve my embarrassment. That's when I remembered some Grade 10 physics about water and refraction. (Stop looking cynically; I really did do this!) Again observing the experts, I now saw that they were applying the principle. I did too and I contributed the biggest, well, a big fish and two smaller ones to the extended family's dinner. The men casually nodded approval after I demonstrated I could replicate the skill. I actually strutted a few steps! (Coombs, personal communication, 2003)

His initial mental model of the action did not allow him to succeed. Success occurred only when he retrieved the concept of water refraction stored in long-term memory and included it in his current mental model, while simultaneously discarding the incorrect assumption that the fish would be where he thought he saw it, instead of where it really was. He had to reformulate his mental model in order to predict, correctly, that he should throw his spear further out from where he perceived the fish to be. With repetition, he confirmed the accuracy of his predictions and stabilized his new mental model. The act of calling on their mental models while planning a lesson or working through a problem that arises when teaching that lesson is an everyday occurrence for teachers,[1] yet we do not consciously perceive that we are utilizing mental models. As teachers, complex factors, including our views and belief systems, shape the formation and use of our mental models. These factors color our thinking and influence our interpretations (Szabo, 1998) concerning ourselves as teachers and learners, our students as people and learners, our capabilities and prior experiences, our desire and ability to incorporate information computer technologies effectively in our curriculum, and so forth. Our mental models profoundly influence how and why we act, teach, and learn in the ways we do. Barker, van Schaik, Hudson, and Meng Tan (1998) go so far as to claim that "mental models are important because they are assumed to form the basis of all human behavior" (p. 104). Many of our mental models produce worthwhile outcomes. Others do not; they are inaccurate or stagnant and need re-evaluation and modification (Halford, 1993; Norman, 1983; Szabo, 1998). Mental models are the root for success and failure.

Such strong contentions raise obvious questions: If we are unaware that we use them, what are the indicators that mental models exist? Indeed, what is their purpose? What are their characteristics? In what ways are they different to schema? Where do they reside in our brain? Is there one mental model per situation or are there multiple mental models? What is their value as an analytic tool in teaching and learning, particularly when working with information communication technologies, and in research?

WHAT ARE THE INDICATORS
THAT MENTAL MODELS EXIST?

Craik (1943) advocated that we reason and predict outcomes of situations based on our construction of cognitive models of that situation and, just as a model plane is a replica of the real object, our mental model need only have a similar representative structure to that which it mimics. Given this, we can infer and predict what may happen before carrying out a task; for example, taking account of students' preferences when planning an online class activity in order to dissipate behavioral problems before they arise.

Johnson-Laird's (1983) seminal work largely involved experiments in formal types of deductive reasoning that required participants to deduce a conclusion from a set of premises. His argument that reasoning needed to take account of semantics rather than the syntactic approach currently dominating cognitive psychological theories triggered animated debate. He and his followers (see Byrne, 1992, and the website devoted to this topic; also see Chater and Oaksford, 2001; Manktelow and Fairley, 2000;

Markovits and Barrouillet, 2002) have provided further empirical evidence to support the mental model theory. According to Evans (1996), research in reasoning demonstrated that the mental model theory captured "within one framework, an account of deductive competence, biases, and pragmatic effects. [In contrast, the] mental logic account can only explain biases and pragmatic influences by referring to factors *external* to the theory of deduction" (p. 323; author's emphasis). Three experiments by Meiser, Klauer, and Naumer (2001) and those by van der Henst (2000) corroborated the mental model theory rather than mental logic theories and pragmatic reasoning schemata. We examined the teacher-librarians' mental models to ascertain if they had the power to make deductions and, if so, whether these were influenced by their biases and pragmatic interpretations of their world.

Published in the same year as Johnson-Laird's work, Gentner and Stevens' (1983) collection of articles focused on the types of knowledge and commonsense understandings we develop from our experiences with the physical world in particular domain areas, such as electricity, artifacts, liquids, and mechanics. Most of the articles in Rogers, Rutherford, and Bibby's (1992) book continued this focus. These particular domains of empirical research have been taken up with enthusiasm by those in the artificial intelligence, human-computer interaction, human-device interaction, and instructional design communities. The editors pointed out that "from basic theoretical cognitive psychology to applied problems of human-computer interaction and human-machine systems, mental models are being utilized now to explain a range of psychological phenomena" (Rogers, 1992, p. 1). The purpose of examining mental models in workplace contexts is that the researcher's description and analysis would consider both the theoretical and practical implications while taking into account the complexity of the environment (e.g., see Wilson and Rutherford, 1989). This is compared with the constrained unauthentic laboratory investigations of mental models that necessitate limits on the type of task investigated (Rogers, 1992).

Our study was conducted in the "messy" context of the schools' libraries. For instance, three lessons were halted to listen to the principal's notices on the intercom; in two separate incidents, one in Australia and one in Georgia, classroom teachers did what was obviously normal practice when they ignored the fact that the teacher-librarian was teaching a student and asked for help with their problems. In another instance, the teacher-librarian responded to a child's query and left the research participant student to carry on with his search on the encyclopedia CD-ROM database. These were authentic incidences and through our research instrument, the stimulated recall interviewing protocol (see next chapter), we were able to capitalize on what was happening in the teacher-librarians' teaching mental models before, during, and after the interruption.

Norman's (1983, 1988) work has been seminal in the area of human computer interaction. Indeed, the computer user's mental model has a long history and is still a current topic for research (e.g., Cole and Leide, 2003). Especially important in Norman's work was his emphasis on the fact that mental models can be inaccurate and incomplete. His delineation of mental models and their characteristics fall just short of deification! Norman argued that there were differences between the user's mental model of the software and the computer programmer's and instructional designer's mental models of the system and interface, and their mental model of the user's mental model. Different labels were attached to these various models.

If Norman's (1983) categorization were adopted, a teacher-librarian's mental model would be labeled the "conceptual model" when explaining the system and software to students. We argue that the rationale for renaming a mental model a conceptual model when it is verbalized or written is misguided. This holds true when the programmer's or instructional designer's mental model, of what the user's mental models would be, is relabeled a conceptual model. This also applies to its non-contextual use by subsequent authors (e.g., van der Veer and Puerta-Melguizo, 2002; Wild, 1996; Williamson, 1999) who usually resort to simply referring to Norman's pronouncement rather than examining whether a conceptual model exists in terms of his definition. Naturally, we cannot transfer or implant our mental model into students' and users' brains. They create their idiosyncratic mental model. We do, however, teach our mental model in the sense that our mental model represents our understanding of the procedural and conceptual structure of the computer system and software and this is what we impart in guided discovery activities with students.

The following are examples that help to demonstrate the viability of mental model theory and application. The mental models of various aged students within diverse domains are a favored topic. One of these topic areas centers on discourse comprehension. We utilize mental models, for instance, when drawing inferences that the language of the text alone does not allow us to do (e.g., Taylor and Tversky, 1992; van Dijk and Kintsch, 1983; Zwaan, Magliano, and Graesser, 1995).

It took some time before teachers' and pre-service teachers' mental models received attention (Barker, van Schaik, and Hudson, 1998; Barker, van Schaik, Hudson, and Meng Tan, 1998; Strauss, 1993; Szabo and Fuchs, 1998; Williamson, 1999). A professional development project (Bolanos, 1996) used mental model theory to guide teachers to reconstitute their mental model of intelligence to one that incorporates multiple intelligences. Their gifted and talented program is now available to all students. Szabo and Fuchs (1998) offered techniques to help teachers and trainers articulate and challenge their own mental models, particularly about the processes of teaching and learning. Our study is informative in its novel examination of the teacher-librarians' mental models and the intersection of these mental models, before, during, and after a lesson. In the post-lesson sessions, the majority of teacher-librarians examined their mental models; a few did not.

Library and information science has been another focus of note. Marchionini and Liebscher (1991) found that users using a full-text CD-ROM encyclopedia could function adequately even when their mental models were flawed or incomplete. However, Pitts (1995) and Dimitroff (1992) established that users with mental models that contained conceptual understandings tended to have better search results than those with incomplete mental models. Slone (2002) reported that the mental models of thirty-one public library users helped influence their search approaches, the websites they visited, and the sources they used. Michell and Dewdney (1998) examined the librarians' mental models through interviews that sought to obtain the librarians' reasoning behind their actions when helping users with their search inquiries.

Further, Stripling (1995) warned teacher-librarians and other educators that they "will not succeed in changing students' limited or incorrect mental models unless the mental models themselves are addressed" (p. 164). From their studies, Cole and Leide (2003) and Brandt (1999) also argued that librarians should ascertain the user's mental models, because teaching a search strategy that is too complicated for the entry level of the user is not effective. One of the teacher-librarians in our study changed her strategy when she found out that the student lacked information literacy skills; the student's mental model in this domain was barely in existence. Notwithstanding the importance of students' mental models, our study demonstrated that mental models of teacher-librarians affected each part of the information literacy learning process.

Despite the utilization of mental models in pure and applied research, there remains a controversy about whether people reason by relying on models or on mental logic rules. Nor are mental models the only construct for examining how we learn and understand. Evans (1996) cautions that there is no cognitive psychological theory that is complete or correct in all aspects. Nevertheless, we cannot ignore the fact that mental model theory has been extensively and experimentally tested. International researchers have published over 350 papers on mental models and reasoning alone (Johnson-Laird and Byrne, 2000). These experiments and qualitative applied research corroborate the existence and viability of mental models. Our study follows an accepted and long tradition in mental model research.

WHAT ARE MENTAL MODELS?

Understanding human mental processes is a centuries-old endeavor. Mental model theory and research, however, are relatively recent entries in the field of cognitive science. Craik (1943) is acknowledged as the originator of the concept with his contention that, because all mental representation mimics the physical world, we operate on our mental representations in order to simulate real-world behavior and generate predictions. Since Craik, there have been numerous studies in various disciplines, with the result that the mental model literature contains varied and often vague definitions and terminology. This prompted O'Malley and Draper (1992) to claim that "talking about mental models can be a dangerous thing" (p. 73) and Wilson and Rutherford (1989) to propose that, because mental models seem to be intuitively appealing, they are all things to all people. Such statements are perhaps made for effect. Nevertheless, the lack of a single definition reflects the strength of mental model theory and application (Moray, 1998; Rowe and Cooke, 1995; Schwamb, 1990; Turner and Belanger, 1996). It highlights the diversity of researchers whose research approaches and interpretations are influenced by their own differing disciplines.

Additionally, there is a diverse range of tasks for which mental models can be used. The following discussion draws from a wide literature in an attempt to synthesize the essential components. The section concludes with a workable classification for mental models that is particularly relevant to our study, always mindful of Norman's (1983) conclusion that mental models are inherently problematic to define.

Johnson-Laird (1983), one of the most influential mental model researchers, explained that we model reality by means of manipulating internal mental symbols. This notion derives from Craik's (1943) assertion that thought models reality. In the fishing story, related at the beginning of the chapter, the image of the way that the Aboriginal men threw the spear and the rule of water refraction were two such symbols being manipulated in Coombs' mental model.

Simplistically, we understand the world by constructing working models of it in our minds. This does not mean that we put a "copy of the world in our heads" (Halford, 1993, p. 26). Mental models are not replica scaled models like those that architects make showing what the actual building will look like. A mental model is a cognitive representation that reflects the structure, or a segment of the structure, of the real environment, situation, event, task, problem, procedure, concept, or phenomenon (Halford, 1993; see figure 2.1). The representation can also be of "assertions and relations between abstractions" (Newton, 1996, p. 205); that is, we can create mental models of concepts like truth and justice and the relationship between them—though one might say that truth and justice rarely co-exist!

However, negative or counter-factual states as well as those that are possible and those that actually exist should be constructed for understanding (Johnson-Laird, 2001; cf. Evans, 1996). Mental models can also contain imaginary situations, events, problems, and stories (Byrne, 1992; Santamaria and Johnson-Laird, 2000; Senge, 1992; see figure 2.1). We map segments from the situation (Ehrlich, 1996; Gentner and Stevens, 1983), such as spearing a fish or using the advanced search function in a search engine or reading about the definition of a mental model, to the structure being built or modified in our mental model. Our mental model mimics the situation that we are experiencing. To understand something is equated with having a mental model of it (Halford, 1993; Johnson-Laird, 1983, 1987).

Newton declared that "understanding is a mental state, a product of mental processes which infer relationships between elements of information" (Newton, 1996, p. 201). Johnson-Laird (1983) clarified this relationship between understanding and mental models:

> Understanding certainly depends on knowledge and belief. If you know what causes a phenomenon, what results from it, how to influence, control, initiate, or prevent it, how it relates to other states of affairs or how it resembles them, how to predict its onset and course, what its internal or underlying "structure" is, then to some extent you understand it. The psychological core of understanding, I shall assume, consists in your having a "working

Cognitive representations of:

Our world
Ourselves
Others
Tasks
Ideas
Concepts
Activities
Artifacts
Situations
Procedures

Figure 2.1. Mental Models as Cognitive Representations

model" of the phenomenon in your mind. If you understand inflation, a mathematical proof, the way a computer works, DNA or a divorce, then you have a mental representation that serves as a model of an entity in much the same way as, say, a clock functions as a model of the earth's rotation. (p. 2)

The clock analog is powerful and helps us understand, or get a handle on (Krieger, 1992) the notion of a mental model. However, this representation is a single direction process in which we form our mental model based on—or mapped from—our understanding and interpretation of the real situation or task or concept. Based on the literature and our research, mental models are much more powerful than this, although the literature does not organize the following distinctions as clearly as we have.

A mental model's structure must show a relationship to the reality it represents (Poirier, 1994). For example, a number of teacher-librarians in our study possessed mental models that contain a "show-and-tell-then-copy-me" strategy for teaching access to computer databases. They automatically adopted these with their students. An artifact can, however, be a reflection of the mental model. A simple example is the artist's mental model reproduced in the actual sculpture. In an Internet information literacy example, our mental model of a lesson for teaching online search skills using Boolean logic would be replicated as the written lesson plan.

Additionally, mental models can direct the way a lesson precedes. We have all witnessed novice pre-service teachers who remain faithful to their mental model of the lesson plan, even when the lesson falls apart. In other cases, if students become restless when watching a projected enlargement of the online steps for accessing, searching, and assessing information on a particular topic, the teacher may call up the "what-to-do-when-students-are-not-listening" mental model. So, from a talking-at-students' strategy, the lesson becomes interactive by asking students to suggest and debate the course of action. The students' inattentiveness to the lesson is the catalyst to modify the original mental model in order to implement a workable solution to student disengagement.

Thus, mental models are autonomous. This means that they can mirror the lesson plan, steer the lesson's progress, and modify the same lesson. The opposite can occur, too: a lesson can mirror the mental model; the lesson can steer the mental model; and the events within a particular lesson can alter the mental model.

Further, because mental models are autonomous and idiosyncratic, they are able to place constraints on the representation of the external world but not vice versa (Fischbein, Tirosh, Stavy, and Oster, 1990; Norman, 1983). For instance, in information communication technologies, innovators have a mental model that identifies the inevitable technical problems as minor hiccups that are solvable. In comparison, the laggard's mental model exploits the problems as a ploy for evading the meaningful inclusion of technology in their curriculum. The laggard's mental model restricts and constricts action. Mental models "belong to the mental structure of the individual, well-integrated into this structure, reflecting its requirements and its particularities" (Fischbein et al., 1990, p. 29). Our mental models continuously activate our deeply ingrained assumptions and generalizations. Their influence can be either liberating or stultifying (see chapter 7).

A mental model is a mediating intervention between perception and action. It provides a mapped representation of a situation, or of a segment of that real or imaginary situation. In turn, the mental model offers the means to conceptualize, remember, interpret, and communicate information as well as to predict, interpret, and control performance (Gentner and Stevens, 1983; van der Veer and Peurta-Melguizo, 2002; Wild, 1996). A mental model is "what people really have in their heads and what guides their use" of artifacts, ideas, tasks, situations, and concepts (Norman, 1983, p. 12). Mental models are fluid and autonomous, with reciprocal consequences for either, or both, the real task and the mental model. A mental model is both process and product. A mental model is a mechanism that functions to help us understand, as well as act in and on, the world.

WHAT IS THE FUNCTION OF MENTAL MODELS?

We create mental models for a purpose; they are not optional extras (Green, 1990). Their purpose is to facilitate understanding so that we can grasp problem situations, choose potential solutions, and predict outcomes as a consequence of our actions (see figure 2.2). They help reduce memory overload. Mental models act like tools; therefore, they allow us to accomplish things. They facilitate cognitive and physical interactions with the environment, with others, and with artifacts.

Mental model theory provides the means for us to attempt to explain human understandings of various aspects of our world (Johnson-Laird, 1983; see figure 2.2). As teachers, our mental models provide the mechanism for creating and recreating an understanding of how the interweaving of components such as context, content, pedagogy, culture, theory, cognitive development, research, and so on, permit us to grasp the process of how one teaches and learns most effectively, particularly when working with computer technologies. Our mental models provide an explanatory function for understanding the complexities involved in teaching and learning interactions.

Besides this explanatory function, another role of mental models is pre-

Functions:

Reduce mental effort
Similarity
Generative
Recall tasks
Generalizability
Analogy
Patterning
Images
Enables action
Explanatory
Prediction
Troubleshooting
Task performance
Metacognition
Memory device
Organization device

Cognitive representations of:

Our world
Ourselves
Others
Tasks
Ideas
Concepts
Activities
Artifacts
Situations
Procedures

Figure 2.2. **Mental Models: Cognitive Representations and Functions**

diction (Gentner and Stevens, 1983; see figure 2.2). Initially, in the fishing story, Coombs' mental model was deficient; he was unable to correctly predict where he should aim his spear. When the concept of water refraction was added to his mental model, his prediction was successful. Prediction is a common cognitive task we, as teachers, continually ask of students. For instance, we ask students of all ages to predict possible scenarios. We urge them to predict what happens next in a story, how certain variables will affect their science experiment, or, as occurred in our study, what types of hits they will retrieve if they use the search statement they just typed into the search engine. These processes extend the predictive power of the mental model. If the learner's mental model is elaborate and accurate enough, it permits them to predict situations before they arise and to react by utilizing knowledge from past experiences to try out various alternative actions.

In such ways, an additional role of mental models is to provide us with troubleshooting capabilities before, during, and after the event (see figure 2.2). For example, when setting up the library media center for parent visitation day, we activate a mental model to help us run through various scenarios that have the potential to go awry. If, in this scenario, two hours into the day, the computer with the interactive software that parents are invited to use freezes, then the teacher-librarian mentally runs through possible causes and solutions and proceeds to put into operation the mental model with the most promising solution. If that solution fails, another mental model can be implemented with success. That night, the first mental model is re-launched and its reliability critiqued in order to decide whether the mental model needs to be discarded or whether it still remains useful for solving other problems. There have been numerous studies of expert and novice mental models when troubleshooting breakdowns in various types of machines or activities. Cohen et al.'s (2000) study of army personnel when in simulated battle exercises is particularly valuable. Such research attests the usefulness of the troubleshooting role and the existence of mental models.

Mental models also have an active role in effective task performance (see figure 2.2). Barker, van Schaik, Hudson, and Meng Tan (1998) maintained that their research confirms this hypothesis: "Indeed, it is our contention that the richer a student's mental model, the better will be his/ her performance" within a given domain (p. 201). Jih and Reeves' (1992) study provided further support with the additional caveats that both awareness and management of the mental model will allow better control over experiences and proficiency in specific tasks. They argued that mental models affect such factors as effort devoted to tasks, persistence, expectation, prediction of results, and levels of satisfaction after task execution. Van der Henst (1999) contended that mental model theory provides a critical role in clarifying the relative difficulty of reasoning tasks applied to the mental effort involved in solving the task. The theory provides a way to examine the amount of effort that is expended by assessing the number of models required to test the viability of counter-examples of the initial task.

Later, we discuss that the difficulty of processing multiple mental models over-extends the capacity of short-term memory to process them. It appears to be a cost-effective issue. The choice is whether to expend more mental effort to reason through the task or to decide that we have exhausted our current cognitive limits in this particular context and should take a different approach, end it, or start over. In one of the lessons, a teacher-librarian solved any chance of conflict between mental effort and task by minimizing the cognitive effort. She simply ignored the student's advanced abilities and delivered her standard information literacy instruction. In subsequent chapters, we explore the mental models brought by our participants to the lesson in order to ascertain the ways in which their mental models were managed during the lesson and how these models affected their mental effort in relation to the number of parallel tasks. Also examined is their reaction to, their control over, and satisfaction with their respective computer database teaching experiences.

An important function of mental models is to serve as memory and organization devices (Williamson, 1999; see figure 2.2). We can chunk—

that is, group—parts of a larger whole. We can actively update, organize, and re-organize as well as discard information, thereby controlling cognitive processes, sometimes consciously but more often unconsciously (Nelissen and Tomic, 1996). There are times when we consciously realize we are controlling our mental models, such as when it is important to use appropriate discourse to induct students into a community of praxis, or in a lesson when our first explanation was unhelpful to the student, and we purposely retrieve an analogy to provide a clearer picture of the concept. Because of its automaticity, processing our thoughts, beliefs, and actions is usually of no conscious cognitive concern unless we are engaged in metacognitive activities. We concur with Rogers and Rutherford (1992) that part of the fascination with mental models is this aspect— the unconscious processing of mental models that allow us to predict, infer, solve problems, and understand.

Another function of mental models is its usefulness for metacognition (see figure 2.2), simplistically defined as thinking about our thinking, and then employing strategies to enhance and problem solve solutions when there is understanding failure. "A mental model is a convenient mechanism with which to consider how we acquire knowledge, achieve understanding and generalize problem-solving skills to make them available to different situations, and develop metacognitive skills" (Haycock and Fowler, 1996, paragraph 5). As we cognitively toil to comprehend concepts, we attempt to find and assimilate similarities from our older mental models and add new understandings and intuitions about the domain being studied (Schoenfeld, 1987). Hopefully, we include metacognitive strategies managing the degree of certainty we feel about various aspects of our knowledge and understanding (Norman, 1983).

Importantly, mental models can help reduce mental effort (see figure 2.2) and thus free working memory to handle and troubleshoot new problems, ideas, situations, and domain-specific content (Gualtieri, Fowlkes, and Ricci, 1996). Reduction of information overload as one role of mental models is shown in the following six instances.

1. One function of a mental model is that it can be quickly retrieved from long-term memory where a particular representation has been associated with that situation in the past (Halford, 1993). Thus, having "a certain degree of generality in the sense that they are transferable from one situation to another" (Halford, 1993, p. 8) ensures that mental models can usefully diminish mental load.
2. Mental models utilize prior experiences. A mental model contains prior experiences that help analyze the new situation and help determine that just the new parts of the current situation or task need to be incorporated in the model. Information about the environment is

"essential to mental models . . . [but] not all the information relevant to a problem will be activated at any one time" (Halford, 1993, p. 143). This was particularly so in the Coombs' fishing example.

3. Mental models are functional in recall tasks because they allow facets of a situation to be predicted, thereby reducing the amount of information that has to be recalled (Halford, 1993). Put another way, once a situation has been experienced and a mental model constructed, it does not have to be processed or mapped bit by bit, but can be recalled as a whole or just a fragment of the whole and then used to predict new aspects of the situation.

4. Mental models can possess a generative attribute so that predictions made from them can operate outside the information given. Once we experience a situation and a mental model of it has been constructed, "it can be used to predict new aspects of the situation" (Halford, 1993, p. 8). If we had continued the Coombs' fishing saga, he explained that he was able to predict where to throw the spear when he later began fishing in running water, in comparison with where the fish would have been if the water were still, and maintain a pleasing degree of success. The generative characteristic helps reduce the mental effort required to create a new mental model to replicate every situation.

5. Mental models can be transferred from one situation (or domain) and used by analogy in another situation (or domain) (Halford, 1993). Gentner (1998) provided four sequential sub-processes of analogy. First is retrieval: "given some current situation in working memory, the person accesses a prior similar or analogous example from long-term memory" (p. 108). The second is mapping: given two cases in working memory, this process derives their commonalities so that one case is employed to explain and predict another (e.g., a clock and earth's rotation). The third is an evaluation of the analogy (see figure 2.2) and its inferences that occurs mainly through working out the structure common to both analogs. The final sub-process that may occur is that of "re-representation" (p. 108) whereby one or both situations and analogies are adapted to improve the match.

"Of all the learning structures, analogy is the only one that offers a mechanism for the acquisition of substantial knowledge structures in a brief span of learning" (Gentner and Forbus, 1996, paragraph 3). The clock is a satisfying analogy for the earth's rotation. Flowing water or teeming crowds are popular analogies for electricity (Gentner, 1998; Halford, 1993; Suzuki, 1998). We do not need to expend mental effort teasing out every aspect of each of the two parts, clock and earth's rotation, in the analogy. For instance, we do not need to understand each component of the clock's mechanical mechanism and what to do if it stops. Regardless of whether you are the original creator of the analogy or been told it by a teacher or read it in a book, only those elements of each part that are appropriate to the analogy are interrogated to create an adequate building block to help understanding. Not only is less short-term memory needed to create or adopt the analogy but also the time taken to retrieve and understand is considerably shortened.

6. Mental models can be constructed out of components obtained from both the situation and analogy embedded in an earlier mental model (Halford, 1993). A teacher's mental model of his teaching with the Internet (situation) incorporated the same analogy, a museum, at the beginning and at the end of his post-graduate online course (Henderson, Putt and Coombs, 2002). What changed in his mental model was the type of pedagogy attributed to the museum guide (i.e., the teacher). At the beginning, the "guide" implemented behaviorist pedagogy, directing the tourists (i.e., students) to various exhibits (websites), narrowed to particular artifacts (retrieved hits) while ignoring others he deemed unnecessary for consideration. At the end of his course, now as the social constructivist guide-on-the-side, he advised each small group of "tourists" to meet him back at the entrance in forty-five minutes (fifteen minutes short of the duration of the lesson) or if his help were needed (student groups were given responsibility for searching sites and hits relevant to their part of the group project).

In effect, rather than creating a totally new representation or retrieving every single bit of content and teasing out what each word or concept means, the mental model makes use of various memory-saving strategies: analogy, similarity, patterning, and imaging (see figure 2.2). For example, one of our ten teacher-librarians patterned her teaching after the models of her own teachers, whether or not it suited the teaching situation. Thus, she avoided the planning and mental work necessary to adjust her teaching to each situation.

Analogy provides a shortcut function. It allows transferring or mapping the analogy used in an existing conceptual structure to current tasks, even if new. Similarity's function is to extract principles from repeated overlapping experiences and apply them appropriately in new situations (Gentner and Forbus, 1996, paragraph 4; Johnson-Laird, 1983). The role of patterning is utilized for simple and more complex tasks (Dreyfus and Dreyfus, as cited in Rouse and Morris, 1985; see figure 2.2). For example, if someone asks for the five-digit pin number for the photocopier at work, Lyn (one of the authors) cannot remember it without using her finger to create the pattern placement of each digit in the pin number in the air.

The expert's mental model consists of "highly-developed repertoires of pattern-oriented representations" (Rouse and Morris, 1985, p. 35). Familiar cues trigger patterns possessing expectancies, objectives, and typical responses (Cohen et al., 1995).

The advantage of the imaging role of mental models is that imagery allows "a lot of information to be integrated economically into one representation" (Halford, 1993, p. 30; see figure 2.2). It also plays a role in promoting recall. When tired, recalling the pattern is sometimes inadequate for remembering the photocopier's pin number. Lyn then resorts to visualizing the image of an actual number pad and, because there is a generic setting out (for the telephone, computer, printer, fax machine, and calculator), she taps out the numbers on the imagined number pad on a flat horizontal or vertical (e.g., wall) surface. It is interesting that this strategy of visualizing the number pad does not produce the correct number when she taps out the digits in the air. It would seem that her mental model has combined the usual placement of a number pad—desk, shelf, or wall—with its image. When tired, support is drawn from the spatial-functional constraint (physical location and artifact) in order to replicate the real situation (Glenberg, 1997). Like the other strategies, images help us by utilizing less working memory to create, activate, delete, or modify mental models.

CHARACTERISTICS OF MENTAL MODELS

The role of mental models is "not just a mental state to be built and maintained; it is a platform for making decisions and solving problems" (Williamson, 1999, p. 15). The role of mental models is to enable cognitive action. Given their complexity, it is not surprising that mental models have numerous characteristics (see figure 2.3). Many are immediately obvious, such as accuracy and functionality. However, they can also be naïve and incomplete. Additionally, mental model terminology can be specialized, such as "running a mental model." This section examines the many characteristics that seem particularly relevant to this book.

Runnability

The concept of "runnability" is a core defining characteristic of a mental model (see figure 2.3). A simple example will help conceptualize this term before embarking on an extended explanation. If asked the following question at a staff meeting, "How many sections are there in your library media center?," invariably, most teacher-librarian media specialists would have executed a mental "walk-through" the library checking off

Functions:

Cognitive representations of:

Reduce mental effort

Our world

Similarity

Ourselves

Analogy

Others

Recall tasks

Tasks

Generalizable

Ideas

Generative

Concepts

Patterning

Activities

Images

Artifacts

Enables action

Situations

Explanatory

Procedures

Prediction

Troubleshooting

Task performance

Metacognition

Organization device

Memory device

Characteristics

Naïve	Idiosyncratic
Mature	Contradictory
Accurate	Propositional
Incomplete	Analogic
Disorganized	Analytic
Recursivity	

Changeable
Obstacle to change

Inconsistent with behavior   ***Defining Characteristic***
"Runnable"

Figure 2.3.   Representations, Functions, and Characteristics of Mental Models

the computer section, the journal section, the junior fiction section, and so on. They may have visualized each section on that "walk." They may have written each section down as they passed by in their imagined journey. Regardless of these latter differences, the mental model would have been in a state of flux; you would be running it in order to produce the answer.

When we are mapping, creating, interrogating, and adapting mental models, we do these cognitive tasks in short-term memory. Thus our mental model becomes active in short-term working memory while we are engaged in the mapping phase or developing an analogy (Halford, 1993). Mental models are processed for each situation as a runnable event, or, essentially, the model has to be run to be useful for internal or external actions.

When working with various artifacts such as computers or printers, various authors (deKleer and Brown, 1981; Forbus, Nielsen and Faltings, 1991; Gentner and Stevens, 1983) argued that reasoning is characterized as mentally simulating or running a mental model of that artifact. For instance, mental models are running when we are problem solving. We can run a mental model to test out possible outcomes in advance of some action or in situ, such as originating and testing strategies to employ if a student does not grasp Boolean logic. As we perform a sequence of actions when working with a computer database or the photocopier, especially if we are troubleshooting, we are running our mental model. When we are looking for similarities between, or creating an analogy using, two mental models, then we are processing or running both mental models simultaneously or in parallel.

Cohen et al. (1995) argued that, as a situation or task is evolving, we can run both the plan (what to do) and action (how to accomplish it) mental models. We do not have to wait until we have run the situation plan analysis completely to then run the action mental model. The results can be variable and are dependent on depth of understanding and familiarity with the problem. Results can also be affected by our ability to reselect a different mental model plan of attack or re-edit our mental model plan by incorporating elements of an alternative action from another mental model. This might happen in a teaching-learning situation where unanticipated events are frequent, as occurred in our study.

Mental models are stored in long-term memory where they are deemed to be static. We convert the dormant mental model into a runnable one when generating new ideas or sequencing "snapshot" images (such as in the Coombs' example). This inert mental model is a product of our cognitive endeavors, whereas runnability is a process in these endeavors, not a product (Jih and Reeves 1992; Randell 1993; Rogers and Rutherford 1992). Running a mental model is a dynamic process of working on or with the internal mental representation of the real external situation or the imagined situation.

Recursivity

Another characteristic of mental models is that they can be "organized recursively, that is, in computational terms a model can call itself during processing, providing both computational power and a mechanism by which the self, and self-reflective aspects of the self, can be understood" (Power and Wykes, 1996, p. 205; see Brand, 1998; figure 2.3). This has relevance for metacognitive assessment of our own understanding and strategies. It also has relevance because our mental models can include an understanding of self.

Analogic, Analytic, Propositional, and Image Characteristics

A characteristic of mental models is that they can be analogic (see figure 2.3). For some teacher-librarians, a bike wheel is an analogy for their media center. Their center is the hub of a bike wheel with spokes representing support, accountability, responsibilities, teaching, advising, and co-planning. Faster spinning represents "it's wanted yesterday" deadlines; getting a puncture represents breakdowns with the technology; a new wheel represents updates and innovations; repainting means band-aid fixes, and so on. Thus analogies are partial similarities capturing the parallels between disparate situations that nourish further inferences (Gentner, 1998).

An analogy differs from a metaphor in that the metaphor does not require structural similarity between its elements. For instance, in the metaphor, "a red rose is love," there is no structural connection as there is between a clock and earth's rotation. An analogy differs from a representation in that the analogy is a mapping from one representation (base) to another representation (target) whereas a representation is a mapping from the representation to the environment and visa versa (Halford, 1993). Using analogies in teaching procedural and conceptual use of complex systems, like the Internet, is a common practice. Schwartz and Glack (1996) and Gentner (1998) support the notion that "learners' models of a domain [can be] shaped by instructional analogies" (Gentner, 1998, paragraph 4). For instance, one way of explaining multiple navigation paths to access the same node in online hypermedia is to offer the analogy of a road map. The map delineates the number of ways, some direct, some circuitous, to drive to a friend's home. The direct way is further aligned with linear navigation and the one that takes branches to non-linear navigation.

Besides being analogic, other characteristics of mental model representations are that they can be analytic, propositional (that is, "if . . . then . . ." thinking), and contain or consist of images (Halford, 1993; figure 2.3). For example, during her lesson preparation, Martha, a middle school learning support colleague, activates her mental model and visually depicts herself as the student carrying out the proposed tasks, analyzes the value of the proposed activities to obtain the lesson's outcomes, formulates propositional strategies with respect to the behaviors of her students, and focuses on specific individuals as she does so.

When we analyze, we break the situation down into smaller parts, or essential features, in order to help action; we can also examine the relationship between these parts in order to understand the whole (figure 2.3). For example, a student has submitted low-level content and arguments for an assignment. We commence our analysis by breaking our diagnostic task into its components: the big picture is the problem of information literacy, then, within that belong the essential features: the adequacy or inadequacy of the search statement, adoption of a surfing (erratic and superficial) rather than a searching (purposeful interrogative) technique, and so forth. In subsequent chapters, we identify where our teacher-librarians utilized analysis in their mental models.

Mental models have variable propositional characteristics (figure 2.3). Rain implies black clouds; no black clouds, therefore no rain (cf. Halford, 1993). This everyday phenomenon is isomorphic to the problem; that is, it possesses a one-to-one correspondence between the elements in the sets, and can also serve as a mental model of it. The following exemplification is not uncommon with teacher-librarians, as our study reveals. *If* I use a "show and tell" strategy when teaching computer skills to a student, *then* I would use the keyboard and *(then)* it would be quicker. *If* I use a "tell" strategy, *then* the student would have hands-on use with the keyboard but *(then)* it would take longer as I would need to wait while the student carried out the instruction; and *(then)* wait longer for the typos and mistakes to be corrected. These propositions are still isomorphic but have a one-to-many correspondence. The planning strategies are further examples of valid "if . . . then . . ." propositions that are characteristic of some mental models.

Mental models can consist of, or include, images (Navarro-Prieto and Canas, 2001; Newton, 1996; Senge, 1992; figure 2.3). The image of Coombs spear fishing is rich in imagery. Actually it consists of an animated simulation of the attempt, failure, puzzlement, attempt, failure, thinking (when recalling prior knowledge), attempt, and succeeding, each with appropriate facial contortions. It is now indelibly etched as a segment within a wider, more encompassing mental model of the various facets of the person, Coombs. Hasselbring (1994) advised that visual images differ in their efficacy when assisting the construction of a mental model. If the image does not contain features of an actual situation, then the construction of the representation of the task, story, or artifact could be severely weakened, particularly in terms of the mental model's usefulness in understanding (Hayes, 1985).

DEFICIENCIES VERSUS FUNCTIONALITY OF MENTAL MODELS

A particular mental model can be complete and accurate (Halford, 1993), which would reflect the expert's model rather than that of the novice or informed novice. For instance, when a lesson is not succeeding the way you had planned, your mental model would interrogate one, several, or all of the following: the difficulty level of both the content and the task; the clarity of instructions and explanations; a generalized summary of students' behavior, attitude, and ability; the usefulness of the pedagogic strategy; the effectiveness of the types of questions and answers; and so forth. Successful teachers and troubleshooters are those who have developed an accurate mental model for the situation presented them.

However, our small-scale mental models of reality need neither be wholly accurate nor correspond completely with what they model in order to be useful (Anderson, Howe, and Tolmie, 1996; see figure 2.3). In fact, mental models can be immature or naïve (Howe, Tolmie, Anderson, and MacKenzie, 1992). They are "apt to be deficient in a number of ways" (Norman, 1983, p. 14). Johnson-Laird (1983) and Halford (1993) concurred that mental models are typically approximate, incomplete, and sometimes inaccurate. They can be "somewhat disorganized" (Anderson, Howe, and Tolmie, 1996, p. 251) and "perhaps include contradictory, erroneous, and unnecessary concepts" (Norman, 1983, p. 14). "The models that people bring to bear on a task are not the precise, elegant models discussed so well" (Norman, 1983, p. 8) in the literature or, indeed, so far in this chapter. All this seems particularly disturbing for us as teachers as it has relevance for our own mental models and for those of our students, yet it is logical.

We cannot "carry all the complex details of our world in our mind" (Senge, 1992, paragraph 3). Hence, errors can occur because we do not activate all our knowledge at one time. Although information about or prior knowledge of the world is essential to mental models, not all the information relevant to a task will be triggered at any one time (Halford, 1993). Coombs demonstrated this characteristic when, as outlined in his fishing story, his initial mental model was inaccurate, and then the theory of water refraction was retrieved from a long-dormant mental model and incorporated into his current mental model. This occurred well into his spear fishing adventure. Teacher-librarians do not activate all their knowledge about information literacy, the Internet, the difference between browsers and search engines, basic versus advanced search functions, student characteristics, and administration costs when advising a high school student to use a particular search engine to find articles on global warming. If this mental model breaks down, however, another, more complete model will be sought in an attempt to compensate and hopefully rectify the situation.

Certain analogies used when teaching, as well as the "spontaneous analogies and implicit similarity comparisons" formed by students, sometimes "lead to models that are wholly or partly misleading" (Gentner, 1998, paragraph 4). Finney (2002) sited the findings of various research studies that "misconceptions tend to override new text information that is inconsistent with the reader's prior knowledge" (paragraph 3). Because naïve and incorrect mental models perform sufficiently well enough in the real world for most situations (Halford, 1993; Norman, 1983), their inaccuracies—and consequences—endure.

"People maintain superstitious behaviors" and such "idiosyncratic quirks" are characteristically embedded in the mental model (Norman, 1983, p. 8; see figure 2.3). We could all cite numerous examples, many of which are deemed "old wives tales." An example concerning technology occurred with one of our colleagues. Although he was correctly regarded as a whiz with computers and could explain that the "cut" function saved a copy to the clipboard, he still copied what he wanted to cut and paste elsewhere, then used the "cut" function. His explanation for these extra actions was his "irrational fear that it would be lost if he just used 'cut'" (his self-description; personal communication). Even though mental models are malleable, they need to be deliberately manipulated by the learner. Some mental models are anchored by deeply held beliefs, some are based on emotional experiences, and some are based upon structured cognitive exercises, this last category being the easier to correct (Williamson, 1999). Simply becoming aware of the concept of mental models and their different categories should help teachers identify and work with their own mental models.

A community of practice, such as that of teacher-librarians, builds up embedded policies and habits of the mind as to the way things are, and should be, done. To change these or to change an individual's deep beliefs and practices is often very difficult. Senge (1992) argued that we possess a strong tendency to see changes we need to make as being abstract, or out there in the world and instead of in the inner world of our mind. To maximize the impact of this, he underscored his message, "We do not 'have' mental models. We 'are' our mental models. They are the medium through which we and the world interact. They are inextricably woven into our personal life history and sense of who we are" (paragraph 6). Teaching and learning to promote change to cherished beliefs, practices, assumptions, and ways of doing and thinking are particularly challenging and disorienting. Changes to the way we teach and learn can create enough discomfort to impose pressure on us to reject the change. Unless we have a strong mental model that such change is critically necessary and are willing to exert the mental effort needed to make that change happen, these changes can be dismissed (see chapter 7).

The notion of what is technically incomplete but yet functional for a teacher's instruction and a student's learning is relevant. For instance, in our study, a teacher-librarian had an incomplete mental model of the dial-up system for connecting to the local library's catalog system, mentioning to students: "I don't know why we use this particular remote dial-in procedure; I just follow the steps that the trainer demonstrated." Nevertheless, her mental model was functionally adequate as a procedural process.

Most non-librarians do not have an accurate mental model of how a library works yet our mental model of how to find a book or journal is functional. After trying unsuccessfully, we readily predict that a visit to the librarian is vital. For some of us who are older, the essential buttons on the remote video or DVD recorders are embedded in the mental model; the others are not. It is as if they did not exist. The mental model's worth is not whether it is imprecise or incomplete, but on how useful it is for each of us. The bottom line is that mental models "must be functional" (Norman, 1983, p. 7). The later sections in Norman's book, dealing with novice and expert mental models (see also pp. 41–43 in this chapter) and the value of mental models as an analytic tool, suggested that the functionality of one's mental models is not sufficient by itself to address the needs of different teaching and learning contexts.

CONSTRUCTION, STORAGE, AND OTHER COGNITIVE REPRESENTATIONS

The findings from pure and applied research have strengthened our understanding of how and where our mental models are created and stored. Mental models are "naturally evolving" (Gentner and Stevens, 1983, p. 7; Johnson-Laird, 1983).

> The "richness" of our mental models usually increases with our growing maturity and exposure to new and varied experiences leading, ultimately, to expert performance. This type of behavior, within a given subject domain, can often be positively correlated with the richness of the mental models involved. (Barker, van Schaik, and Hudson, 1998, paragraph 8)

> Formation and adaptation of our mental models takes place throughout our life. The emphasis in this section involves the mental models' facilitation of information retrieval and their storage and organization of variant knowledge for learning and instruction. (Haycock and Fowler, 1996)

Mental models are formed and processed in short-term or working memory; that is, the internal workspace for our thinking, understanding, and troubleshooting (figure 2.4). This internal workspace is sometimes referred to as the problem space. Because mental models are "active while solving a particular problem, they provide the workspace for inference and mental operations" (Halford, 1993, p. 23). Loosely equating mental models with the cognitive problem space or cognitive work space has also contributed to the ambiguity in mental model literature. Indeed,

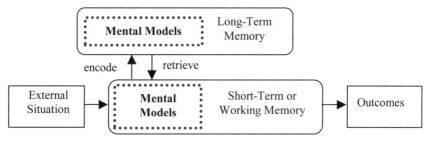

Figure 2.4. Mental Models and Memory

when we first began reading the mental model literature, we based our understanding on literature that identified mental models as episodic and therefore constructed upon demand rather than being retrieved (e.g., Brewer, 1987).

Johnson-Laird (1983) also mentioned that we discard the mental model after we use it when deducing conclusions. We therefore thought that mental models were always transitory; occurring in working memory while being run, then the content being sent back to long-term memory while other aspects of the mental model were discarded. Given this framework, mental models retrieved information from various forms of knowledge, such as schemas, syntactic rules, rules of logic, analogies, and hierarchical propositional networks stored in long-term memory, and *became* the mental model as it was being run in short-term memory.

There are a number of problems with such reasoning. From the exploration of the many facets of mental models in this chapter, it is obvious that mental models contain content, images, and notions of our abilities in and across domains and tasks, and can be propositional, analogic, generative, generalizable, and incomplete. They possess a structure that has a correspondence to that of the external event, task, or phenomenon, as we perceive that reality. We can work with more than one mental model at a time; for example, when we are comparing and contrasting them for similarities or deciding upon an explanatory analogy or predicting the best troubleshooting strategy. In order to engage in such cognitive and metacognitive skills, mental models have to possess some permanence. Thus, creating, deleting, comparing, and modifying mental models occur in short-term memory. The last two cognitive tasks, however, can only be carried out when a mental model is retrieved from long-term memory and brought into short-term memory (see figure 2.4) where the task is executed. Mental models are therefore both transient and permanent, existing in short-term and in long-term memory (Bagley and Payne, 2000; Hambrick and Engle, 2002; Mani and Johnson-Laird, 1982; Rukavina and Daneman, 1996).

Miller's (1956) significant research found that our unaided working memory span has a limit of seven plus or minus two units of information. If we chunk individual items into a larger set, we then increase the number of discrete items able to be stored. For example, there are ten items in figure 2.1, Mental Models as Cognitive Representation: our world, ourselves, others, tasks, ideas, concepts, activities, artifacts, situations, and procedures. However, they can be chunked into four categories: (a) our world, ourselves, others, and situations; (b) tasks, activities, and procedures; (c) ideas and concepts; and (d) artifacts. Another person may reduce this to three chunks of information by putting "artifacts" with the items in (b) as it has a meaning connection because artifacts are used to complete tasks and activities by following procedures. Such chunking therefore permits a much greater likelihood of processing, rehearsing, encoding, storing, and recalling our mental model of the cognitive representation of mental models (Morra, 2001).

The capacity of short-term memory does not increase with age or cognitive development. More efficient use of working memory results from practice at tasks as well as practice when working socially and cognitively at tasks that require small group collaboration (Anderson et al., 1996). With age, experience, and practice we become more adept at building, retrieving, comparing, testing, and chunking mental models, thus maximizing working memory.

Mental model literature distinguishes between mental models and other cognitive representations. Mental models are viewed as complementary to other mental representations and processes such as schema and rules of logic (Halford, 1993; Haycock and Fowler, 1996; Johnson-Laird, 1987; Manktelow and Over, 1992). "Schema represents a general category of [domain specific] things, situations or phenomena rather than specific instances" and, like mental models, "they are flexible and generative" (Halford, 1993, p. 34). A schema of cars represents properties of cars in general rather than each specific make of car. Semantic networks are commonly drawn as concept maps that join items hierarchically from superordinate to subordinate via propositional arrowed links (or relational arcs). For instance, "Internet" could be the superordinate concept linked to the second level categories, such as "WWW" and "e-mail," with separate branches from "WWW" to both the third level categories of "synchronous" and "asynchronous" and a branch from "e-mail" to "asynchronous."

Both schema and mental models involve categorization and compartmentalization; both are able to call on other items within their respective representations. Schwamb (1990) made the point that schemata cannot "account for novel situations, new actions, or new arguments. The fact that mental models are constructed and can mimic relations in the situation at hand, supports their use in representing novel phenomena" (p. 30). This ability of mental models to map the structure of our experiences means that its form is not arbitrary like that of schemata (Halford, 1993; Schwamb, 1990). Mental models are also able to draw on schema and propositional networks to help constrain memory overload. Because mental models possess runnability, or as Haycock and Fowler (1996) labeled it, a fluidity, this gives mental models power in comparison with the static forms of representation (Halford, 1993). Mental models also allow self-reflection, which is not found in schema or in hierarchical propositional networks. Mental models can also include pragmatic and social factors because they are linked to the underlying semantic representations. These are not represented in schema theories (Manktelow and Over, 1992).

A number of researchers (e.g., deKleer and Brown, 1981; Halford, 1993; Johnson-Laird, 1983, 1989) identified how reasoning is accomplished by "manipulating special semantic operations . . . of interconnected components, rather than general syntactic ones" (Payne, 1992, pp. 110–111). We are able to remember the meaning of text or dialogue rather than the linguistic structure of its presentation. For example, while reading, we are creating a mental model. This allows us to recall the meaning of the text and how it was themed, just as you are doing now when reading this chapter. You would probably be unable to recall the text's surface structure, specifically words, punctuation, and sentences. Mental model theory utilizes semantic (meaning making) processes of deduction and induction rather than formalist rules of logic or the inferential rule approach, such as that utilized in Piagetian theory (Boudreau, Pigeau, and McCann, 2002; Halford, 1993; Johnson-Laird, 1983, 1993; Santamaria and Johnson-Laird, 2000; van der Henst, 2002). We are able to derive answers from simulation through mental models of the event, task, or phenomenon rather than applying rules of logic reasoning.

NOVICE AND EXPERT MENTAL MODELS

Based on research (Chi, Feltovich, and Glaser, 1981; Greeno and Simon, 1984; Holyoak, 1991), an expert's mental model is not just more elaborate or accurate than that of the novice; it is fundamentally different from the novice's mental model. Sloboda (1991) defined an expert as "someone who can make an appropriate response to a situation that contains a degree of unpredictability" (p. 108). To accomplish this would necessitate situated task, procedural, and conceptual expertise, such as that of an experienced librarian, a master mechanic, or heart surgeon. Additionally, the expert would have expertise in problem solving in new situations and also when solving unforeseen problems while unraveling that new situation's problem. Expertise in complex tasks is distinguished by flexibly switching among these alternative expertise strategies embedded in various mental models (Holyoak, 1991). The expert's mental models contain understandings from prior problems and solutions. Common events in differing situations are generalized while dissimilar events herald possible problems to be solved. They also contain content and metacognitive knowledge with strong links within and across multiple mental models in order to generalize to novel problems (Haycock and Fowler, 1996, paragraph 5; Schank and Cleary, 1995).

Research (e.g., Puerta-Melguizo and van der Veer, 2001; Roschelle and Greeno, 1987) indicated that experts' mental models include, but are not limited to, informal commonsense knowledge. This would include the visualization of objects in particular situations, as well as the interactive links between these mental models and those that contain technical and theoretical knowledge. In essence, experts think in terms of concepts and analogies. Novices, in comparison, think in terms of formula or a series of steps to solve educational problems. Holyoak (1991) argued that action, and the conditions that apply to an action (e.g., stopping for a red traffic light), can be "flexibly re-coupled" (or re-linked or re-embedded) by experts (p. 310). Clement (1985) also emphasized this "bridge," which was defined as testing out an analogy linking the proposed mental model and the problem situation. Newton (1996) maintained that the expert's mental model in a particular domain "tends to be hierarchically organized with broad strategies at the top and narrower tactics below. [It also links] useful actions and declarative knowledge to form clusters that tend to be deployed simultaneously" (p. 206). To do this, the expert would be engaged in running multiple mental models, or sections of the multiple models, in parallel.

In comparison, the mental models of novices "lack a repertoire of relevant clusters" (p. 206). Novices are more likely to respond by commencing with a narrow stratagem and by responding to surface features and detail first. Being novices, much of what they need to be able to function in problem solving, or even in procedural tasks, will be relatively newly embedded in their mental models and may be only weakly connected to other parts of their knowledge within these mental models. "This can place an increased burden on processing capacity [in their short-term memory] and novices may not make an economical or efficient use of the capacity they have" (Newton, 1996, p. 206). Novices who have had some practice solving tasks generally describe strategies that are mechanistic and procedural in their application. When trying to find a fault, a common strategy is to check all possibilities in a sequential manner until the fault is identified. The more expert the individual is, the more the individual shifts to efficient strategies that utilize heuristics. This results in only having to check one particular sequence as the other possibilities seem to be unconsciously discarded as irrelevant or unlikely to be correct (Anzai and Simon, 1979; Bibby, 1992b; Newell and Simon, 1972).

Bibby (1992b) and Williams (1996) pointed out that more practice is only one factor. The initial instructions provided the student or user is another crucial factor. As we explained in the sub-section discussing the value of mental models, this has implications for whether teacher-librarians provide procedural instructions or engage the student in conceptual activities. "The expert's model incorporates tighter constraints on action based trajectories derived from experience" (Glenberg, 1997, p. 19); this would have been a factor with the Aboriginal men in Coombs' fishing story. Coombs mentioned that the older men did not provide him with any help. Nor does their traditional culture of informal education and socialization give instructional directions or directed guidance to young Aboriginal boys, and this was the case with spear fishing. Coombs wondered how long it took the boys to work out the concept of refraction in water from observation and trial and error to allow them to spear accurately. Given the same text or problem, the expert is able to take actions that can leave the non-expert baffled.

MULTIPLE, DISTRIBUTED, AND
SHARED MENTAL MODELS

Multiple Mental Models

Taking advantage of the language of the Internet, Haycock and Fowler (1996) cleverly declared that "there are dynamic links between and among mental models that permit navigation to proceed sequentially, in parallel, or in hypermedia mode as needed in any particular situation" (paragraph 1; we substituted "hypermedia" for the original "hypertext" as hypermedia is now a more accurate description). Their conceptualization is appealing. "Dynamic links" recognizes that within mental models we have embedded a trigger that reveals their connectedness for navigation between and among them. Each of us can provide examples for the systematic retrieval of one mental model, its subsequent discard when it cannot fulfill requirements or has exhausted its ability to meet our needs, and linear sequential path navigation to another mental model needed to complete the exercise.

We previously alluded to the notion that mental models can be processed individually or in parallel within short-term memory. When our study commenced, we hypothesized that teachers would necessarily possess multiple mental models as they prepared, taught, observed, managed behavior, explained, elaborated, questioned, probed, guided, used the computer, manipulated the software, reacted on the fly to student questions and unforeseen problems, evaluated, and reflected. If a system, such as a classroom, library, or teaching in its broadest conceptualization, is used in multiple ways, then it is logical that multiple mental models are likely to be constructed (cf. O'Malley and Draper, 1992).

Another way to conceptualize the relationship between dynamic linkage and multiple mental models can be found in DiSessa's (1988) notion of "knowledge in pieces." She concluded from her studies that knowledge is fragmentary and seems to exist in pieces, dispersed over several partial models rather than one comprehensive coherent mental model. This view proposes that we have mental models for different purposes. For instance, when working with computer software, we may have strategies for diagnosing a mistake in our HTML coding in a "diagnosing error strategies" mental model, while the "routine action" mental model would store those actions we have habituated and thus result in unconscious usage of the mental model. Examples include using "shift F7" to bring up Microsoft's built-in thesaurus; another could be for error correction, as occurred with two of our teacher-librarians using Telnet dial-in procedures. Each mental model would need to incorporate a "binding" or linking mechanism to allow for adequate parallel processing to manipulate each mental model in working memory (Randell, 1993; Stenning, 1992).

The hypermedia analogy suggests that when searching our mental models, we can either search meaningfully for appropriate, jump haphazardly to inappropriate, or randomly surf to mental models or sections of mental models. It "encourages a view of knowledge use as an active process" (Bibby, 1992b, p. 168), even if sometimes it is incorrect or our links are in need of repair. This re-emphasizes the dynamic nature of using embedded links to interact with multiple mental models or parts of multiple mental models.

The number of mental models or parts of mental models that can be processed in parallel simultaneously appears to be dependent upon whether there are built-in linkages; semantic, situational, or analogical similarities; and our ability to chunk such similarities to free working memory to utilize multiple models for the current task.

Distributed and Shared Mental Models

So far, our explanation of mental models has included the notion that mental model construction occurs as an individualistic enterprise when interacting with the world, people, artifacts, or imaginary situations. Notwithstanding the general uneasiness between Piagetian and mental model theories, this has echoes of a Piagetian perspective where social interaction or socio-cognitive conflict between individuals is the catalyst for individual conceptual growth (Anderson et al., 1996).

In contrast are theories that advocate an unequivocal social origin for conceptual growth. According to Vygotskian theory, mental models would be socially constructed in interaction with more capable others (Vygotsky, 1978; Wertsch, 1991). In our study, the teacher-librarian was usually the "more capable other" guiding the student. There were instances, for example, when two students, one in Grade 4 and one in Grade 10, were the more capable other during the lesson. During a stimulated recall interview, there was another case in which the student could have been the more capable other at a particular point in the lesson, but the teacher-librarian did not invite it, and the student did not know if his input would be welcomed.

In social constructivist theory, our conceptualizations derive from the internalization of socially structured activities and experiences. This suggests that mental models are either socially constructed and then internalized, or are jointly constructed products so that each person's mental model would be a compromise of their negotiations. Ideally, the jointly shared mental model would be superior to any individual's mental model (cf. Anderson, Howe, and Tolmie, 1996; Doise and Mugny, 1984). Mental model activity in situ provides an account of mental models as constructed individually as well as distributed or shared among the various players and artifacts in any community of practice (e.g., Banks and Millward, 2000; Bibby, 1992a; Cohen et al., 1995; Rogers and Rutherford, 1992).

Bainbridge (1992) explained that "no part of a complex task is done in isolation" (p. 40; see also 1978). In education, we use teaching and learning artifacts, such as diagrams, pen and paper, handout worksheets, computers, pictures, and concrete manipulables. These are fundamental to numerous activities, especially those requiring inference or problem solving. Indeed, the literature in cultural psychology emphasizes the importance of artifacts in shaping our thinking (Cole and Griffin, 1980; Payne, 1992; Vygotsky, 1978). Teachers interact with teachers and students, who interact with other students and teachers. All interact with artifacts. All three—teachers, students, and artifacts—are situated within a particular social, historic, cultural, economic, political, and institutional community (hereafter, socio-cultural community) (Vygotsky, 1978; Wertsch, 1991). The literature talks about two sorts of distributed or shared mental models: one between the person and the artifact, the second between students or within teams. The following discusses these two types.

Distributed or Shared Mental Models between the User and the Artifact

O'Malley and Draper (1992) contended that some forms of knowledge can be seen as distributed between users' mental models and representations embodied in the artifact itself. Their conclusion is based on research indicating that the user's mental model of a word-processing package is incomplete. This supported Hammond, Morton, Maclean, Barnard, and Long's (1992) study emphasizing the fragmentary nature of the user's mental model of computer systems as well as DiSessa's (1988) knowledge-in-pieces explanation. This means that the user's internalized mental model consists of what the computer interface display does not provide combined with the information required to access what the computer does present to us.

For instance, Microsoft Word users may not be able to list sequentially the titles of the drop-down menus in Word. Test yourself! What about PowerPoint? How long did it take you to remember that to create a footer, header, or footnote you need to go to "View" rather than "Insert"? Rarely used functions tend to be habituated very slowly. The reason is that our mental models contain not every function and its position in each pull-down menu, but rather the procedure to find the function (e.g., select the menu topic that seems to be the most relevant and survey the function options; if incorrect, choose the next most relevant menu topic, check its options, and continue this process until you find the function you want to use). What is also embedded in the mental model is our confidence that, through using this method, we can find what we do not remember or do not need to remember. As Payne (1990) reminded us, the computer and its interface is a resource to be exploited rather than a gully to be bridged. In fact, we argue that users choose to create a mental model that is purposefully fragmented. They realize there is no need to incorporate information that is easily triggered by the interface.

What is intriguing is the ability for English speakers to use Microsoft Word and Microsoft PowerPoint when in Japan and the Middle East (where the interface reads from right to left and is in their own westernized languages). For instance, one of the author's productivity was generally at an acceptable level. There were five reasons for this. One was the virtually identical keyboard configuration that presented few problems for Lyn's mental model, particularly as a touch typist. A second was the standardization of MS Office products, including a majority of the icon graphics, across various language groups. A third reason was that she needed to use only a small amount of the capacity of her working memory. She merely ran her current MS Word mental model and embedded within it a mental model that placed the menu items from right to left for this particular language context. The fourth reason again related to Microsoft's standardization as it maintained the ordinal placement of the essential functions in the pull-down menu topics, such as open, save, copy, paste, insert graphic, and print. A fifth reason confirmed findings that we have stored in our mental models more about the menu topics and certain function items in them than we realize (Bibby, O'Malley, and Waterson, as cited in O'Malley and Draper, 1992). Again, the procedure was to embed this standardization factor into her mental model.

In such ways, information in a mental model is distributed between "knowledge in the head" and "knowledge in the world" (Norman, 1988; Jonassen and Henning, 1999) or, as O'Malley and Draper (1992) put it, some "knowledge is left out in the world rather than being 'in the head'" (p. 77) because the interface clues are enough for satisfactory outcomes (Mayes, Draper, McGregor, and Oatley, 1988; Payne, 1991). The distributed information is accessed and used in parallel, thus researching mental models in the context that we used could not be understood independently of the interactions between the person and computer (Banks and Millward, 2000, p. 3). Our research is a case in point.

Distributed or Shared Mental Models among Pairs, Groups, and Teams

Distributing or sharing mental models in a class, group, or team situation can occur through integration of two or more mental models and through collaborative critiquing and correcting of a single shared mental model. When individuals' mental models are dissimilar, or do not contain elements that overlap, then integration entails joining the parts that do not overlap to the other mental model or embedding both into a larger mental model (Cohen et al., 1995). Collaborative critiquing of one's own and other's mental models requires simultaneous work on a single model. In our study there were three actors—the student, the teacher-librarian, and the computer database. There were some cases of genuinely shared mental models between the student and teacher-librarian where the outcome reflected a mental model that incorporated both the student's and the teacher-librarian's incorrect and correct solutions to a particular problem.

The act of sharing or distributing mental models between group or team members involves social discussion and debate. According to Anderson et al. (1996), this presupposes that all participants socially negotiate a transitory mental model. In turn, this requires the representation of a mental model, or segment thereof, containing one's beliefs, as well as a comparison of that model with another's beliefs, and the execution of various manipulations of those beliefs as new information is revealed during the ongoing session. Such cognitive actions are dependent on the capacity of working memory. Johnson-Laird (1983) maintained that we are able to embed a mental model of another person's beliefs within our own mental model of a relevant domain. This—embedding one mental model within another—is a form of chunking that frees up working memory. This is particularly crucial for younger learners who may find it difficult to cope with the social and cognitive processes of negotiation.

In the teaching-learning situations there are multiple partners for differing contexts: whole class-teacher-artifact; individual student-teacher-artifact; and within student groups-teacher-artifact. A possible explanation for student failure could be overloading working memory to handle mental models of social cooperation (with particular individuals within the working group) running in parallel with a mental model about the content and yet another that provides arguments for a solution or having to "drop" one mental model to run another to predict an answer, and so forth. Perhaps, this is why a student sits back and allows another student to monopolize the interactions, or why students opt out in our lessons and provide meager responses.

Anderson et al. (1996) found that, with primary school children, small group discussion was the catalyst for change that clearly took place subsequently in each individual's mental model. The same findings replicate those found by Howe, Rodgers, and Tolmie in their 1990 study. Young children "do not appear capable of negotiating and manipulating a transitory, jointly held mental model as a prelude to integrating the results of those manipulations into their more enduring model of the domain" (Anderson et al., 1996, p. 269). Howe et al. (1990) believed the reason was lack of working memory because of the number of mental models that had to be activated in order to solve the problem. The article did not include the added difficulty that the social aspects of group work may have created.

Secondary school children demonstrated some ability to construct transitory mental models jointly and internalize the results of testing them (Anderson et al., 1996). They failed, however, to integrate some relevant information into their long-term mental models: the male groups dealt with each problem and did not engage in abstraction, whereas the female groups coordinated across problems without generating explanations for each individual problem. Interestingly, teenage mixed-gender pairs did not engage in any dialogue when inputting their solution into the computer and dealt with conflict between predictions by simply alternating agreement with the other's answer. The positive change in each student's mental models occurred as a function of their private reaction to what happened on the computer screen. These findings have implications for the role and outcomes of distributed and shared mental models for differing ages and genders when involved in paired and group activities.

MENTAL MODELS AS AN ANALYTIC TOOL IN TEACHING, LEARNING, AND RESEARCH

We implement many tasks without understanding. For instance, our mental model of the computer's filing system is that folders, and the files within them, are stored in a hierarchical directory structure because the operating system has been programmed to present them in this way on the computer screen. The hard disk, however, does not save files in this hierarchy. We do not need to understand how they are actually "filed" in order to use and save our computer files and folders. Limits to our understanding do not necessarily set limits to performance. If this is so, what benefit are mental models in teaching and learning?

Developing mental models is "the underlying 'driving force' that forms the basis for all teaching and learning activities. [They] play an important and fundamental role in dialogue and communication processes (including: reading, writing, talking, and listening), thinking and problem solving activities" (Barker, van Schaik, and Hudson, 1998, paragraph 4). When we provide our own, elicit students', or reveal the experts' mental models as part of our lessons, the result is more likely to be characterized by sophisticated performance, faster execution of procedures, and improved performance for novel problems (Rowe and Cooke, 1995). Because of their importance to our own and our students' success and failure, critiquing our mental models is a first step. When did we last question how we arrived at our preferred mental model of implementing procedural or conceptual strategies in information literacy lessons?

> New insights fail to get put into practice because they conflict with deeply held internal images of how the world works, images that limit us to familiar ways of thinking and acting. That is why the discipline of managing mental models—surfacing [bringing to the surface of our consciousness], testing, and improving our internal pictures of how the world works—promises to be a major breakthrough for building learning [communities] and organizations. (Senge, 1990, p. 174)

Ascertaining our own and our students' mental models of the content and strategies to employ is a worthwhile starting point.

Teachers can support the construction of mental models. Newton (1994) demonstrated that providing pictures that directly correspond to the initial state of a situation that they describe can help students. Even "children as young as five years construct an appropriate mental model that is used for articulation as events proceed" (p. 208). The example Newton provided was a picture of a plank next to a box; this image in the child's mental model was enough to facilitate understanding when they were told that the plank was placed on the box; other images were embedded in the mental model of the picking up and placement of the plank. They were then told that the plank on the box was used as a see-saw. Further images were embedded so that the mental model could run and be interrogated to provide accurate recall and description of the process.

In another study, providing diagrams or pictures of an initial state and an end or opposite state, and verbally describing the action that occurs between them, was adequate for students to embed appropriate links into each mental model so that recall and predictions for improving reliability or troubleshooting a fault were high (Mayer, 1989). In our research, one teacher-librarian required her student to make step-by-step predictions about certain attributes in the database. Research shows that this strategy of forced prediction requires the learner to articulate a mental model of a situation, rather than remain passive and cognitively inert (Friedler, Nachmias, and Linn, 1987; Newton, 1994).

Ohtsuka's research (as cited in Newton, 1994) revealed that genre type affects our mental models, with or without specific instructions. For instance, readers constructed a one-dimensional mental model and a two-dimensional mental model when they were told to expect inference questions about order and global perspectives, respectively. The same results were produced when these questions were asked at the end without prior warning. This suggests that students may construct one-dimensional mental models when they are given procedural (ordered) step-by-step instructions to make an online search of a database, but construct two-dimensional mental models when provided with the global how-it-works conceptual information about linking to other computers within cyberspace.

An expository genre study of 173 fourth, fifth, and sixth graders by Troyer (1994) ascertained that the group provided with mental model instruction outperformed the control group (read/answer group) in the immediate writing samples. Both the mental modeling and graphic organizer conditions outperformed the control group on the delayed writing sample. The graphic organizer proved to be the most effective strategy for reading comprehension. The implication for teacher-librarians is that the use of graphic organizers together with mental model instruction based on students' elicited mental models could encourage students to create useful transitory and long-term mental models.

Bell and Johnson-Laird (as cited in Johnson-Laird, 2004) discovered that, when engaged in reasoning, we are "faster and more accurate in inferring that an event is possible as opposed to necessary, but are faster and more accurate in inferring that an event is not necessary as opposed to not possible" (paragraph 9). Apparently, this arises from a failure to take into account information about what is false. This signals to teachers that we have to look to concept attainment theory. We need to provide instances of non-exemplars as well as exemplars. Making use of errors as learning opportunities (Carroll, 1990; Henderson, Patching, and Putt, 1994), as occurred with three of our teacher-librarians, assists students in the building of mental models that draw on both what is false and what is valid.

Alternately, "inadequate instruction can cause lasting problems" (Rogers, 1992, p. 187). Duff's (1989, 1992) research is important with regard to this. He maintained that the how-to-do-it or procedural information literacy instructions enable faster and more accurate performance during the session. However, this results in an "inert" mental model (Renkl, Mandl, and Gruber, 1996) because students demonstrate poor accuracy under novel conditions. This means that if something is learned in a single context, then the ability to transfer and use that theory or strategy in new situations is not high. For example, learning how to use the search function may bear fruit, but then trying to use the underlying principles in the advanced search function proves too difficult for satisfactory success. How-it-works or conceptual-type instructions require students to deduce certain inferences during task performance. Duff found that teaching for conceptual understanding often produces mediocre accuracy during the session but permits the development of a robust mental model, thus facilitating transfer of problem-solving strategies to novel situations, a requisite for lifelong learning. Price and Driscoll (1997) also emphasized that knowledge transfer of problem-solving abilities "does not arise spontaneously" and warn that it cannot be left to chance (p. 491).

Teacher-librarians and other instructors assume that telling or showing someone how to do something in a step-by-step matter will make learning quicker and easier. Conversely, making students work something out for themselves will be much more taxing and time-consuming (Rogers, 1992), not just for the student but importantly for the teacher. This was a relatively common finding with some teacher-librarians in our research. Duff (1992) and Duke and Reimer (2000) concluded that it is more effective in the long run to have a conceptual understanding of how computer databases and other devices operate. Seel (1995) recommended a mix of both. Learning a complex cognitive skill should be regarded as incrementally developing more complex mental models that include both procedural and conceptual understanding in order to solve problems effectively at each stage of acquiring that skill.

A number of researchers (e.g., Cannon-Bowers, Salas, and Converse, 1991; Langan-Fox, Code, and Langfield-Smith, 2000; Newton, 1996; Redish, 1994; Senge, 1990; Szabo and Fuchs, 1998) stressed that teaching, training, organizational restructuring, and team efficiency fail if the teachers, leaders, or team members do not ascertain, respectively, the students, staff, or individuals' mental models. This would involve brainstorming their content knowledge, ascertaining the relationships and types of relationships (e.g., prepositional and analogic) that they have or have not constructed linking the relevant sections in their mental models, and their self-concept with respect to the tasks in hand. If we do not, their mental models may not be generative. Based on our research, we argue that teacher-librarians, and by extension, other teachers, need to examine critically these aspects of their own mental models, as well as the mental models of their students and how learning occurs.

Even when these suggestions are implemented and accurate information and data are provided (for instance, to do with many scientific concepts or gender and race inequalities in education), we need to recognize that we and our students may construct generative mental models that satisfy our own interpretations of the world. Rather than face the mental challenges posed by minimizing cognitive dissonance, we continue with hard-core misinformed mental models (Newton, 1996; Vosnaidou, 1994).

Halford (1993) urged us to examine whether we correctly categorize students as understanding concepts, particularly "at younger and younger ages, in an all-or-none fashion, and . . . especially on the basis of success in a very restricted set of tests. We should examine precisely what the student understands in that domain" (p. 477), how that understanding is stored and utilized, and what will be entailed in further manipulation in different learning situations. Tools such as mental models allow us to deal with such questions educationally and scientifically.

CONCLUSION

The literature we researched emphasized the complexity of mental models and their many uses in various disciplines to identify how people think and respond to the situations presented to them. In a sense, mental models serve as belief and knowledge systems that guide the thoughts and actions of teachers and learners.

When we activate or create a mental model, we run it in short-term or working memory. We can purposefully link a mental model or a section thereof to one or more mental models. We do this when we run two or more mental models in parallel. By identifying similarities or differences in our old mental models based on prior experiences, we only need to embed a link, perhaps an analogy if a similarity exists, to them in the current mental model we are using or creating. In these ways, mental models are a product when they are stored in long-term memory and a process when they are being newly constructed in short-term memory or are being applied after their retrieval from long-term memory.

We draw on our stored knowledge, strategies, and beliefs; that is, the knowledge in our head, and also deliberately leave certain knowledge out in the world, such as that embedded in a computer database. Through using the computer interface clues, we help reduce working memory overload because we run fewer mental models. This allows us greater scope for efficiently and effectively searching, predicting, troubleshooting, and metacognizing. However, mental models can be naïve, incomplete, or inaccurate, and can be stubbornly difficult to change. The holder of the mental model can choose to let the mental model control the situation or manipulate the mental model to respond to the situation.

If the mental model is based on procedural how-to-do-it understandings, it will not be easily transferred to new situations. If the mental model is based on conceptual how-it-works understandings, it is more difficult to manipulate but possesses greater transferability to new situations, particularly as conceptual understandings change and develop. If the mental model is based on both conceptual and procedural understandings, the holder has the opportunity to control, manipulate, troubleshoot, and transfer the mental model to explore and solve new, potentially unpredictable situations. In these ways, mental models can be potent tools for teachers and learners.

Mental model theory and research continues to seduce and intrigue us with its complexities. Mental models have the potential power to control a teaching-learning session, to maintain the status quo, or to respond innovatively to the situation. It was also clear that this aspect has received too little research attention. This research study therefore aimed to ascertain how teacher-librarians' mental models affected their teaching, thinking, and responses to their students and the computer database. The issue became how to identify their mental models before they began their teaching-learning session, during their lesson when the mental models would be in action, and post-session when the teacher-librarians were invited to reflect on their mental models. During the pre- and post-sessions, we knew we could ask a set of probe questions and follow the participant's interests and our research goals. During the lesson, we employed a methodology that permitted us insight into the teacher-librarian's thinking at that time as well as the justification for her thinking and actions. The following chapter explores our choice of methodology, stimulated recall, and why we realized it was the most effective methodology to use for our purposes.

NOTE

1. From this point forward within this chapter, "teachers" will include "teacher-librarians" and "library media specialists." It also incorporates lecturers, instructors, trainers, coaches, and those in various types of instructional settings.

3

Stimulated Recall
Methodology

A teacher-librarian and the two researchers were viewing a videotape of her information literacy lesson. It had been taken sixty-five minutes previously with one of her elementary students. They were working with the dinosaur section in the *International World Book* encyclopedia database software. Five minutes into the replay of the lesson, one of the researchers paused the videotape after noticing that in the video, the teacher-librarian was nodding her head.

The researcher prompted her to access her memory and reveal what had been going through her mind: "I noticed you nodded your head. Can you tell me what you were thinking at that point in the lesson?"

The teacher-librarian replied: "Well, I was thinking, 'I don't want to show him, so how am I going to get out of him that I want him to scroll and, as he is scrolling the text [on different aspects of the dinosaur's habitat], look at the headings in the text and at the same time look at the headings in the left menu, so that I can get him to match headings?' Then I nodded as I confirmed my strategy. I thought, 'Yes. I want him to work out how they are related. Let him do it.'" (Marie's stimulated recall interview)

This research scenario is a glimpse of what occurs during a stimulated recall interview. Stimulated recall is an introspective method that can be used to elicit people's thought processes and strategies when carrying out a task or activity. Accessing cognitive processes gains entrée to "a private and personal storehouse of myriad public performances, edited and replayed" through memory (Lyons, 1986, p. 148). Mental models are our

55

private cognitive representations of our public world. In the scenario, the teacher-librarian's verbalization was realized as a stream of consciousness. It allowed us into the step-by-step running of the mental model of her pedagogy-in-action.

The chapter places stimulated recall within an appropriate theoretical and methodological framework and proceeds to discuss its strengths and limitations. Comparing stimulated recall methods with other data collection tools allows a privileged exploration of our various mental models.

THEORETICAL AND METHODOLOGICAL FRAMEWORK

The theoretical and methodological foundation of stimulated recall rests on a framework that connects information processing theory, the mediating process paradigm, and introspection methods. The information processing theory explains how learning and remembering occur by examining the way we take in, act on, and recall information (Atkinson and Shiffrin, 1968; Craik and Lockhart, 1972). The mediating process paradigm specifically targets the various thinking processes participants engaged in during a task (Anderson, 1970; Doyle, 1975; Rothkopf, 1966, 1970). Introspective process tracing methodology is used to access those processes based on the assumption that we can activate our long-term memory to recall and report past mental processes (Lyons, 1986; Vermersch, 1999). The stimulated recall interview is a tried and tested information process tracing tool that allows the interviewer to elicit, identify, and explore participants' cognitive processes and strategies, including their mental models. The diagram (figure 3.1) and the associated discussion help explain the relationship of these theoretical and methodological elements as contextualized within our study.

Information Processing Theory

Information processing theory emerged as a coherent branch of cognitive psychology in the late 1950s and 1960s. It was influenced by artificial intelligence research that used the computer as a metaphor for learning in order to model how humans store and retrieve information. This theory particularly focuses on the cognitive operations of receiving, encoding, storing, and recalling information in our memory system; in essence, how we learn.

According to the most widely accepted theory, labeled the "stage theory," our memory system comprises three types of memory: sensory, short-term, and long-term memory (Atkinson and Shiffrin, 1968; see figure 3.1). However, mental model theory could also draw on Craik and Lockhart's (1972) "levels of processing" theory and borrow from Rumelhart and McClelland's (1986) "parallel-distributed-processing" theory. Modified from various diagrammatic models of information processing (Center for Advancement of Learning, 1998; Doolittle, 1999; Herrmann, Raybeck, and Gutman, 1993; Huitt, 2000), the top part of our diagrammatical model illustrates how these components relate to each other (figure 3.1).

Each component performs a specific task in the learning process. The initial task in the information processing system is performed in our sensory memory. In this study, the participants received information from an external stimulus, the information literacy database lesson, as sensory experiences (Atkinson and Shiffrin, 1968). The teacher-librarians used their eyes, ears, mouths, and hands to obtain and process the information through sensory memory. Although the sensory register receives information constantly, much of the information is unconsciously discarded, replaced, or remembered for only a brief period of time (Sperling, 1960). For example, some of the teacher librarians would have registered the feel of the keyboard and heard the hum of the computer's hard drive, but if such peripheral input were not consciously focused upon, it would have been discarded by sensory memory.

Indeed, the key to moving any incoming instructional stimuli from sensory memory to short-term, or working, memory involves involuntary and selective attention (Herrmann, Raybeck and Gutman, 1993; Treisman, 1969; see figure 3.1). Involuntary attention occurs reflexively; for instance, when searching a CD-ROM encyclopedia database, we hear the "you-have-mail" sound and process the information for immediate or later action. Selective or purposively self-directed attention is more crucial for learning. If we do not give focused attention, for instance, to each procedural step involved in conducting a Web search, then sensory memory will not transfer each step to short-term memory for processing (see figure 3.1), and without further selective attention it will not remain in short-term memory to be embedded in a mental model. Attention is the ability to concentrate mentally during the rehearsal, coding, and retrieval stages. The quality and quantity of attention is vital to the learning process.

The information transferred from sensory memory to short-term memory can remain active for about fifteen to sixty seconds without rehearsal. Otherwise, it will be forgotten or discarded from short-term memory (Rudolph, 1996; Doolittle, 1999; Huitt, 2000; see figure 3.1). Some research suggested that with rehearsal it can remain active for up to twenty minutes (Goldstein, 1999; Huitt, 2000). However, only a limited amount of information can be stored at any one time in short-term memory, also

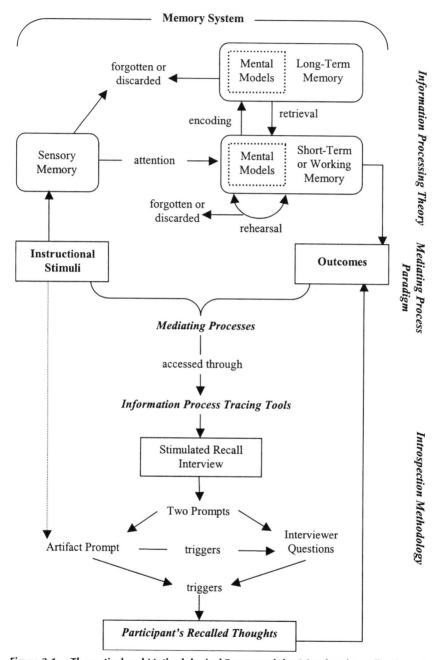

Figure 3.1.   Theoretical and Methodological Framework for Stimulated Recall (adapted from Pausawasdi, 2001)

called working memory, because it involves what we are thinking about at any given moment in time.

Unfortunately, rehearsal alone cannot increase the number of items currently held in working memory; it only increases the duration that items remain in short-term memory. As we mentioned in the previous chapter, Miller's (1956) research established that our unaided working memory span has a limit of seven plus or minus two units of information. If individual items are chunked into a larger set, the number of discrete items able to be stored increases. For instance, if each individual number and letter in a meaningless eight digit non-word log-in password (q2#90Cx8) were purposely grouped into smaller chunks (q2#—90C—x8), these three chunks would be represented rather than the initial eight chunks in working memory. Such chunking therefore permits a much greater likelihood of the information—that is, the mental model—being processed, rehearsed, encoded, stored, and recalled. What we pay attention to in working memory is more likely to be sent to long-term memory. A type of task common to our short-term memory would be the running of a mental model, often simultaneously, with information passed to it from sensory memory and information embedded in one or more other mental models passed back to it from long-term memory.

A number of operations occur during the movement of information from short-term memory to long-term memory. Mapping, or encoding (see figure 3.1), looks for similarities when comparing the recently arrived information with a mental model retrieved from long-term memory that is currently held in short-term memory. The learner then discards or integrates the new information into an existing mental model or other knowledge representation, such as a schema, in long-term memory. The formation of meaningful associations between the new and prior knowledge while focusing on unique features of the new information, the transfer to and storage in long-term memory appears to be accomplished more effectively for later retrieval from long-term memory back into short-term memory. This we describe as an "output" (see figure 3.1). One output example would be the answer to the question about the relationship between the various headings in the dinosaur database in the opening excerpt from the stimulated recall interview.

According to the Atkinson and Shiffrin (1968) model, long-term memory is unlimited, but information can be forgotten or discarded. Information can also be stored inaccurately and in fragments as well as with illogical linkages in our network of mental models. This would ensure difficulty in retrieval as well as the poor quality of what is retrieved, such as an inaccurate mental model of how to troubleshoot connecting to the Internet when something goes wrong, which occurred with two of our teacher-librarians. Additionally, Craik and Lockhart (1972) posited that the length and quality of retention in long-term memory are dependent on the level of initial processing during the rehearsal and encoding phases. For instance, if the amount of attention or level of processing was at a shallow level, then the recalled mental model would most likely be of the basic steps of how to access Netscape, type in the URL that the teacher had written on the board, and press the enter key on the keyboard. If, however, it was processed at the deepest level, then we would have a conceptual rather than a procedural mental model of information access, retrieval, and evaluation.

Once retrieved from long-term memory, short-term memory then processes and delivers the information contained in a mental model as an outcome (see figure 3.1). When we activate our mental models, we "run" them in working memory. They can then be verbalized for researcher identification and examination as outcomes of the memory system. The mediating processes paradigm and introspection methodology help explain why and how our mental models are accessed.

Mediating Processes Paradigm

The mediating processes paradigm has considerable explanatory power with respect to "the knowledge utilization process" (Doyle, 1975, p. 12). Specifically, it focuses attention on the importance of ascertaining the thinking skills, strategies, and processes as well as the mental models of participants when carrying out a task. The purpose is to understand more fully the cognitive processes that mediate instructional stimuli and learning outcomes. As shown in figure 3.1, the mediating process paradigm helps situate aspects of what occurs in the information processing theory. It is not focused on how stimuli are processed within the sensory, short-, and long-term memory system. Rather, the value of the mediating process paradigm is finding out what is actually going on in teachers' and students' heads in a learning and teaching situation, an important aspect in understanding teaching-learning connectivity (Anderson, 1970; Doyle, 1975; Glaser, 1972; Marland, Patching, and Putt, 1992; Rohwer, 1972; Rothkopf, 1970). These mediating processes can be viewed as "the fine-grained elements of cognition through which, and by which, learning outcomes are realized" (Henderson, Putt, Ainge, and Coombs, 1997, p. 103).

The mediating processes paradigm was a response to dissatisfaction with the process-product paradigm because it failed to identify what occurred in the participants' minds and because it interpreted what occurred in their minds based on the input-output variables (see figure 3.1). For instance, after an information literacy lesson (input or stimulus), the student used the Boolean "and" function in a Web search (output or outcome). The teacher-librarian could assume that the student had a mental model that contained conceptual understanding, such as "I want information to do with both dinosaurs and meteors but I don't want information about everything to do with dinosaurs as well as everything to do with meteors. I should use 'and' as it will only give me hits with both terms mentioned." However, the student reported that she was merely engaged in a "If I want information to do with dinosaurs and meteors then that means I type in 'dinosaurs and meteors'" thinking process. As with the teacher-assumed mental model, propositional thinking was utilized in the student's actual mental model but it was certainly inaccurate. To reiterate, although the process-product paradigm can be utilized by researchers (or teachers reflecting on a lesson) to focus on the cognitive processes that underline the results, they assume the cognitive strategies used by participants based on matching the learning stimuli with the outcomes (Carroll, 1971; Marland, Patching, and Putt, 1992; Snow, 1974). Thus the process-product paradigm is not suitable for a detailed consideration of participants' mental models in situ.

The issue concerning the two paradigms is partly one of emphasis. Cognitive mediating processes play a minor role in process-product research designs in contrast to their central function in the mediating processes paradigm (Doyle, 1975; Marland, Patching, and Putt, 1992). Variations in teaching and learning outcomes are a function of the mediating processes (information processing) employed by both the teacher and students during the teaching-learning process itself. This means that instructional stimuli are not as directly related to outcomes as previously suggested in the process-product paradigm, but rather are mediated by information processing mechanisms, such as mental models, employed during the teaching-learning process.

Because mediating processes come between instructional stimuli and outcomes, they can provide an answer to questions about in-action and reflective mental models. Indeed, because he focused on teachers, as this book does, Shulman's (1986, 1996) assessment is pertinent: behaviorist process-product methodology is inadequate to explain the choices, decisions, and judgments made by teachers during lessons. It was particularly inadequate to elucidate the cognitive processes through which the teachers selected their actions and problem solved. What was needed was a methodology that allows researchers to study teachers' thought processes before, during, and after teaching-learning episodes. This is precisely what our book does through its use of stimulated recall, an introspection process tracing tool.

Introspective Process Tracing Methodology

Introspection is an approach in which the use of, and access to, memory structures are enhanced. However, as Gass and Mackey (2000) pointed out, this is not always guaranteed even with a stimulus that aids in the recall of information. In the scenario at the beginning of the chapter, the tangible reminder (delineated as the "artifact prompt" in figure 3.1) was a videotape of the lesson. Running the tape prompted the teacher-librarian to recall thoughts she had during the actual lesson. In most research, the tangible reminder is a video taken of each participant executing the activity. Audiotapes (Beaufort, 2000), computer software (Henderson, 1996), the World Wide Web (Henderson, Putt, Ainge, and Coombs, 1997), and written documents (Gass and Mackey, 2000) can be used as alternative artifact prompts. During the stimulated recall interview, the participant and researcher together re-engage with the event by watching the video (or revisiting the artifact prompt). The purpose is to expose the participant's thought processes at the time of the original task through verbalization of those thoughts.

Introspective methods, or the use of reflections on mental processes, can be traced back at least to Augustine (Lyons, 1986). Nevertheless, introspection has had a variable reputation as a viable research method. Its "golden age," as Lyons (1986) termed it, was between the 17th and early 20th centuries, with Descartes as a prominent proponent. As behaviorism gained favor, introspection fell into disfavor as a methodological tool as did consciousness as a legitimate field of research. Introspection methodology was seen to lack the scientific objectivism of behaviorism, whose goal was the control and prediction of behavior through observation, measurement, and interpretation (Lyons, 1986; Watson, 1913). Ericsson and Simon (1993) also observed that introspection lost ground, not surprising because much of the early research lacked critical self-scrutiny even when introspective research findings were inconsistent.

In the 1950s, cognitive psychologists (e.g., Bruner, Goodnow, and Austin, 1956; Chomsky, 1959; Newell and Simon, 1956) became disenchanted with the research emphasis on public observable behaviors and began to focus on private inner cognitive processes. Gass and Mackey (2000) pointed out that, although their comment is a simplistic interpretation of the complexity of Skinner's (1953) theory of the relationship between private and public behaviors, "Skinner acknowledged that inner events could be observed by the possessor of them" (p. 8). Bloom's (1954) work was also seminal. Based on his research to verify the reliability of recall, he argued that the recall method was a valid method to recollect "one's own private, conscious thoughts" (p. 26) about an event. He reasoned that this allowed the "subject to relive an original situation with great vividness and accuracy if he is presented with a large number of cues or stimuli which occurred during the original situations" (p. 25). Such theorizing and research from respected researchers went some way toward legitimizing introspection as a research tool.

Introspection has been criticized because it requires simultaneous introspection of one's experiences, thoughts, or actions and introspection on oneself introspecting (see Lyons, 1986; Vermersch, 1999). This duality therefore modifies what is being introspected. However, such duality does not need to, and often does not, occur simultaneously when introspecting. Retrospection introspective techniques, of which stimulated recall is one, merely demand the former, which is verbalized "observation of the presentification of past lived experience" (Vermersch, 1999, p. 3). For instance, when watching a video replay of a lesson in which we obtained 2,000 hits on a Web search, we can recall and verbalize what we were thinking and feeling without consciously and simultaneously verbalizing our thinking about ourselves thinking about and verbalizing that recall. Indeed, the goal of stimulated recall and other introspection tools is to record the participants' recalled thoughts, not to require them to become knowledgeable about their own subjective experience of reliving and reporting the initial experience.

The following sections explore additional aspects and issues concerning the methodology of introspection. Various methodological tools are compared and contrasted with that of stimulated recall. What stimulated recall reveals in terms of the mediating processes is then examined. The strengths and limitations of stimulated recall are further scrutinized.

Introspective Verbal Reporting Tools

Shavelson, Webb, and Burstein (1986) described three types of "process tracing," another term used to categorize methods of introspective verbal reporting. The three methods—think-aloud, self-observation, and a prompted interview—allow the researcher to trace the mediating mental model processes of participants as they work through a task. Think-aloud, also called talk-aloud, self-revelation, or protocol analysis, reporting occurs when individual participants articulate their thought processes while simultaneously performing a task. A good example of the think-aloud process would be an individual's running commentary of what they are thinking as they conduct a search on the Web. Self-observation occurs without a visual, aural, or written prompt of the previously performed task. This type of verbal reporting or reflection usually occurs in a post-interview when, based on the interviewer's questions, the interviewee attempts to recall thoughts and strategies from memory. It is a retrospective activity as is the "prompted interview," which is more aptly labeled "stimulated recall" interview. However, in contrast to the self-observation interview, stimulated recall interviews rely on a visual prompt, usually a videotape, of each interviewee carrying out the task in order to aid participants' recall of their thoughts and strategies during that task.

The obvious advantage of verbal reporting methodological tools is that researchers gain access to mental models that are otherwise unavailable. All three process-tracing procedures do not and cannot capture all of a participant's thoughts and strategies, as participants can only report what is in their consciousness. Nevertheless, researchers (e.g., Bloom, 1954; Ericsson and Simon, 1980; and Lieberman, 1979) have shown that stimulated recall and think-aloud reports "are reliable measures and that results obtained using verbal reports do correspond with the actual behavior" (Gass and Mackey, 2000, p. 17). Langer (1986) found no significant differences between think-aloud versus stimulated recall to elicit students' overall reading and thinking strategies. She concluded that the two procedures were qualitatively similar. According to Meade and McMeniman (1992), their research established the robustness of stimulated recall methodology and that its use was particularly salient for examining the relationship between teacher beliefs and classroom actions. Given these findings, a question begs exploration: What advantages does stimulated recall offer that the other introspection methods do not?

COMPARISON OF STIMULATED RECALL WITH OTHER METHODS

Think-Aloud versus Stimulated Recall Methods

Think-aloud is alleged to be the more "invasive method" (Karasti, 2000) of the three process tracing methods. It is perceived to interfere with a participant's normal thought processes and routines as it creates an artificial situation (Afflerbach and Johnston, 1984; Ericsson and Simon, 1984; Langer, 1993). According to these researchers, think-aloud participants are unable to match the extent of their thinking with what they are simultaneously verbalizing. Stimulated recall methods, in comparison, appear to elicit more of that thinking. Think-aloud participants are unable to communicate as fast as they think and act, unless a specific problem arises that slows them down and allows them time to verbalize their thinking processes. Researchers are vitally interested in the comparison between what is happening cognitively during each problem situation and during problem solving that the participant finds difficult. Think-aloud process tracing can then capitalize on these problem situations. Obviously, being able to stop a videotape during stimulated recall interviews allows participants time to report as full an account as possible of their thinking during all situations.

Think-aloud has the added disadvantage of proving difficult for participants; specifically, to perform simultaneously a set task and verbalize their thinking as they are problem solving that task (Ericsson and Simon, 1998). Training and a model to follow are stipulated to help counteract this. Last century, Wundt's (as cited in Gass and Mackey, 2000) clinical participants had to practice at least 10,000 separate introspections before being deemed reliable enough to participate in verbal recall interviews and activities. Yet, that level of practice would certainly have altered their thought processes by establishing patterns of behavior! It is not surprising that introspective methodology fell into disrepute. Nevertheless, training remains an issue of validity. Think-aloud researchers need to be conscious of the amount and type of training they demand of the participants in order to minimize adverse effects on data validity.

Think-aloud techniques are an effective cognitive apprenticeship modeling tool for teachers and teacher-librarians when verbalizing their thought processes as they demonstrate, for example, when and how to use Boolean terms to make effective database searches. However, they are inappropriate as a research tool in a classroom or lecture where the participants have to carry out a speaking task (that is, teach or lecture) and talk about their thinking simultaneously. The process of thinking aloud would, of course, affect their task talk. This alteration of the primary process (that is, the classroom or, as in our study, one-on-one teacher-student talk) by verbalizing what is being thought is another problem of validity with the think-aloud method (Russo, Johnson, and Stevens, 1989). This specific issue is not as problematic for stimulated recall research because it employs a retrospective technique.

Self-Observation versus Stimulated Recall Methods

The retrospective self-observation method relies heavily on the participant's memory without a triggering artifact prompt of the event (see figure 3.1). The accuracy of teachers and students reporting the thoughts that they had during the teaching or learning event in a post-interview without a visual, aural, or written reminder is more open to charges of non-reliability than that from think-aloud or stimulated recall methods (Ericsson and Simon, 1993; Meade and McMeniman, 1994). For instance, Harris (1993) conducted a study of fifteen undergraduate student teachers to determine the extent to which they could perform unaided recall of deviations from their planned lessons. Results indicated that these student teachers remembered an average of only 42 percent of their deviations, and remembered less than 35 percent of deviations initiated by their students. Another difficulty with retrospective self-observation is that we are "essentially sense-making beings and tend to create explanations . . . for phenomena, even when these explanations may not be warranted" (Gass and Mackey, 2000, p. 6). In their study of 144 university undergraduates, Hannigan and Reinitz (2001) found that the students made increasing inferential errors about causes and events as the time increased from the original event.

Clearly, there is a danger that participants may infer plausible stories for descriptions of mental activity without consciously realizing that they are doing so. This can also occur during think-aloud and stimulated recall interviews. However, as we explain below, maintaining stimulated recall's strict questioning protocols can maximize reporting recalled thoughts rather than the plausible story. There is also a greater likelihood of the interviewer channeling the participant in the direction that the researcher wants to explore in self-observation interviews than with think-aloud and stimulated recall, the other two introspection process-tracing techniques. In spite of this, the self-observation verbal report can be effective with enhancement in certain circumstances.

We enhanced the self-observation interview to function more effectively than either the self-observation interview or a post-interview. The enhancement was that of timing; it occurred immediately after the stimulated recall interview. In fact, the stimulated recall flowed seamlessly onto the enhanced self-observation interview. This ensured that the participant had access to a more reliable prompt—the video and the stimulated recall of the teaching-learning session—than the participant's memory. The enhancement also allowed a directed exploration of our research questions.

The enhanced self-observation interview also granted the teacher-librarians the chance to elaborate, justify, and explain their actions and strategies as well as their retrospective and current thoughts triggered by the stimulated recall interview and video. These hindsight comments were encouraged through open-ended questions, such as "Is there anything else about the lesson that you would like to comment on?" Such open questions were followed by specific research-directed questions, like the following posed to the teacher-librarian: "Were there any instances when you modified your instructions, questions, or actions based on what the student said or did?" and, depending on the answer, followed by "Why?" or "Why not?"

An example of a research-driven question directed to the teacher-librarian that repeated those asked in the pre-interview is "How would you explain a database to someone who doesn't know?" These types of interviewer-directed questions attempted to obtain clarification about the teacher-librarian's thoughts reported during the stimulated recall interview, their rationalizations for what they did or did not do during the lesson, their evaluation of what had occurred during the lesson, what could be improved in the lesson, and some comparative measure of pre- and post-interview understandings. The enhanced self-observation post-interview thus allowed us to identify the participants' reflective mental models that were then compared and contrasted with their espoused mental models obtained through the pre-interview and their in-action mental models obtained through the stimulated recall interview.

Non-Verbal Reporting versus Stimulated Recall Methods

Researchers (for instance, Barrows, 2000; Karasti, 2000; McMeniman, Cumming, Stevenson, and Sim, 2001; Suchman and Trigg, 1991) compared stimulated recall with interviews, observation, and interaction analysis and enumerated the limits of the last three methods for in situ environments, such as our context of teachers' mental models-in-action.

Meade and McMeniman (1994) bluntly argued that, based on their current (1994) and previous research (Meade and McMeniman, 1992), a particular strength of stimulated recall over structured interviews is that it can "successfully avoid the 'pious bias' of self-report data devoid of context, and the associated problem where the researcher 'leads the witness' in discrete interviews unrelated to observed classroom actions." Thus, because interviews are not based on a specific event, they can be unreliable predictors of actual teaching-learning behaviors, strategies, and mental models-in-action.

Work practices, such as teaching, may not be readily reached through interviews, as the interviewees may not articulate aspects of their work processes. Karasti (2000) found that teleradiologists were unable to articulate their way of working with the new technology through interviewing, but could do so in stimulated recall interviews with a video of them working as the prompt. Such a situation also arises when work practices are so familiar, and therefore habituated, that participants perceive their practices to be unremarkable (Suchman, 1995). This relates to the novice-expert research that has pointed out the difficulties experts have in explaining their problem-solving processes and judgments. The expert's numerous experiences facilitate the automation of procedural knowledge, as well as the consequent freeing of working memory for utilization in the higher-order thinking necessary for conceptual understanding of new knowledge. Thus, many experts lose the ability to articulate their knowledge because the habituation of their procedural knowledge supplants their declarative knowledge (Anderson, 1990; Bereiter and Scardamalia, 1992; Sternberg and Horvath, 1995). Barrows, Norman, Neufield, and Feightner's (1982) research on physician reasoning-in-action, Gilbert, Trudel, and Haughian's (1999) work on sport coaches' decision-making-in-action, and McMeniman et al.'s (2001) research on teachers' knowledge-in-action are just a few that have found stimulated recall methods to be extremely useful to elicit recall of those habituated processes.

The criticisms concerning the reliability of interviews for obtaining participants' thoughts about their actions notwithstanding, certain interviews, such as pre-interviews and the enhanced self-observation post-interview, have a vital role to play in supporting stimulated recall. In our study, the structured pre-interview allowed us to obtain introspective espoused mental models. From the transcript of the videotaped lesson and the stimulated recall interview transcripts, we identified in-action mental models. Reflective mental models were extracted from the enhanced self-observation post-interview as well as from the hindsight thoughts mentioned during the stimulated recall interview. In this way, the stimulated recall interview provides two categories of data.

What is also being highlighted is the further usefulness of stimulated recall when it is combined with other data collection methods. Together, the methods provided profound insight into the relationship among (a) what the teacher-librarians said were their beliefs, theories, and preferred pedagogy, (b) if and how these were utilized when running their mental models during their lessons, and (c) whether their post-evaluative mental models reflected or contradicted their espoused mental models and what they did and thought during the lesson; that is, their in-action mental models.

Researcher observation of teachers and students during lessons does not permit access to their mental models in what Nespor (as cited in McMeniman et al., 2001) had aptly called a "complex and entangled environment." Yet researchers often identify these processes and strategies based merely on the behaviors and outcomes they observed. Also, activities in the field may occur so quickly that observers may miss details and implicit components of the work. Without the possibility of replay, as occurs with videotaped sessions in the stimulated recall method, these data are lost. Observations are especially problematic when the researcher is unfamiliar with the traditions, in-house language, and workplace practices that are automatically interwoven with the activity. Karasti (2000) used this argument as part justification for adding stimulated recall to her team's data collection methods in their study.

McMeniman et al.(2001) were more disparaging of another type of observation, interaction analysis, in which teacher and student behaviors are recorded at pre-determined intervals (based on the conventions of Bellack and Davicz and Flanders, as cited in McMeniman et al., 2001). McMeniman et al. argued that this method "provides only a crude and superficial record of [participants'] actions and little, if any . . . of the interactive decision-making of teachers-in-action" (p. 388). This argument was used to support their use of stimulated recall methodology to explore the links between the findings of educational research and the reasoning for what teachers did in the classroom. It also supports our study's use of stimulated recall to provide data from which we could identify the various in-action mental models of teacher-librarians in the teaching-learning situations.

Discourse analysis of the transcript of a videotape of a teaching-learning episode, such as the ones in our study, helps overcome some of the problems associated with observations and interactional analysis. Because this example of discourse analysis is based on a visual and aural record of what occurred, the video can be replayed so that nothing is missed. It has, however, the same major limitation as a research tool because the data are confined to the teachers' or learners' verbalizations, actions, and non-verbals; the cognitive thinking processes are not available for scrutiny. As is the case with observations and interactional analysis, researcher interpretations of teacher and student reasoning are assumed from this data.

Data from observations, interactional analysis, and discourse analysis of video transcripts accommodate the observable fraction; it is the hidden data—the participants' thoughts—that stimulated recall can elucidate.

What Stimulated Recall Methods Reveal

What follows is an excerpt of the dialogue between a teacher-librarian and a Grade 8 student taken from the transcript of a videotape of their information literacy lesson. A discussion of various interpretations follows the dialogue. Then there is a comparison of the dialogue matched with stimulated recall transcripts of the teacher-librarian's reported thoughts. From this dialogue that occurred close to the beginning of the lesson, we can identify crucial elements. In terms of the teacher-librarian's input, we can demarcate her strategies. First, the teacher-librarian checks that the student will go to the local council library to use and borrow books if their search locates relevant sources. Next, she tells the student what curriculum projects the student's class will be undertaking for the current and subsequent term, that they will be having a new teacher, and that the student will use computer databases again with the project. The student confirms that she will go to the library with the one word response "Yeah." She does not reply to the teacher-librarian's comments about further projects, change of teacher, and subsequent use of computer databases.

Teacher-librarian: So, you will be able to go to the public library if we find some books of poetry by her [the author] to be able to check out a book or make a copy of a poem to use in your presentation?
Student: Yeah. On Saturday.
Teacher-librarian: Okay.
Teacher-librarian: Besides this project, you're going to be getting ready to do the research report on a woman before Ms. Petty goes on maternity leave. Then Ms. Mullins is going to be taking over the unit on women. And at these points, we will come back and work with computer databases.

If we were analyzing the data from the transcripts using interactive analysis or discourse analysis, we would argue that the teacher-librarian was ascertaining whether her intended electronic information literacy objective would be useful in terms of follow-up by the student before progressing with the intended lesson. Conversely, if the student indicated that this would not be possible, she would change the lesson to teach something else. With respect to the teacher-librarian's consequent utterance, we could surmise that the "Okay" demonstrated her full acceptance of the student's intention of going to the library, or that the teacher-librarian remained skeptical but pushed on with the lesson as planned. We would interpret the teacher-librarian's next statement as her wanting the student to know that she, the teacher-librarian, was on the ball because she had liaised with the classroom teacher and was aware of the projects the class would be undertaking and what computer resources would be useful. We would further claim that she wanted the student to take the current lesson seriously as the student would be using the database again, even with a substitute teacher. As non–stimulated recall researchers, we could take the explanations that best suited our research aims.

Table 3.1 provides an example from our data revealing the "hidden" thoughts obtainable through stimulated recall interviews. Table 3.1 repeats the excerpt from the transcript of a lesson using Telnet to access the local public library from the school's media center. The excerpt is matched with the teacher's reported thoughts obtained during the stimulated recall interviews. What became apparent in our study were the differences in the thoughts reported as occurring during the task performance by the teacher-librarian in comparison with those verbalized during that teaching-learning session. Table 3.1 helps clarify this point while simultaneously revealing the volume of thoughts. Additionally, table 3.1 provides a clear example of the benefits of stimulated recall interviews as a research tool for understanding teacher actions and interactions.

The stimulated recall interviews confirm some of our earlier supposi-

Table 3.1. Comparison of Teacher-Librarian's Verbalizations and Thoughts

Excerpt Video Transcript	Transcript of Teacher-Librarian's Reported Thoughts
TL[a]: So, you will be able to go to the public library if we find some books of poetry by her [the author] to be able to check out a book or make a copy of a poem to use in your presentation? **S[c]:** Yeah. On Saturday. **TL:** Okay.	**TL:** Okay, right here I was thinking, "Is she really serious about the project or does she just want to participate in learning about the technology?" That was when I asked the question. I wanted to be sure that when she was trying to locate the materials that she really was approaching this in terms of it's something I'm going to use. **1st I[b]:** So you said you wanted to be sure. Did you think that? Did you think: "I want to be sure that when she . . ." or what were you thinking [pause]? **TL:** I was thinking: "Is she really going to use what we find today or is this just an interesting little thing that she's participating in?"
TL: Besides this project, you are going to be getting ready to do the research report on a woman before Ms. Petty goes on maternity leave. Then Ms. Mullins is taking over the unit on women. And at that point, we will come back and work with computer databases.	**2nd I:** What were you thinking at that point? **1st I:** When you were watching the student's face? **TL:** I was thinking she didn't know she was going to do this. I know that I was thinking that I was still glad I was telling this because my reasoning behind it was that I wanted her to know that she was going to have another opportunity to use this [database]. So I was thinking that I wanted to be sure that she knows that I want her to remember what I'm fixing to show her because she's going to use it again and again and again.

[a] TL indicates teacher-librarian.
[b] 1st I and 2nd I indicate two interviewers and the order in which they asked questions.
[c] S indicates student.

tions but certainly not all. Let's examine the teacher-librarian's reported thoughts.

The teacher-librarian did not report thinking of changing what she had decided to do in the lesson if the student had not answered "yes." Rather, her initial thoughts centered on her intention to find out about the student's commitment to her project versus wanting to know how to conduct a search via the Internet. (This lesson's objective, using the Internet to access the public library, was established earlier in the lesson.) Her thoughts then returned to the seriousness of the student's commitment to using any resources found during the search.

After our interview prompt querying whether her statements were what she had been thinking, the teacher-librarian reiterated these thoughts; they reveal that her "Okay" was not an acceptance that the student would go to the library. She remained undecided about what the student intended. This affected her next statement (see table 3.1). She reported thoughts that stressed her aim was to reinforce the student's awareness that the Internet access skills taught during the lesson would be used by the student repeatedly, and that the student should remember those access strategies.

After interpreting the surprise on the student's face, the teacher-librarian reported being aware that the student had had no prior knowledge of future projects. She remained convinced, however, that her strategy of advising the student was sound as it met her purpose of reinforcing the necessity to take the lesson seriously. Without a stimulated recall interview with the student, researchers would have no way of knowing if the teacher-librarian's aim was interpreted correctly by the student. We could only assume that the student would have clued into the teacher-librarian's message—you will use the skills I teach you today so take what we do today seriously!

The focus of this book is the identification of the teachers' mental models to help inform our understanding of the teaching role of teacher-librarians. We leave the cause-effect combination of the teacher-student interactions to another book or articles. However (in case you are curious), the student did report that the she went to the public library nearly every Saturday morning and that she took no notice of the teacher-librarian's admonishment. Her thoughts were focused on whether Ms. Petty would have a girl or boy, whether her new teacher would be as good as Ms. Petty, and, crucially, whether she and the new teacher would get along.

From table 3.1 and the above exploration, stimulated recall allowed us to identify the teacher-librarian's mental models, as outlined in the next chapter, from coding and categorizing what they reported as their thoughts during the actual lesson. As we can see in table 3.1, these cause-effect relationships do not necessarily stand alone. They can, and usually do, interconnect. For example, the teacher-librarian's last statement was influenced by the skeptical thoughts she had during the first interchange with the student. Her thoughts about her last statement were also influenced by the student's non-verbals as well as her own thoughts rationalizing her continued efforts to make the student aware of the forthcoming projects even though she realized it was new information for the student.

It is timely to reiterate a number of strengths of stimulated recall process tracing methods that we have surveyed before examining concerns voiced about stimulated recall methodology. The stimulated recall method:

- has theoretical support as it is embedded within an information processing-mediating processes-introspection theoretical framework;

- is useful as a research tool to elicit mental models utilized during task performance;
- strengthens reliability in that the data correlate well with behavior;
- is less intrusive on thought processes than the concurrent verbal reporting of think-aloud methods;
- helps overcome problems associated with eliciting expert knowledge-in-action;
- assists in keeping pace with the participant's thinking through pausing the video;
- diminishes researcher misrepresentation because data are not based on assuming what is going on in the participant's head through observation or discourse analysis of participant actions and verbalizations.

ISSUES OF VALIDITY AND RELIABILITY

It is worth remembering that no methodology is without critics and no methodological tool without limitations (see Gass and Mackey, 2000). It would be as foolish to claim infallibility for introspective reports as it would for other perceptual reporting such as various types of questionnaires. Because stimulated recall is a particularly useful research tool, its full potential is obtained when it is used with knowledge of not only its strengths but also its limitations. Stimulated recall has been criticized most notably on the issue of reliability (see Ericsson and Simon, 1993; Lyons, 1986; Nisbett and Wilson, 1977; Smagorinsky, 1994).

Validity

According to Schwandt (1997), arguing that the findings of a study have validity is to say "that the findings are in fact (or must be) true and certain"; that is, that "they accurately represent the phenomena to which they refer" and "are backed by evidence—or warranted—and there are no good grounds for doubting the findings or the evidence for the findings in question is stronger than the evidence for alternative findings" (p. 168). In our study we follow the position of "fallibilistic validity" where validity is "a test of whether an account accurately represents the social phenomena to which it refers. Yet, no claim is made that an account actually 'reproduces' an independently existing reality or that a valid account is absolutely certain" (Schwandt, 1997, p. 169). We maintained the plausibility of our account through our rigorous data collection procedures, our double-recording of all interviews through audio means, and videotaping the actual teaching/learning session. We also used triangulation of the two researchers' observations and debriefing thoughts; separate coding of the transcribed interviews and lesson with consultation on the analysis or elimination of data in case we could not agree, which rarely happened; multiple interviews (pre-, stimulated recall, and post-) based on comparable probes for the pre- and post-interviews; and the videotaped teaching/learning episode. For the videotaped episode, we used two-camera technology that allowed us to film and audio record the participants' speech, actions, and reactions along with the events on the computer screen via a split-screen format for replay of a matched set of data. Finally, we claim the use of extremely strict protocol for the stimulated recall retrieval of in-action thoughts, which was repeated for all of our stimulated recall interviews, as an additional safeguard for the validity of our study and findings.

Additionally, Merriam and Simpson (1995) discussed validity in internal and external terms. They described internal validity as the measure of congruency that research findings have with reality. They indicated that qualitative inquiry assumes that "there are multiple, changing realities" (p. 101). To their thinking, "reality is constructed by individuals. Thus in qualitative research the understanding of reality is really the researcher's interpretation of someone else's interpretation" (pp. 101–102). Further, "because qualitative researchers are the primary instruments for data collection and analysis, interpretations of reality are accessed directly through observations and interviews" (p. 102). Researchers are closer to reality not having the quantitative instrument interjected between them and the researched. They suggested that researchers could use several methods to "get as close to reality as possible." As indicated above, we triangulate our data and use multiple methods to confirm the emerging findings. We also immersed the "member-check" within our data collection by providing participants with multiple chances to reflect on their actions and resulting events during the teaching/learning sessions.

Recall Accuracy

Recall accuracy is a reliability issue. Bloom's (1954) stimulated recall study is particularly relevant here. He found that if recalls were prompted with aids within two days of the task, recall was 95 percent accurate but declined to 65 percent two weeks later. Reder's (1982) and particularly Gardiner and Parkin's (1990) experiments supported Bloom's findings. Reder's research revealed that when memory traces are fresh, then retrieval of the exact memory is easier and faster than if memory has "faded" due to an intervening time gap. Gardiner and Parkin found significantly fewer cognitive events were recalled two days following the event than were reported on the day of the event; the longer the gap, the greater likelihood of plausible and explanatory statements.

As researchers have revealed, schematic and causal-inferential gap-filling errors occur the longer the time frame between the event and the recall (e.g., Friedman, 1979; Hannigan and Reinitz, 2001; Waldmann, Holyoak, and Fratianne, 1995). Such errors occur when we compensate for failing to recover specific details about a past episode by drawing inferences and then mistake these inferences for something that we had experienced. Errors also occur when we fill in omissions that were not present because they are typical of that kind of situation (Friedman, 1979; Hannigan and Reinitz, 2001). For instance, we incorrectly recalled that "www" appeared in the following Web address, http://imp.jcu.edu.au. Because "www" nearly always appears in Web addresses, we expected it to be there. Jenkins and Tuten (1998) postulated that such memory inaccuracies occur because a fundamental goal of cognition is to make coherent sense of the world.

Recall accuracy is also a neural issue. Posner (1992) pointed out that some memory types could decay after thirty minutes. Given the focus of the book, it is unnecessary to elaborate this neural issue here. Its importance for our discussion is that it provides further evidence that recall accuracy diminishes as a function of the intervening time between the event and the recall.

In summary, stimulated recall methods have a satisfactory degree of reliability for obtaining data about the thoughts participants had while performing that task if the stimulated recall interview is conducted within a forty-eight-hour time frame. In our wider study, all stimulated recall interviews commenced within fifteen minutes of the videotaped teaching-learning episode for each student and within seventy minutes for each teacher-librarian (see table 3.2 later in this chapter). Based on Færch and Kasper's (1987) categorization, both these stimulated recall interviews are designated as "immediate consecutive recall" because of the short time lapse between the videotaped lesson and the stimulated recall interview. Depending on the intervening time span between the event and the stimulated recall, researchers are open to criticism in terms of what is being accessed and the claims they make about their findings in their analysis.

Ericsson and Simon (1987) contended that their model predicts that the immediate consecutive retrospective reports on the preceding cognitive activity can be accessed and recalled without the interviewer providing specific instructions about what to retrieve. The participant will have the necessary retrieval cues in short-term memory once a general instruction is given. The type we used in our study was, "We are interested in what you were thinking. What we want you to do in this interview is to tell us everything you were thinking during the lesson. If you cannot remember what you had been thinking, that is okay." This instruction conforms to Ericsson and Simon's recommendation. In effect, this type of instruction should help ensure that "the retrospective verbal report would give the closest approximation to the actual memory structures" utilized by the teachers and students during the lesson (Ericsson and Simon, 1987, p. 41).

Russo, Johnson, and Stevens (1989) also addressed this issue of instruction versus training, and cautioned that instructions given by the interviewer need to minimize any threat to the methodology itself. More specific directions, such as "Please tell me your thoughts about what strategies you used and why you used them," are open to claims of recall contamination. In Ethell and McMeniman's (2000) study, the instructions required multiple tasks of the male teacher who was asked "to walk the researcher through the lesson, stopping the video at any point where he would like to elaborate on what he was thinking, how he was feeling, or what thinking, beliefs, knowledge, or theories influenced any in-class decisions and observable teaching practices" (p. 93). Ericsson and Simon (1993) warned that by asking participants to vocalize their thoughts as well as to explain them, the additional cognitive load may interfere with memory and recall. We previously noted that the think-aloud technique requires training to enable the participant to verbalize their thoughts as they complete a task. Stimulated recall requires a simple generalized instruction of the type used in our study rather than participant training.

Types of Prompts and Thoughts

Artifact Prompt

The use of an artifact prompt (figure 3.2) is supported by experimental research. For instance, Bloom (1954) and Ericsson and Simon (1987) asserted that the accuracy of participants' recall is maximized if they are presented with all possible cues or stimuli that occurred during the original situation. Thomson and Tulving (1970) argued that memory is better when the conditions that existed at the time of the task (or event) are reinstated at retrieval because "memory consists of storing information [e.g., a mental model] along with a retrieval plan. The retrieval plan is constructed during learning so that when provided with certain elements of the original learning context it can determine the location of the stored information [in a mental model]" (Shulman, 1997, paragraph 5). In our case, such research strongly suggests that when our teacher-librarians were vividly reminded of the information literacy computer database lesson by means of the video of the lesson, then the event itself, and many of the thoughts that occurred during the event, were recalled. Figure 3.2

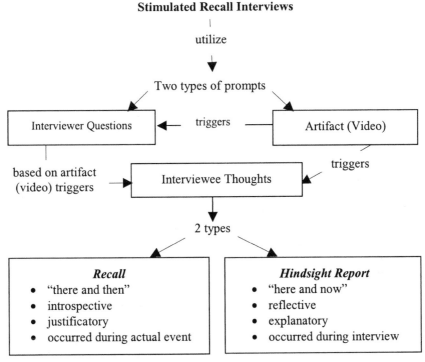

Figure 3.2. Types of Prompts and Thoughts Accessed in Stimulated Recall

delineates the types of prompts and the types of thoughts triggered by stimulated recall interviewing.

We used a video of each lesson as the artifact prompt (figure 3.2). Other artifact prompts can be an audiotape of the event, a replay of the computer software used during the event, or the writing sample produced during the task activity. Our use of a video replicated common practice. Pausawasdi's (2001) representative survey of research utilizing stimulated recall between 1995 and 2001 revealed that the artifact prompt is usually a video of the event. Like most stimulated recall interview researchers who use videotapes, we typically employed split-screen techniques to stimulate recall. One camera recorded what was on the computer screen while the second camera captured both the teacher's and the student's verbal and non-verbal actions. The two cameras were connected to a special videotaping apparatus. The images from the two cameras were put through a video mixer so that they both appeared on the same TV monitor that was used to replay the videotape during the interview. Each camera's images covered half of the TV monitor's screen and were positioned vertically side by side on the screen so that the cause-effect relationship between the participants and what was happening on the computer was apparent. Such a split-screen video prompt—revealing the participants' actions, questions, comments, directions, and non-verbals and what occurred as a consequence of their actions on the computer screen during the lesson—is perceived as a memory retrieval cue with high associative strength and is, therefore, more likely to trigger accurate memory recall. Thus, in order to maximize full stimulated recall, participants need to see and hear both the instructional stimuli and themselves simultaneously on one TV monitor.

The video documents the participant-in-action. When and how they did and said what they did can be triggered by viewing the split-screen video of the teaching-learning session. The video is described as a more reliable instrument to capture the "artful routines" (Karasti, 2000) of the participant than think-aloud, observations, interactional analysis, and discourse analysis. Viewing the video replay renders "the participants' practices as both extraordinary, through distancing them from their daily routines, and yet recognizable to evoke participants' memories of their experiences" during the videoed session (Karasti, 2000). Eliciting participant thoughts based on re-engaging with their teaching-in-action through the video prompt has the advantage of staying close to the actual events in the sequence they occurred. Indeed, a number of studies (e.g., Barrows, 2000; Dunkin, Welch, Merritt, Phillips, and Craven, 1998; McMeniman et al., 2001; Meade and McMeniman, 1992) have indicated that, because the stimulated recall video presents participants with their recent actions, it helps diminish "superficial self-presentation" (Parsons, Graham, and Honess, 1983, p. 95). This maximizes the reliability and accuracy of the interviewee's recalled thoughts (Bloom, 1954; Ericsson and Simon, 1998).

Interview Question Prompt (Figure 3.2)

Gass and Mackey (2000) contended that researchers' questions and responses are "the most serious of difficulties" (p. 89) as they have the potential to compromise the data. Exposure of the participant's thoughts through adherence to tested protocols helps maximize reliability and credibility of recall. These protocols involve attention to non-directive questioning, interviewer versus participant initiation of responses, interviewer training, the timing of questions, and checking to ascertain recall versus the plausible story.

The nature of the interviewer's prompt is an important reliability and credibility issue in participant recall and researcher bias. Prompts are used to focus respondents so that they can access their memory and then vocalize what it was that they were thinking during the activity. If the interviewer's prompts are non-directive, such as in our study ("What were you thinking then?" or "Can you recall your thoughts when you asked that question?"), there is a high likelihood of obtaining reliability and accuracy of recall. If prompts are more directive, such as those used in the McMeniman et al.'s, (2001) study ("What is the basis for your using this technique/directing the lesson in this way?"; p. 389), then the participant is keyed by the prompts to report those thoughts that align with the research focus. There is a greater likelihood of the participant reporting and creating plausible stories as explanation rather than recalling what they actually remember thinking.

Aside from their emphasis on non-directedness, Gass and Mackey (2000) commented that "unstructured situations do not always result in useful data" (p. 55). In our research, this has not been the case. Our prompts followed the strict protocols adapted from Marland et al. (1992) and tested in subsequent research (Henderson and Pausawasdi, 2000; Henderson, Putt, Ainge, and Coombs, 1997; Putt, Patching, and Henderson, 1996). Our data revealed that we avoided keying the participants in the stimulated recall interview (or in the pre-interview) by mentioning "mental models," yet our data are rich and thick; indeed, the in-action mental models identified in the stimulated recall transcripts were grounded in that data. What our experience suggests is that researchers can take confidence in open non-directedness in terms of instructions and prompts rather than trade off reliability and credibility against the fear of not obtaining thoughts about their specific research focus. The enhanced self-observation post-interview provides a solution to such a trade-off.

Even though we have labeled the prompt as "the interviewer's questions" (see figure 3.2), it is not as definitive as this. Indeed, the participant or the researcher or both can initiate the recall. All are accepted stimulated recall practices. Some researchers, such as Ethell and McMeniman (2000), McMeniman et al. (2001), and Ritchie (1999), required the participants to stop the video and report their thoughts. Where the participants stopped the video and the areas of their focus were coded as significant identifiers of what was important or noticeable to the participant. When researchers only control where and when to stop the video to prompt the participant, they could be channeling the participant to areas that are perhaps more meaningful to the research aims.

For instance, Mackey, Gass, and McDonough (as cited in Gass and Mackey, 2002) chose those segments for replay that contained content that was the focus of their study. When both the researcher and participant stop the video, there is greater likelihood of obtaining a more thorough recall of what the participants had been thinking. We advocate that researchers be involved in the process of pausing the video, especially when they realize that the participant is not going to do so. The number of recalled thoughts that ensued from when we stopped the video far outweighed the times when the participants replied that they could not remember what they were thinking. It was not uncommon for a teacher-librarian to say something similar to the following statement as she pointed to the video image at which we had paused: "Hey! This thinking stuff really works. I really did think that there!" Valuable data would have been lost if we had allowed the participant to take sole control.

Further support is provided by Vermersch (1999) who asserted that participants verbalize less by themselves than they would with a media-tor—that is, the interviewer. He argued that retrospection methodology is "based upon a mediator whose aim is to help in the unfolding of the internal act making possible access to the [prior] lived experience" (para-graph 68). In essence, the participant will recall thoughts that occurred during that event through interviewer guidance in the process of prompt-ing the participant's verbalization of these thoughts.

Types of Thoughts Accessed

Both the video and interview question prompts trigger the participant's thoughts. As depicted in figure 3.2, there are two types of thoughts recalled during stimulated recall interviews, which we have labeled "recall thoughts" and "hindsight thoughts." The recall thoughts occurred during the performance of the task, the "there and then" or retrospective thoughts, whereas the hindsight thoughts occurred during the interview, the "here and now" or interpretive thoughts.

The participants report their recalled thoughts. The recalled thoughts are those that they report they had during a preceding event, which in our case was the videoed teaching and learning information literacy les-son. Some of these "there-and-then" thoughts provide their reasoning and justification for what they were thinking at that particular time in the lesson. We label these in-action thoughts. In contrast, the hindsight thoughts are those that are a spontaneous response to what the partici-pants are seeing on the video. They are thoughts that are only now, an hour after the lesson, occurring to the teacher-librarian. Although sponta-neous, they are reflective as they are hindsight interpretations, explana-tions, rationalizations, and descriptions of their actions, verbalizations, and non-verbals during the videotaped event. Sometimes it is about what they did not do, say, or think during that event. These hindsight thoughts necessarily retrieve information from long-term memory as it stores the mental models of past actions, thoughts, and ideas that are drawn upon to argue, explain, clarify, justify, and describe their actions and thoughts during the event. Why, then, have the former reasoning and justification of thoughts not been categorized as hindsight thoughts? The crucial iden-tifier is that the justification of their recalled thoughts had to have

occurred during the actual lesson. If they had, then they are correctly designated as recall "there-and-then" thoughts.

The following stimulated recall interview excerpt from another lesson
with different participants permits an effortless identification of the recall
versus the hindsight thoughts recalled by a teacher-librarian:

> I was thinking that he needed to decide what resource he
> wanted to use, that he knew the assignment, and I was think-   Recall
> ing that I was not really sure as to whether he might possibly
> need some current information. ‖ You know, in retrospect, I
> would not have given him the choice. I would have directed.
> And I think this is a case where knowing the child, I made   Hindsight
> some assumptions about his decision making that were incor-
> rect.

In the example, the teacher-librarian reported two types of thoughts triggered by the video: recall thoughts that had occurred during the lesson
and hindsight thoughts that were only just occurring to the teacher-librarian as she was being interviewed.

As we have seen, trusting the reliability of verbal data is partly dependent on the amount of the participant's interpretation versus pure content
of memory (Pressley and Afflerbach, 1995). It is important to determine
that there is recall as opposed to a verbal report; this, after all, is the basis
of stimulated recall. Interviewees in stimulated recall sessions often seek
to evaluate, rationalize, and reflect on their behaviors, generate alternative
strategies, indicate their goals, or outline their beliefs (Marland, Patching,
and Putt, 1992). This should not be handled negatively or judgmentally
and, as we elaborate later, these hindsight thoughts are useful to ascertain
the participants' reflective mental models. Even so, there remains an obligation on the part of the researcher to be vigilant about distinguishing
between participants' reports, which provide hindsight reasons and justifications for their thoughts or thought sequences, and those that simply
report those thoughts and reasoning that occurred during the lesson. For
instance, during one of our stimulated recall interviews, a teacher-librarian justified her teaching strategy: "So, at that point I realized he was not
searching properly, so I took over . . ." after which we nodded under-
standingly and prompted: "Can you remember what you were actually
thinking then when you realized he was not searching properly and you
took over?" Of course, if participants reply that they cannot recall what
they were thinking, we accepted this without question. As we mentioned
earlier, all thoughts are not obtainable for recall.

Both types of reported thoughts—the recall and hindsight thoughts—
can be profitably utilized (see Pausawasdi, 2002). We treated the hindsight

thoughts during the stimulated recall interview in the same way we did the participants' statements during the enhanced self-observation post-interview. The major stipulation is that during discussion about the participants' thinking, researchers must acknowledge the type of thinking accessed and reported—recall or hindsight—to maintain reliability and credibility of the researcher's assertions.

Interviewer Training

The discussion of the interview prompts (the video and questioning) and the types of thoughts and mental models obtained during stimulated recall highlights the crucial role of the interviewer. Vermersch (1999) argued that researchers (rather than interviewees as with think-aloud methods) undergo training in the conduct of stimulated recall interviews in order to maximize accuracy and reliability of recall. Vermersch sees this apprenticeship as essential in retrospective introspective methodologies. A number of researchers have enumerated guidelines for the conduct of stimulated recall interviews (for instance, Ericsson and Simon, 1999; Gass and Mackey, 2000; Marland, Patching, and Putt, 1992). These guidelines also provide structure for the neophyte researcher. Our research paid particular attention to the recommendations by Marland et al. (1992) who advocated that certain protocols and question types are asked at different stages during the interview.

First, to promote effective recall, participants need to feel comfortable enough to report their thoughts during the interview. Proficient implementation of the interviewer role depends on establishing rapport, mutual trust, and respect through being supportive and non-evaluative. This type of methodology demands good listening skills and non-verbals that demonstrate engagement with what the participant is saying. Participants should correctly believe that they are capable of telling the interviewer about their thoughts and cognitive processes. They, after all, are the authority on their cognitive processes during the task or activity. The researcher is learning from them.

Second, the timing of the question prompt is triggered by what is occurring in the video replay of the actual event. For instance, a change in task, a question asked by the teacher-librarian or student during the lesson, obtaining or not obtaining relevant WWW hits, hiccups with the technology, and non-verbals all provide an observable point of reference that may prompt recall. The first question prompt, something like "Can you tell us what you were thinking as the lesson was about to begin?," usually occurs during the first few seconds into watching the video replay. This is because, at the commencement of any lesson, there is a marking-time phase when both teacher and student are settling down.

The purpose of asking this type of question at this point is to lessen any tension that might exist for the participants. It is also important to mention that they should report any thought even if it is not related to the lesson. This is to help ensure that the interviewee does not censor and select "appropriate" comments for reporting. In our study, we had incidences where teacher-librarians reported such things as "I was thinking about the computer technician coming." Naturally, such reporting allows analysis that reflects the laps in attention that is a normal feature of people's attention span (Gilroy, 1998; Middendorf and Kalish, 1996).

Third, subsequent invitations to verbalize their thoughts are prompted by questions such as: "What were you thinking about as you did that?"; "What were you thinking about at that point?"; and, once the participant is familiar with the type and range of questions, the prompt can be occasionally truncated to: "Any thoughts?"

Fourth, confirmatory questions are used in stimulated recall interviews when the interviewer wants to confirm that the answers are thoughts that occurred during the learning session, but not during the interview. Questions in this category include: "Were you thinking that back then during the lesson or did you just think that now?"; "That is what you were thinking about during the actual lesson?"; and "Did you think all that during the lesson or some of it then and some of it now?" If the latter, probe to clarify what part was a recall and what part was a hindsight thought. Of course, other studies would substitute the relevant activity instead of "lesson."

Fifth, during the interview, there might be some silent moments when interviewees do not report any thoughts. In these situations, the interviewer needs to encourage the interviewees to report their thoughts and feelings. Prompts like: "Was your mind a blank?" lead the interviewee to opt out rather than try to recall their thoughts. However, questions such as "Can you tell me what you were thinking during those last one or two minutes?" can help trigger the line of thought during the silent moments.

Sixth, self-disclosure of the accuracy and quantity of their thoughts at the end of the stimulated recall interview assists in providing some, albeit subjective, gauge of the participant's recall processing. For example, questions like "About how much of your thinking during the lesson do you think you reported?" resulted in teacher-librarian comments like: "I really think about 90 percent" or "Most" or "I know I thought some things but I couldn't remember them to tell you." "How accurate has your self-reporting been?" obtained the following answers from the teacher-librarians: "Pretty accurate; I remember thinking that I was surprised at how accurate" or "I think I didn't do too badly." When we asked, "Is there anything about your thinking that you want to tell me about now?," it brought forth statements like: "Well, I know I was supposed to report my thinking but, being a teacher, I couldn't stop giving you some reasons for why I was thinking that." Obviously, such self-reporting is susceptible to respondents providing answers that they think will make them "look better" or those they surmise the researcher wants to hear. Nevertheless this type of self-disclosure can be used by the researcher when interpreting the data and making claims about the level of recall and its accuracy. Validating introspection in multiple ways is a fundamental issue of reliability.

At the end of the interview, the interviewer may ask questions to confirm the accuracy of the reported thoughts and to trigger thoughts that the interviewees might have forgotten to report. Questioning in this situation should include some of the following sorts of questions: "Were there any thoughts that you did not tell us?"; "Were there any occasions when your self-reporting was inaccurate or partly inaccurate?"; and "Is there anything else about your thinking during the lesson that you would like to tell me about now?"

These types of non-leading questions help the participant to ensure that reports are as complete and accurate as possible. As Pausawasdi (2002) pointed out, this is because students' reports are used as raw data for analysis and discussion. Thus, implementing appropriate steps to help ensure accuracy and completeness is a central part of maximizing validity, reliability and trustworthiness of the research.

Participant Fatigue

Participant fatigue can also affect data reliability. We were conscious of this, given the sequence of consecutive data collection instruments as delineated in table 3.2. Although the book explores the mental models of the teacher-librarians, the inclusion of the students' research commitments in table 3.2 allows a holistic overview of this crucial part of the total research process. The purpose of chatting with the student participants while they played with the videotaping equipment (table 3.2) was to establish a degree of rapport for the interviews and comfortableness when videoing the lesson. The teacher-librarian's pre-interview occurred before the student arrived in order to shorten the time the student would be out of the classroom. For this reason, as well as to maximize student recall and alertness, the teacher-librarian's stimulated recall interview always occurred after that of the student. After the fifteen- to thirty-minute teaching-learning episode (whose length depended on the nature of both the student's task and the teacher-librarian's interpretation of what information literacy strategies she would target), the stimulated recall interview (with variable times dependent on the length of the videoed lesson), and a ten- to forty-five-minute post-interview (with the longer

Table 3.2. Sequence and Physical Location of Interview Activities with Participants

Pre-interviews with Teacher-Librarians	Introduce Students to Research	Pre-interviews with Students	Videotaped Lesson	Stimulated Recall Interview with Students	Stimulated Recall Interview with Teacher-Librarians	Enhanced Stimulated Recall Post-Interview
15 minutes	10 minutes	10 minutes	15–30 minutes	20–45 minutes	60 minutes	10–45 minutes
• Location in library office	• Location in library • Chatting • Showing students cameras and tape decks • Allowed students to use the camera	• Location in library adjacent to where lesson occurred • Semi-private to put students at ease	• In section of library where computers located, replicating normal practice • Backs to other users to avoid distractions	• Located in library office • Isolated from outside distractions • Privacy for replaying the lesson video and audiotaping the interview • Set-up split-screen videotape and TV monitor equipment		• Continued directly after stimulated recall interview in same location and with the same isolation

times recorded by teachers) occurred. The following strategies helped our participants to prevent or diminish fatigue.

We kept the pre-interview questionnaire to the essentials; trialing the instrument proved beneficial. Administering the questionnaire in a different location from the teaching-learning videoed session location offered a mental space that was quiet, calm, and away from what was to come (see table 3.2). The participants were very aware of the two cameras and other technical equipment involved with the stimulated recall interviews. Using an alternative location for the pre-interview also provided for some physical activity in moving to another location. After the videoed lesson, the teacher-librarians had time in which to move around or go to the rest room before the stimulated recall interview while the equipment was set up (see below for details) in the glassed-in office. The enhanced post-interview obtained some psychological distance to mark its difference from the stimulated recall interview simply by the participant and interviewer turning away from the TV monitor to focus on each other. The enhanced post-interview was now the "final leg" and, if fatigue was noticeable, balance occurred between asking the essential questions as determined by the researcher and deep exploration of the participant's answers. Finishing the session or asking participants if they needed a break was another possibility. The teacher-librarian participants reported that fatigue did not become an issue in our study.

A particular advantage of having two researchers was the ability of one researcher to rectify the situation if the other researcher prompted the participant with a leading question. The strategy was simply to ask after the participant's reply what the participant had been thinking during the event (that had triggered the first researcher's biased prompt). We had a few examples of this in our data. Another advantage of having two researchers during stimulated recall occurred when, as occasionally happened, the participant appeared to bond with one researcher more than the other. The latter then deliberately "blended into the background" and allowed her research partner to adopt the dominant role.

Even with researcher vigilance, stimulated recall interviews could go awry (Gass and Mackey, 2000). Being aware of participant fatigue and its relationship to researcher prompts and recall accuracy helped us buttress data reliability and fallibilistic validity. Considerations of fatigue with respect to the length of the recall support—that is, how much of the video was replayed—was a further issue considered by the researchers. The aims of a study dictate whether the whole videotape was replayed, just segments were played, or sections were fast-forwarded so that researcher and participant could still see what was happening and have the option to stop or, if necessary, to rewind. The rule of thumb was thirty minutes of a videoed session equated to sixty minutes for the stimulated recall interview. In our study, we replayed the video in its entirety because the research did not have a priori mental model categories. The stipulation was that how the video was played was standardized for all participants.

Transcription Protocols

Once the stimulated recall data were collected, there were a number of steps involved in the analysis process: transcription of the video and stimulated recall audio tapes, coding the data, reporting the results, and discussion. Transcripts were word-processed verbatim from audiotapes of the stimulated recall interview. It was not uncommon for the videotape to be included in the transcription, particularly if the talk during the lesson was important to the research aims, as it was in our study. If the task involved computer software, it was advantageous to include any voice-overs or sounds from the software that were heard on the audiotape in all transcripts. Another notation method was to include the beginning and end of attributed quotes from the videotape. This was helpful, particularly if the coder (or rater) was not present during the interview. An example from our research is as follows: "L on video: xxx . . . xxx." This made it easier for the researcher to match the participant's transcribed stimulated recall interview comments with the transcripts of the video. Without the computer cues or the participants' voices embedded in the transcripts, trying to align exactly the specific videotaped event or nonverbal with the researcher's prompt and the participant's thoughts in the stimulated recall transcripts could have been a difficult task. This was particularly so with multiple participants and, as in our case, different database software was used as well as a delay between the interview, transcription, data coding, and analysis. Researcher memory was fantastic but not perfect!

Coding

The stimulated recall transcripts were then divided into episodes or interactional features, if that were appropriate for answering the research questions. An episode or turn boundary consisted of the dialogue between interviewer and participant relating to one point or idea unit in the videotaped episode. Episodes or segments are broader categories than coding identification. It is often a preparatory stage to coding. It also avoids counting a repetition or continuation of the same mental model or teaching strategy twice and inflating their occurrences in the data and analysis. They are usually easy to identify and can be confirmed jointly by the coders before each takes the transcript for coding. This can assist with inter-rater coding reliability.

Coding schemes are also determined by the research focus and aims. Sometimes the coding scheme adopts a top-down technique based on established categories from previous research. Instances of this are the studies concerned with identification of the mediating processes used by students and teachers when learning with various mediums. The mediating processes were based on the nineteen identified in Marland, Patching, and Putt's (1992) research and added to by Henderson (1996) and Pausawasdi (2002). McMeniman and colleague's (2001) coding used Shulman's (1987) general pedagogical knowledge categorization of teacher knowledge as refined and extended by Meade and McMeniman (1992) to include management, planning, and strategic applications. These two examples highlight the importance of flexibility when coding.

To emphasize the difference from the top-down scheme, "bottom-up" coding schemes emerge from the data as the categories are identified from the data themselves. For instance, from the stimulated recall transcript of one teacher-librarian we categorized her mental model of the student as a procrastinator based on her reported thoughts when she realized that the student had not conducted any research for her class assignment:

> I was thinking that she would have had most of this done and that this [the information literacy lesson to access the public library online catalog] would be frosting. . . . I was thinking that I had assumed that she had already explored everything here because the classroom teacher had brought them to the media center and I thought that she would have tried to locate all that was available.

Our categorization was confirmed through checking her other thoughts about the student that were articulated during the remainder of the stimulated recall interview and against her reflections during her post-interview.

Coding participant thoughts is not just a matter of the type of scheme implemented and corroboration of categories from supporting data sources. Examination of the nature of the interviewer's prompt and rater and inter-rater reliability are central to the accuracy of researcher claims and analysis of the stimulated recall data. As much as it is painful to do so, if the coding reveals a leading prompt that directed the participant's thoughts in a specific direction, then the participant's thought is discarded as an instance of that category.

Rater and Inter-Rater Reliability

On the one hand, if the researcher conducts the interviews, codes, and analyzes the data, this could cause concern about the subjectivity of the interpretation. One problem may be that researchers could read too much into the data because of their expectations about the data and their research aims. On the other hand, because the transcriber is usually not the researcher and therefore not present during the interview, the transcripts would lack inclusion of non-verbal indicators, such as the smile and thumbs-up sign when the computer connected with the Internet after a number of false starts, as occurred in our study. Then, compounding the transcription problem, if the coder or "rater" had not participated in the stimulated recall interview, categorization would not reflect these nuances that changed the meaning of the participant's words. Gass and Mackey (2000, p. 65) described such a scenario. However, because the non-verbal data would be part of the recall criteria used by the researcher when coding the data, the coding and analysis should be more accurate than the objective outside rater.

Employing independent raters to code the data is common practice with stimulated recall (and think-aloud) studies. The coders are given training that can take up to three days, according to Gass and Mackey (2000), who detailed an intensive sample training program. The purpose of independent raters is to instill confidence that the researchers' coding will also be found by the outside raters. Inter-rater reliability is then carried out by randomly assessing the coding of all raters for consistency. We adopted a method that has been tested for coding reliability in the studies by researchers at James Cook University based on the Marland, Patching, and Putt (1992) protocols. It is a method that can be used when funding is not available for intensive research support and training, as is so often the case.

As the researcher-coders, we jointly coded one transcript, deciding on the episodes and negotiating the categorization based on a priori mental model categories as well as categories that emerged from the data. We next decided on the episodes in a second transcript before coding them individually. Returning to a joint session, we matched our categories and provided rationales for any coding that differed. A categorization was accepted when we agreed. When after a long debate we could not agree, the data and category were discarded, like those obtained from researcher prompts that "led" the participant.

Identification of new categories received the same treatment. We next met after we had coded two to four transcripts to check the full coding for these transcripts. We revisited previously coded transcripts to double-check what we had coded and if the original or the new category were correct or acceptable. In this way, we also increased standardization of coding that occurred over time. We found that our coding achieved very high inter-rater reliability (95.6 percent) as we progressed. It was time-consuming but we argue that this process of authentication helped secure a high degree of inter-rater reliability and less subjective interpretation.

Summary of Protocols and Reliability

Counteracting potential limitations when conducting and analyzing the data strengthens reliability and credibility of data results, analysis, and interpretation. We advocate the following procedures as summarized in stimulated recall research and note how our study matched these.

- If the stimulated recall interview is conducted immediately after the event being recalled, but definitely within forty-five hours, it strengthens accuracy of recall. We conducted consecutive stimulated recall interviews (within seventy minutes of the lesson) with the teacher-librarians. (We conducted the stimulated recall interviews first with the students, hence the delay with the teacher-librarians.) This time frame helped capture recall thoughts before an unacceptable level of memory decay and contamination by intervening events.
- Rather than requesting simultaneous justification, explanation, and/or specifically targeting the research questions, minimalized generalized instructions about what is required of the participant during the stimulated recall interview diminishes researcher bias. We provided a simple instruction to our participants to tell us what they had been thinking about during the lesson.
- Maintaining the integrity of interviewer prompts is a further strategy that strengthens the quality of data. Our prompts reiterated our instructions nearly verbatim, using the participants' actions, directions, comments, and non-verbal cues to prompt for their thoughts during the lesson. Our prompts checked that the thoughts they were reporting had actually occurred during the lesson rather than what they were now thinking. We thereby strengthened our confidence that our participants were recalling rather than engaging in verbal reporting.
- The purpose of stimulated recall data analysis is "to identify and classify the verbalizations that shed light on the phenomena being investigated, yet to capture them in a way that is as low in subjectivity as possible" (Gass and Mackey, 2000, p. 100). We identified the categories of mental models empirically from the stimulated recall data to determine the teacher-librarians' mental models-in-action. We strengthened inter-rater coding reliability and lessened subjectivity through, initially, working jointly then individually, confirming our coding on all of the full transcripts and negotiated differences and new categories either of us had identified. We revisited pre-

viously coded transcripts to double-check that our coding was standardized. Whenever a leading prompt was identified, we discarded the participant's response from our data analysis.

CONCLUSION

"Although generating some interesting criticisms . . . stimulated recall is, in general, a methodology that has been subjected to both empirical testing and theoretical review" (Gass and Mackey, 2000, p. 35). The stimulated recall methodology allowed us to identify the thought processes of teacher-librarians and their students during computer information literacy one-on-one lessons that we would have been unable to elicit with the same degree of reliability, credibility, and validity using other introspection methods, lesson observation, or interaction analysis of the lessons. We were able to identify the categories of mental models from the stimulated recall data to ascertain the teachers' mental models-in-action. We then utilized these to compare and contrast with the pre-interview espoused mental models and the reflective mental models from the post-interview. We agree with Barrows (2000, paragraph 4) that, notwithstanding the growing number of studies, "stimulated recall is underutilized because its existence is not generally recognized and its usefulness not appreciated."

4

Mental Models Emphasizing Procedural and Product Goals

It sounds interesting but is it going to be something that will help you with your report? Because I would really like for you to take something away today that you will have written down that you can use for your research. (Anne, videoed lesson)

I prefer not to stand up and, although my background [pause] when I went through teacher training, instruction was delivered and learning took place somehow, was more in a lecture format. I don't think that I was nearly as aware of student response and was not nearly as aware of focus when I began as a teacher. I think the period I grew up in, it was lecture and regurgitation, much more than today. I'm much more comfortable with teaching this way [student-centered] than I was with [the lecture format], and I think it's because I think learning takes place this way. (Anne, post-interview)

Anne is the teacher-librarian in an urban middle school, grade levels sixth through eighth. She received teacher training when lecture and testing was the primary pedagogical model and had spent many years as a classroom teacher and teacher-librarian in other schools. Her training was evident in her mental models, although she espoused a constructivist educational philosophy. Her mental models contained her desire to retain status as the knowledge expert and to retain control of the teacher-student learning sessions. When mistakes and the unforgiving nature of computer operating system commands permeated her second lesson, the one that she assumed would be the easier of the two lessons, she lost her composure and would have preferred to quit the lesson. She did not possess adequate problem-solving skills with electronic technologies to troubleshoot the problems comfortably. Instead, she had to admit to an incomplete mental model that conflicted with her desire to retain her image as knowledge expert. Our stimulated recall sessions with Anne emphasized her deep emotional disappointment with the second lesson and opened her up to a philosophical discussion in the immediate stimulated recall post-interview as to her self-perceived identity as a teacher-librarian and who she would like to be as a teacher and learner.

ESPOUSED PRE-INTERVIEW MENTAL MODELS

From her answers to our open-ended pre-interview questions, we were able to categorize the various mental models Anne espoused. The majority were concerned with her work, the students, and her concepts of herself.

Roles of Teacher-Librarian Mental Models

Table 4.1 demonstrates the espoused mental model categories, labeled appropriately, that we identified from a section of the interview transcript. The italicized parts of the transcript data align with the mental model or models identified in the mental model column. There were a number of mental models being run in parallel during a short time within a particular part of the lesson. It is likely that Anne created a mental model linking fragments of mental models that were distributed in various mental models (DiSessa, 1988). The identified fragments are represented as the mental model dot points in table 4.1 within the overarching mental model. An example of a fragment would be the "finder and provider of resources mental model" embedded as a fragment within the larger mental model of the "teacher-librarian as a resource mental model" (table 4.1).

Anne's pre-interview responses in table 4.1 highlighted her espoused mental models concerning the role and characteristics of the teacher-librarian. One mental model related to time management, as Anne felt that the job "sometimes controlled her" to the extent that tasks were left uncompleted at the end of the day. A second mental model identified responding to on-the-spot emergent needs as a priority, regardless of pre-scheduled tasks. This mental model also alluded to the service role of teacher-librarians. Additionally, besides highlighting the service aspect of her role, one of her mental models demonstrated the importance she attached to her leadership role in the school. We noted from other comments in her pre-interview that the integration of the teacher-librarian

Table 4.1. Espoused Mental Models from the Pre-interview Transcript

Interviewee Transcript	Identified Mental Models (MM)
I come in with an *agenda of things to do* in the morning, and when I look at it in the evening, *nothing has been marked off* of it because my *job has taken me elsewhere*. So, sometimes I'm not as in control as I would like to be.	Time management MM
Nevertheless, I find this very stimulating because often it ends up being totally unplanned. I *go with the moment and what happens, and respond* to it. I have to be a very *flexible* person.	Role as teacher-librarian MM: • Respond to emergent needs MM Self-concept MM • Flexible MM
Sometimes I'm *disappointed* in the *quality of service* that I have given and perhaps in the *quality of leadership* that I have given. There are days I feel very frustrated.	Self-evaluation MM • Characteristic of teacher-librarian MM Roles as teacher-librarian MM: • Service to staff and students MM • Leadership to staff MM
But, I'm finding that the teachers are not just coming to me *to pull books* anymore. They ask, "Do you have any *suggestions of how we could approach* this and *how we could tie it in* with literature?" I'm gradually beginning to get the faculty to accept me as a resource in multiple areas so far as *planning of instruction*.	Role of teacher-librarian as a resource MM: • Finder and provider of resources MM • Instructional curriculum co-planner MM Teacher-librarian as expert MM

into classroom curriculum planning was embedded in this leadership mental model. The comments about her role also suggested that she perceived herself to be an expert in her field and wanted staff to make more use of her skills in a variety of ways. Conversely, she had a mental model of herself as sometimes lacking in areas of her expertise, "I sometimes feel disappointed in the quality of my service and leadership." Her comment indicated a mental model in which self-evaluation was a requisite tool in a teacher's profession.

Product-Oriented Mental Model

A significant mental model within her role as the teacher-librarian focused on the uncompromising need to produce a product (table 4.1). To Anne, this meant providing students with books, journals, a printout of information from, and call numbers of, hard copy resources. Anne believed that to students "something printed out from an electronic data-base seemed more valuable than material from a print resource." This was aligned with another of her espoused mental models, which was the importance of educating students and staff that print and electronic aca-demic sources both had relevance. She advised us that this educative goal was a reason for her participation in the research.

Interestingly, providing printouts, books, or call numbers seemed to be equal priority for her with teachers as it was with students. Anne's co-planning of curriculum, as well as finding resources for her teachers, had an important function in her mental model (table 4.1) with respect to her interactions with a growing number of classroom teachers.

Self-Concept Mental Models

Self-Concept as Teacher-Librarian Mental Model

It appeared that Anne had linked the teacher-librarian role mental mod-els of time management and meeting emergent needs through validating her prioritization of responding to emergent needs. This linking gave emphasis to a self-description of flexibility. This personal characteristic was embedded in her self-concept as a teacher-librarian mental model (table 4.1).

Self-Concept as a Novice with the Internet

Anne had embedded into her espoused mental model of working with the Internet a self-label of being a novice but reported becoming more comfortable with online practice over the two weeks prior to this inter-view. Clearly, her mental model of being "on show" in the videotaped teaching-learning session necessitated practice in order for her to have a greater degree of procedural control with the online database protocols than, perhaps, a complete novice would. Her mental model of the teacher-librarian as the knowledge expert supported the need for practice.

Mental Models of the Participating Students

Anne did not ascertain information about the students from the class-room teachers other than comments that Frances had worked harder recently on her assignments and was one of the brighter students in the class. Rather, her focus was on supporting the student's assignment through the public library online access catalog and having the students walk away from their respective sessions with a product. Individual learner characteristics, especially concerning the student's experiences with online learning, did not appear to be relevant to her mental model of what a teacher-librarian needed in order to support students' class work.

Teaching Strategies Mental Models

Although Anne advised us that when she was learning to use computers she preferred demonstrations and then practice, she favored a different strategy when teaching with computers. Anne's teaching-using-computers mental model incorporated a student-hands-on strategy while carrying out her directives: "If they don't have that concrete touching interaction that's personal, then I think the retention is just minimal." Her mental model reflected Piagetian theory where using concrete manipulables is important for novices. It was interestingly different, however, from the other teacher-librarians' reported espoused mental models of appropriate strategies when using computers. There was an embedded link in Anne's mental model between the kinesthetic "touching" and "personal" and these were then coupled to cognitive retention of procedures. Another espoused mental model in her suite of appropriate teaching strategy mental models was the importance of scanning students for nonverbal cues. The cues would prompt her "to re-explain or move forward" because students appeared to be lost or to have understood.

IN-ACTION VIDEOTAPED
LESSON MENTAL MODELS

Analysis of the data revealed the variety and number of mental models used by Anne during the two videoed lessons. Many were common to both lessons and some confirmed the reliability of certain espoused mental models, but there were also significant differences between the two sessions. This section in the chapter is themed according to the mental models we identified from the functions and characteristics revealed by her verbalizations and strategies.

The teaching-learning lessons occurred seven days apart. Both lessons involved dial-up procedures to access the public library. Both lessons utilized the public library's online catalog, with the second lesson also accessing one of the public library's online CD-ROM databases. Our discussion of the mental models identified from the videotapes and video transcripts of these lessons attempts to remain within the limits of what went on during and before each lesson. It attempts to avoid hindsight identifications, statements, and judgments about Anne's mental models from her subsequent stimulated recall and enhanced post-interviews. However, we have referred to any mental model in Anne's first lesson

with Frances that had relevant links to, or effects on, the series of interviews in the second lesson with Allen. Through utilizing only what preceded each videoed lesson, we hoped to maximize credibility of our
analysis.

Teaching Strategies Mental Models

Lesson Introduction Phase Mental Models

Figure 4.1 is a diagrammatic representation of Anne's mental models during this introductory phase of her lessons with Frances and Andrew. It
shows the linked fragments of the various mental models Anne activated
during this phase. For instance, Anne appeared to hold a "how-to-com-
mence-an-online-database-lesson" mental model as she initiated each
session by asking the student to tell her about their respective assignment
(see figure 4.1). Anne had begun building two mental models labeled
"Frances" and "Andrew," respectively, before each lesson and continued
to embed new information in fragments within each. The lesson mental
model is linked by arrows to various mental models that Anne activated
or created during this phase of the lesson (figure 4.1). Within her mental
model of each student was a link to their respective assignment. In both
lessons, Anne had decided upon the online public library catalog resource
after asking the students' teachers about their projects. Her recent access
to the tool played heavily in her choice. With Andrew, she considered a

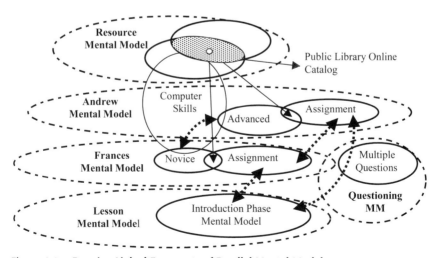

Figure 4.1. Running Linked Fragments of Parallel Mental Models

further tool, the WWW, but decided by herself which tool they would use first. They did not get to the WWW.

After admitting, "I haven't started yet," Frances said her assignment was an oral presentation on a poet and her work. Anne asked no further questions. In comparison she asked Andrew questions to do with how much he had already found, where he had found it, and how much he still needed to find (see figure 4.1). Perhaps this was either influenced by Anne's introspective comments in the earlier post-interview research lesson with Frances or it was Anne's normal practice at the beginning of any session. If Frances had started researching her project, perhaps Anne would have asked the same sorts of questions.

Her question to Andrew about his familiarity with the computer access screen and whether he could get access from home seemed to be prompted by her reflection about what she would do differently in her enhanced post-interview after Frances' lesson. (Andrew answered yes to the first and no to the second.) The reflective thoughts from Anne's stimulated recall and enhanced post-interviews after Andrew's lesson may support the deduction that she changed her mental model to include these computer literacy questions. Anne did not, however, ask about either student's information literacy skills. We wondered if Anne would replicate what happened in Frances' lesson; that is, that she would concentrate on procedural information access skills with minor sojourns to promote conceptual understanding. This and our previous suppositions are located within the process-product paradigm in which the researcher assumes what occurred inside students' heads based on the video (Marland, Patching, and Putt, 1992).

Conclusion Lesson Phase Mental Model

Even though she had prioritized obtaining book call numbers, at the end of the session Anne asked Frances if she could repeat what she had done during the lesson. Frances expressed doubt with a hesitant response, "I might." Both appeared to have left the session with mental models that acknowledged Flower's weak procedural understanding of accessing the public library online. As her session with Andrew ended, Anne told him that he could come back, use the online library catalog whenever he wanted, and get the software from the library to load onto his own computer so he could get access at home if he had a modem.

Hands-On Strategy Mental Model

At the beginning of Frances' lesson, Anne twice verbalized the rationale for her hands-on mental model as she gave Frances control of the keyboard. She did not control the keyboard at any time during the lesson. She implemented this strategy with Andrew until her growing non-verbal frustration with the number of errors, glitches, and her inability to find relevant resources resulted in, "Okay. Enough is enough!" as Anne took over control of the keyboard. She did not give control back to Andrew.

Questioning Strategies Mental Model

The majority of Anne's questions were closed questions demanding a yes-no response or a single correct answer. Anne eschewed deeper-level questioning, thereby preventing various learning opportunities for both students. For instance, she could have asked both students to provide predictions and then provide reasons for the results obtained. Virtually all her questions concentrated on giving the students choices as to where to go rather than providing opportunities for understanding. During the session with Andrew, Anne sometimes asked a string of questions without giving him a chance to answer until the last one. For instance, "So what do you want to try? Do you see anything? Have you used this CD-ROM database?" When Andrew chose a category, Anne asked, "It sounds interesting but is it going to be something that will help you with your report? Because I would really like for you to take something away today that you will have written down that you can use for your research that you could go to the public library."

We could interpret this as providing a hint to the criteria he should use to assess his choice. If so, it would have demanded higher-level thinking skills from Andrew. On the other hand, it could be interpreted as a rhetorical question because of the "but" between her feel-good statement about his "interesting" choice and the rationale.

Once they began searching for specific resources, Anne's questioning mental model tapped into a habituated "teaching catalog literacy skills" mental model that allowed her to ask some questions demanding higher-level prediction skills. Demanding higher-level prediction skills would have been influenced by Anne's "my expertise with teaching catalog literacy skills" mental model pushing the dreaded "novice with online dial-up protocols" mental model to the background. Her change in mental model emphasis was a result of her normal self-confidence as a teacher of catalog literacy skills once they entered the actual catalog.

Directives Mental Model

Anne maintained a strategy of telling the student what to do. An example from each lesson will suffice to demonstrate this mental model. With time running out in the session, Anne directed Frances to "back out. Keep backing. Back some more. Okay. Uh, back again. The other thing you could have done is, you could have typed 'SO' for 'start over' to take you back to the beginning [to exit the program]." Again, this strategy seemed appropriate to a procedural mental model of how to teach technology literacy skills. Although the tedious backing got them there, it should have served an educational purpose. It provided a visual clue as to where Frances had been that may have reinforced her mental model of exit procedures. Providing the shortcut at the end should have enabled Frances to compare the two mental models of the school and online library command as well as embed a link to this similarity within both mental models (Gentner and Forbus, 1996; Johnson-Laird, 1983).

Anne read the on-screen directions and interpreted them for Andrew, telling him what they could do in the database related to his topic, what options he would have for finding information, what the database would allow him to do, what to do to expand the titles to full text, and where he could find out what commands to use. Anne was utilizing "knowledge-out-in-the-world" from the computer (Jonassen and Henning, 1999; Norman, 1983). She appeared to run with her mental model of the mechanistic and procedural-level directions rather than attempt to develop a new conceptual mental model of the way the database worked. Instead, she transferred her previous experience working with generic database commands to show him generic procedural commands; for example, Boolean search terms.

Trusting Students with Computers Mental Model

Anne strongly voiced her anxiety about allowing students unsupervised access to conduct Web searches through instructions to both students. She explained that they were not to go online independently without her supervision when next they came in to search the public library online catalog. Nevertheless, Anne told Andrew that he could also get the software from the library and load it on his own computer for access at home, if he had a modem.

Mistakes and Technical Glitches Mental Model

Other mental models emerged when unintended mistakes and inconsistent computer responses to the inputs occurred. Two examples are provided, one from each student's lesson. When Anne gave Frances an incorrect series of letters for one of the connection protocols, she laughingly said, "Oops, that isn't what I wanted you to type. Messed up. Let's backspace it out." Anne's ability to admit a simple mistake reveals part of her mental model of herself as teacher-librarian; such a common error did not challenge her status. Her mistake may have resulted from translating her mental model of the entry procedure from its patterned sequence to a verbal command, thus breaking the pattern (see chapter 2). Patterning of numbers and login protocols seemed to be a consistent mental model strategy as a similar mistake occurred in her lesson with Andrew. On retrying the number dictated by Anne, the modem did not dial the number and would not let Andrew escape. The login protocol then needed a password. Anne was frustrated: "Let's start over. I don't know what happened. . . . I don't remember it ever asking for a password!" Her personification of the computer, exemplified by the use of "it" in the previous quote, reflected a degree of powerlessness in her self-concept-with-online-technologies mental model while the full quote acknowledged her novice mental model of the database. These mental models did not allow her to predict what solutions she might try, other than the basic repetition of their actions and then starting over when that repetition did not work. A reason for this would be that Anne's mental model of the database contained procedural "how to do it" rather than conceptual "how it works" knowledge.

Anne's response to the phone number mistake with Frances was to provide a simple conceptual "how it works" description of what was happening within the computer and the connection attempt (cf. Dimitroff, 1992; Marchionini and Liebscher, 1991). She gave a summary of what had happened and the outcomes of their mistakes to Andrew (e.g., "We misspelled 'library'" and "We made a mistake in the dialing and it wouldn't let us redial"). Anne's responses to both students demonstrated the "if . . . then" prepositional function of mental models. Her lack of conceptual understanding, however, prevented her from providing better explanations to Andrew. Nevertheless, her comment, "It always says it's bad at the beginning and then it lets us go ahead and connect," would permit Andrew not to be anxious about this message the next time they connected online as this glitch would be embedded in his mental model. Perhaps, influenced by her mental model concerning time constraints as well as her self-concept mental model, she did not take the time to work with Andrew to attempt to discover other ways rather than starting over with the connection process. As a result, she was unable to add some conceptual understanding to Andrew's and, importantly, her own mental model. This reinforces the mental model literature. Novices are likely to embed simplistic procedural actions in their mental models (Anzai and Simon, 1979; Bibby, 1992b; Newell and Simon, 1972; van der Henst, 1999).

Product Oriented Goal Mental Model

With both students, Anne's mental model demanded products. For both, this meant call numbers and book titles of materials that Frances could borrow and Andrew could read at the public library. For example, Anne suggested to Andrew, "I really do hope you'll have something to take with you [to the public library]. So let's try again going back into the keyword and doing Peru in conjunction with another term and see if we can find a book title to write down." Based on the videotape transcript, Anne's mental model of the session goal was to find an acceptable resource for each student rather than to develop conceptual understandings of the database. Procedural understandings were less complicated and would allow quicker examination of the electronic resource. Our supposition that Anne's time constraints' mental model impacted her goal mental model with Frances was confirmed in her lesson with Andrew.

Teacher-Librarian as Expert Mental Model

When Anne and Andrew finally got into the catalog, and as she had done with Frances, Anne drew on her self-concept mental model to claim more expert status because of her work as a teacher-librarian. With both students, Anne focused their attention by drawing a comparison between the online CD-ROM catalog and the catalog they had seen on the screens at the school library. She told Frances that the catalogs were similar. This strategy appeared appropriate, although it may have been clearer to Frances if the teacher-librarian had also mentioned that it functioned like the school's system and quickly explained the functions of the extra four menu items, as she did with Andrew. Of course, Andrew was going to use one of these extra items and Frances was not. If both students were able to, they could have used their current mental model of the school catalog to note only the essential differences between it and the public library's automated catalog. This action should have helped to minimize any working memory overload from running two mental models in parallel. Each student could add the new parts as Anne told them what to do.

When Frances entered the author's name where Anne told her to, but in a way that would have caused an error on the school library catalog, Anne learned with Frances that the public library catalog was more forgiving. They shared the new knowledge that they each added to their mental models of the public library catalog. When Andrew answered that he had not used the newspaper database before, Anne confessed, "Now, I have to tell you I have not used this database before. I have not gone into it before so we're going to be learning this together." Once away from dial-up procedures for entry into the catalog and the new database, Anne took back her novice status openly, preparing Andrew for any mistakes that she might make by telling him they would be learning it together. These instances would be examples of what the literature refers to as shared mental models (Anderson et al., 1996; Cohen et al., 1995). Anne was also demonstrating an unvoiced embedded mental model of lifelong learning to her students.

Summary

If we used the process-product paradigm with Anne, from her teaching-learning sessions, we would assume that Anne held a weak procedural mental model for using the technology that did not hold up under the pressure of these teaching-learning sessions, that she had a rudimentary conceptual mental model of how the computer operated with the tele-communications software, and that she was not experienced enough with the telecommunications software to have developed a problem-solving mental model. We interpreted the videoed data as showing that her espoused mental model of herself as a student-centered teacher appeared early in the lessons, when she probed both students for their perspective on their assignments and asked them to be hands-on with the keyboard. This mental model also became apparent late in both sessions when they were in the catalog database, and when she felt comfortable asking questions that demanded more than a yes/no answer. However, we further interpreted that her teaching mental model rapidly changed to teacher-centered when problems that she could not solve kept reoccurring with the software. In both sessions, her overriding mental model seemed to be the time it was taking to find a viable information product. She shared some conceptual understandings with her first student, but did not stop to give conceptual explanations to her second student until the open-ended questions, once they began using the catalog. While she shared some small problems as opportunities to learn with her first student, Anne did not do the same with Andrew. She seemed more intimidated by the problems. Essentially, during the major part of both lessons, Anne's teaching strategies mental models appeared predominantly directive, teacher-centered, procedural, and product-oriented, which was in conflict with some of her espoused mental models.

IN-ACTION STIMULATED
RECALL MENTAL MODELS

Analysis of the stimulated recall interview data highlighted conflicts with, and confirmations of, Anne's espoused and in-action videoed mental models. Without stimulated recall methods, this would not have been possible. We cannot assume that without the stimulated recall we would have found these same data from a post-interview. Our research paradigm contained two elements that supported this assertion. First, we did not skew the stimulated recall interview data by focusing on a priori research questions. As pointed out in chapter 3, after we, or the teacher-librarian, paused the video replay, we asked non-directive questions, such as "Can you tell us what you were thinking there during the lesson?" We also asked the participants whether their reported thoughts had occurred during the lesson and or were just occurring now during the stimulated recall interview. We did not exclude the latter from our analysis but they were identified as reflective hindsight reports (see chapter 3, figure 3.2). Second, the post-interviews were enhanced post-interviews as the teacher-librarians relived their experiences through the video and, crucially, the stimulated recall interview (see chapter 3, figure 3.2).

Teaching Strategies Mental Models

Beginning the Lesson Phase Mental Model

As we pointed out in the videoed section, Anne was running her mental model of "how to start a lesson" when she checked on Frances' understandings of her information needs for the assignment.

> I thought, "Okay, this is very valuable information for me; it has to be just some type of presentation." . . . I had assumed it would be a research project. What I was thinking, right here, I was feeling relief because all of my thoughts were revolving around her success on the assignment, and a presentation didn't need as many resources.

We find that Anne had misinterpreted the teacher's description of the assignment. She linked the new information to the number of resources needed within the time limit of the lesson. This brought a sense of relief as it made her job during the session seem more manageable. Stimulated recall revealed the inaccuracy of our previous assumption that Anne always probed students about their assignment. It was having misinterpreted the task that influenced her lack of questions to Frances. Anne was rearranging her mental model of what to do and accomplish in Frances' session. In this process, her product-oriented goal and time constraints mental models were run and adjusted.

Hands-On Strategy Mental Model

In the pre-interview, we revealed one of Anne's espoused mental model strategies for successful retention; that is, students should have hands-on control of the keyboard. Anne reinforced this espoused mental model by verbalizing it twice to Frances during the lesson and giving Andrew control of the keyboard at the beginning of the lesson. However, we obtained a different picture when we tapped into what she reported she had actually been thinking during the lesson: "Originally I had thought, 'Well, I'll just show her how to do it and let her sit there.'" Anne's initial mental model of her plan for the lesson validated a "demonstrate and tell" teaching strategy and not a hands-on strategy. Remember, this was Anne's espoused mental model of how she, herself, preferred to be taught.

However, because Frances had not searched for any resources, the session with Anne was

> no longer going to be an extra; it had become essential. . . . When I got with her and she told me about not starting, I thought, "Naw, this [demonstrating as I controlled the keyboard] isn't the way to do it. She needs to do it." So, that was what I was thinking, "She needed the hands-on and she would remember it better."

Hands-on provided the stronger learning situation for the learner. She wanted her student to experience actual control of the computer by typing in the commands. In this way, Anne argued, Frances could construct her own memory of the procedural steps and the key commands. Anne hoped that this would help Frances recall when she next used these information access skills. Her thoughts and actions reflected Anne's mental model about learning and teaching. Rather than stay with a mental model strategy that meant an easier time for herself (cf. Rogers, 1992), Anne adopted the "hands on the keyboard while I direct you" approach, which she did with Andrew until too many problems occurred. At that juncture, "I started taking over the typing because I was thinking, 'We've got to move on and find something.' And I did think this. 'Yes, I'm having one of those very bad days. It continues!'" Anne linked three mental models: time constraints, product lesson goal, and, within her role as teacher-librarian, the store of a "bad day at the library" situations. Her final "It continues" groan had echoes of reliving Groundhog Day (as occurred with Bill Murray's character in the movie *Groundhog Day*). This resulted in her taking control of the keyboard and reverting to her preference for demonstration with accompanying explanations and directives.

An important difference between the two lessons was that in her lesson with Frances, Anne appeared to have control initially over her mental models and, hence, changed her teaching strategy. Her mental models in Andrew's lesson controlled her, hence the reversion in strategy when she took over the keyboard (see chapter 2).

Seizing the Teaching Moment Mental Model

Anne used her mistakes as teaching opportunities (Carroll, 1989) on three occasions, all with Frances.

Table 4.2 provides the videoed discourse and Anne's stimulated recall thoughts plus our comments to enhance exemplification of the first example of this seizing-the-teaching-moment mental model. When she had given Frances the incorrect numbers to type in the online dial-up protocol, Anne tried to pass on to the student her partial understanding that was a rather useful, if simple, conceptualization of how one computer linked to another computer (table 4.2).

This strategy of imparting just so much (table 4.2) would not overburden the student's working memory. In this way, Frances should have been able to embed this into a conceptual mental model. Research demonstrates that also providing an actual diagram or graphic of the linkup, such as an image of the linked computers, would have been more beneficial to mental model creation (Mayer, 1989).

Second, while Frances was typing in a command she made an error. Anne explained her decision to allow Frances to make this error rather than correcting it.

When she was doing the actual typing and I noticed that the space wasn't in there, I thought, "Should I let her go ahead and finish typing the name or should I correct her here?" I thought, "Let's go ahead and let her do it and then maybe if she sees that there's a difference she will remember to look at these example screens because I didn't say, 'Pay attention to the example screen.'" I had covered it up and said, "Even though there's an example, you tell me what you type." Then I thought as I uncovered the example, "By looking at the screen to find her own error, that will make her examine the

Table 4.2. Comparison of Videoed Discourse and Stimulated Recall Thoughts

Videoed Discourse	Stimulated Recall Thoughts
What we're trying to do is, we're connecting up with a computer program in this computer. It has a telephone line hooked into it. The computer is going to dial out and talk to another computer over the telephone line. That is, it is going to talk to the other computer that speaks its language. If the line is busy, this may mean we will not be able to connect.	Okay, I was doing a kind of decision making here. I was thinking that I couldn't explain a whole lot of the technical part, but I wanted her to realize that we were going outside of this building. I thought, "What she really needs to know is that there's a reason for typing in those letters and that reason involves the communication between the computers." I thought, "I only need to give her enough information so that she feels comfortable."
Our Comments:	
This was expressed confidently.	Demonstrates "don't let students know my novice level" mental model.

example screen and utilize it in the future." . . . When she didn't see the space error, I was a little bit concerned that she didn't see the difference.

This provided another teaching strategy mental model embedded in Anne's repertoire of teaching library information computer literacy: you learn best from recognizing your own mistakes. Anne's mental model for using the examples often provided in databases as guides for the correct way to enter commands had not become a part of her student's cognitive processing. Frances did not know how to compare what she had typed with what the example showed, thus she did not see her error.

Third, the added space did not make a difference to the database protocols. The database correctly interpreted what Frances wanted. Astonished, Anne commented in a mixture of "there-and-then" thoughts that occurred during the lesson as well as reflective "here-and-now" thoughts that were only occurring due to the video and interviewer prompts.

> I thought, "I was wrong." I remember thinking that I was really surprised that it worked and that I didn't know why that computer was not sensitive to the spacing. I felt surprised that it worked. I thought, "It's real interesting" at this point. I really felt kind of in tune with Frances; I felt it was okay for me to be wrong. But, yet part of me, I guess, did say [as a "there-and-then" thought], "Well, I goofed again." But for some reason I wasn't quite as concerned at that point [a "there-and-then" thought, as is the next one, as they had actually occurred during the teaching learning session]. I'd thought that this mistake is a teaching opportunity because it will allow me to tell her that this works on our computer and there was just a difference between the two computers. [From this point, the thoughts are "here-and-now" explanations as to why she thought and felt as she had during the lesson.] Another time I think I said I was a little concerned about my image and what I was projecting so far as competency to her. I wasn't then, because it was a teachable moment.

Anne was running two mental models here. Using the spacing error as a teachable moment was accepted and acted upon by Anne, but the parallel mental model that was also running, that of status and projecting competency with the technology, was discarded. Previously, she had not been able to discard this because her self-image of her status as a teacher-librarian was uppermost then. She did not avoid sharing with Frances that the database was unpredictable for her. Anne communicated her sense of pleasure in finding out something new to Frances. In addition, perhaps an unacknowledged (or unreported) element—learning is a lifelong process—in her mental model was also unintentionally transmitted. When she learned something new with Andrew—for instance, that the database would not let them back up to correct the typing—she did not turn it into a teaching moment or allow Andrew to see her joy in learning.

Using Comparison Mental Model

When Anne compared the school's automated catalog with the public library's CD-ROM database menu, which had a different menu structure and interface, she said she was thinking,

> I hoped she had used the school's catalog because I had no idea whether she had or not. And I was thinking if she had, that might help her realize that this screen compared [sic] and it would make it seem less alien to her, make it seem more familiar. [When they went on to the public library's CD-ROM database menu, Anne commented], I was thinking, "I have no idea if this child knows what a CD-ROM database is." Then I thought, "I don't have time to explain it, that's not really part of this lesson."

We now discovered through stimulated recall that when she used the comparison as a learning device during the lesson, she knew that her strategy was not as adequate as it should have been. Her focus on time constraints meant that providing, at the very least, a brief conceptual overview description of the CD-ROM database was discounted because her mental model dictated a product-oriented outcome. It is doubtful that she would have retrieved from long-term memory the "how to explain a CD-ROM database mental model" fragment of the "CD-ROM database mental model" that she was currently utilizing in the lesson.

Nonverbal Cues Mental Model

Stimulated recall methods indicated that Anne executed her espoused mental model that utilized nonverbal cues with Frances. However, with Andrew, there was no mention of reading Andrew's non-verbals. In fact, at one stage she reported: "I did not realize he even looked away until I saw this [on the video replay]." This demonstrates the importance of video replays for critical self-reflection when prompted through stimulated recall. With Andrew, the continuing number of glitches and the inability to find resources that were not out in circulation or in the bindery increased Anne's frustration and concerns about obtaining a resource for Andrew. Her focus was sidetracked from implementing the non-verbal cues mental model. The dominant mental model controlling her teaching strategy was her need for a product outcome to the lesson.

When it came to choosing materials through the public library catalog, both Frances and Anne were using "knowledge-out-in-the-world" when they were engaged with the computer interface (screen). In addition, Frances was interacting with what Anne was saying; that is, using Anne's expertise. It was a case of distributed mental models between the participants and the computer (see Banks and Millward, 2000; Bibby, 1992a; Cohen et al., 1995; Rogers and Rutherford, 1992).

> I made a conscious decision at that point that I was going to try to see how much she knew. I was interested at this point because *she was focused on the screen* and for some reason I *felt I was getting feedback from her as kind of a self-teaching thing* . . . I was thinking, "She is *looking at this screen and is trying to figure out as much as she can.* She's *listening to me* but she's *also reading and learning on her own."* So at that point I made a decision to ask her the choice she was going to make. (our italics)

The italicized sections in the stimulated recall quote relate to identifiable instances of distributed mental models between Anne, Frances, and the computer interface. In the pre-interview, Anne had revealed in an espoused mental model that she did not like to teach classes larger than twelve students because she could not follow everyone's non-verbal responses to her teaching. From Anne's stimulated recall thoughts, she ran her mental models of past teaching experiences, with the same type of teaching, to compare her current student's reactions with past students' non-verbal reactions.

Again, Anne informed us that she had interpreted Frances' non-verbals accurately when Frances demonstrated an understanding of a concept by answering correctly. Anne said she felt

> kind of proud of her, that she did know it because I thought she did but there are so many times that students don't. You'd think they would know that if you wanted a book by someone you're going to type in author, but I've gotten off the wall answers before from students I thought knew. Hey, I really thought all this during the lesson! I also thought, "Good girl, you did know it."

These reported thoughts during the lesson demonstrated that Anne was again running mental models of students' incorrect responses to what she thought was an easy question. She was assuming that students who gave the correct answer would have the conceptual understanding that probably was not embedded in the mental models of students who answered incorrectly. Her surprise at remembering that she had engaged in these thoughts during this point in the lesson demonstrated the ability of the stimulated recall prompts to elicit participants' retrospective thinking.

Decision-Making Mental Model

When they managed to get into the library CD-ROM database, Anne gave Andrew a choice of which category to choose. His first choice was "Newspapers." Anne reported, "I was thinking that he needed to decide what resource he wanted to use, and that he knew the assignment. I thought, 'He is going to be looking for current information and therefore it was a good choice.'" Anne termed this "decision-making." We interpreted her questioning in the previous videoed in-action mental models section as either demanding higher-order thinking or a rhetorical question. From the stimulated recall comments, her intention was the former. During the stimulated recall interview, when Andrew was selecting his category choice, the following took place.

> Interviewer: Okay, when he's articulating all of these choices, what were you thinking?
> Anne: At that point then, I was thinking that I'm okay with this; I really need to do this with this particular child. I need to let him explore and learn about his own decision making.
> Anne: And I think at this point I had made a decision, "I need to lead him in the direction that, what he saw on this particular article, he thought he was going to find information about government." I realized really, at that point, that he possibly was not heading in the right direction with his decision making [all "there-and-then" thoughts]. And that was when I started questioning him ["here-and-now" statement]. And again, I'll go back to what I know about this student [another hindsight comment], that I still felt, at this point, that experience in decision making was possibly more important than the technology ["there-and-then" comment].

In both cases, besides the higher-order thinking skills, it required an "if ... then" propositional strategy in the student's mental model. Anne realized the nature of the tasks when she labeled this teaching strategy mental model "decision-making." It also demonstrated that, at that particular point in the lesson, this mental model (exemplified through their question and answer interactions) was more important to the teacher-librarian than her product-oriented goal mental model.

Questioning Mental Model

Anne's mental model of questioning strategies would appear to require only a yes, no, or a closed-answer (one correct answer) response. Thus most of the closed-answer category questions were recall-type questions. Interestingly, her questioning demanded more open-ended responses or required higher-order thinking skills from both students once they were into the actual database. This was probably because her strengths with this area allowed her to feel less anxious. She had habituated the type of question to ask in this area of information skills and her mental model swung into action.

Product-Oriented Goal

A little after the earlier quote about feeling relief because Frances' assignment was a presentation, Anne reported, "I was thinking, 'Do I have anything in the media center that I can put in her hands before she leaves?' I know my thoughts had nothing to do with how I'm going to teach it, any of that kind of stuff." Her mental model reflected her emphasis on playing the role of information specialist with students, perhaps to the point of not allowing students to cope with the consequences of their own actions. In fact, Anne told us she had followed up the thought that she had had during the lesson, about what resources were currently in the library (first question in above quote). During the break before her stimulated recall interview, Anne found two books that she gave to Frances when Frances exited the room after her stimulated and enhanced post-interviews with us. Anne's last comment in the above quote confirmed another two of her espoused mental models: one of the expert teacher-librarian, in this case, with all types of catalogs, and the other of teacher as self-reflective of the teaching process. Again, we see the interlinking of various mental models or fragments of various mental models.

Abandoning Ship versus Product-Oriented Goal

The newspaper database proved unsuitable for Andrew. We provide the transcript of this section to demonstrate her thoughts, our checks to ensure they were "there-and-then" thoughts, and her reaction to the accumulation of mishaps with the technology and student choices within the database.

> Anne: I didn't want to really take charge, I wish I had, but at this point I still didn't want to really say, "Andrew, we need to get out of here and you need to let me tell you where to go."
> Interviewer: Okay. And that's what you were thinking at that time?
> Anne: I remember at some point, once we were into this database, in which I did think that. I was thinking, "We need to abandon ship." [She continued with two "here-and-now" thoughts.] I don't know why I didn't say, "Andrew, I think we need to abandon ship," unless there's something, just sheer tenacity, "I'm going to find a right answer." To be perfectly honest, had the cameras not been on, I would have probably abandoned ship.
> Interviewer: So you were thinking that during the lesson?

Anne: Yes. At this point [touching the paused TV monitor screen], I was really coming to the realization, "We weren't where we needed to be" and I was thinking, "We need to abandon ship."

Her desire to disband the lesson came as a surprise. Stimulated recall allowed us to see that abandoning the lesson may have been a strategy that Anne used when too many glitches kept occurring. This reaction, which would result in finishing the lesson without a product, was somewhat surprising given the strong confirmation of Anne's product-oriented goal for all sessions with students from the pre-interview, video, and other sections of the stimulated recall interview. It indicated her enormous frustration from the continuing number of problems. However, the comment, "I'm going to find a right answer," should not be ignored. "[Shortly after this], I started taking over the typing because I was feeling we've got to move on and find something. . . . We were bombing out. I just did not want him to leave without something." Her self-concept as tenacious, together with the reiteration of the goal of obtaining a product, meant that the product-oriented goal mental model was stronger and that it dominated the lesson. Perhaps the strength of the product-oriented goal was uppermost in any lesson with students and in any interaction with staff, including the curriculum planning group.

Self-Concept and Status Mental Models

Anne voiced general satisfaction with herself and her student at the end of the stimulated recall session with Frances. In contrast, Anne started the stimulated recall session after her teaching-learning episode with Andrew exclaiming: "I would like to forget the whole event!" She was discouraged by the technical problems they had during the session and she was discouraged by her own teaching performance. Being in front of cameras would have increased this evaluation, although she did not say this. Much of the negativity in her self-concept mental model was due to how she responded to mistakes and technological glitches.

Mistakes Mental Model

Anne was comfortable with the mistake after she told Frances the wrong letters to type into the command: "I was thinking right then, 'Okay, I goofed. Maybe this is the only one [mistake] I'll do.'" As we mentioned in chapter 2, providing non-examples is nearly as important as providing valid examples for creating mental models (Carroll, 1990; Henderson, Patching, and Putt, 1994). Mental models need to include correct information as well as inaccurate methods so that predictions and inferences can be made. Particularly when troubleshooting, we make a prediction and run a mental model to choose a likely action. The more we gain expertise, the more we run other mental models with other possibilities, some accurate and some incorrect, to test our prediction (Haycock and Fowler, 1996; Holyoak, 1991; Johnson-Laird, 2001; Schank and Cleary, 1995).

Anne reported a string of thoughts throughout the ongoing saga of mistakes with the dial-up procedures during the lesson with Andrew. They included, in sequence:

> Probably about this time I was thinking, "Oh my Lord . . . I can actually hear somebody saying, 'Hang up and dial again.'" I thought, "I don't have a clue." I still didn't realize I'd left a digit out [a hindsight thought]. [As the frustration and mistakes mounted, she recalled], I was basically thinking, "Oh, no, this is falling apart. Why is nothing working right now?" I was fighting hard to try to regroup but, you know, I can handle a couple of mistakes but when they keep going, ahhh. [This last sentence was a "here-and-now" hindsight comment]. At this point I was thinking: "Okay, maybe we can get in and we're going to go quickly because we had all these boo-boos."

Anne could not solve her problems because of her lack of a conceptual problem-solving mental model that would have developed from more experienced use and practice with the database, plus more dealings with its problems (Anzai and Simon, 1979; Bibby, 1992b; Newell and Simon, 1972).

Novice Mental Model

As a novice with online technology, she responded to surface features and details (Bibby, 1992b; Newell and Simon, 1972), openly admitting that she did not know the why or how. One mistake was acceptable; more were not because they would draw attention to her novice status. This caused anxiety because she also wanted to retain her belief that students had an image of her as the knowledge expert teacher-librarian.

Anne voiced considerable anxiety and worry about momentary lapses in remembering commands and thought about how she would be perceived. At one point, while trying to remember a command, she told us: "It was something akin to a moment of panic because I couldn't remember! I was concerned a little bit about my own image. I didn't want to come across to Frances as if I didn't know what I was doing." Stimulated recall showed that Anne's confident manner with Frances during the lesson meant that she was again running her "do not show your novice insecurities; maintain the expert's demeanor" mental model. Her mental model also contained the perception that if Frances, in particular, thought otherwise, it would damage Anne's usefulness as a teacher-librarian. The mental model of her technology knowledge of online communication did not include an ability to visualize problem situations in order to make appropriate responses to unpredictable situations (Puerta-Melguizo and van der Veer, 2001; Roschelle and Greeno, 1987; Sloboda 1991).

Her novice status did not allow her incomplete procedural access mental models to cope with the continuing unpredictability of the events in her lesson with Andrew. Anne's mental model of her competency with databases and newspapers in general allowed her to feel some degree of control—but only with her fingers crossed! As in the section on "abandon ship versus product outcome," her demeanor of control continued to be challenged. It was hard won. Reinforced by her need to obtain a product, she did not collapse the lesson earlier than planned. Her mental models of her tenacity over challenges and her product-oriented goals were strengthened, and dictated the lesson. This was a classic example of Norman's (1983) warning that mental models can control actions.

Her status as information specialist appears again and again in her reported thoughts. It is intertwined with other mental models, particularly her self-concept, product-oriented outcome, and students' nonverbal cues as guides for her teaching strategies and comments.

Student Mental Models

Mental Model of Frances

Anne's mental model of Frances included doubt that Frances would succeed with the assignment. Possibly, this doubt was formed when other teachers mentioned that Frances had not always been conscientious about her work. Anne also read Frances' body language as being less than committed to her assignment. As we pointed out previously, Anne told Frances twice that she would use the online database for future projects. We found, through stimulated recall, that her mental model of Frances' lacking genuine interest influenced this comment. Anne's mental model of Frances maintained some of the initial negativity about Frances' seriousness of purpose. However, this mental model of Frances became embedded with Anne's positive attitudes as the lesson progressed. For instance, when Frances anticipated some commands, Anne told us what she had been thinking and her justification for those thoughts during the lesson. Both types of thoughts occurred during the lesson:

> At that particular point when I saw her make the decision, it was like, "We're thinking the same way." That was what went through my mind, "We're thinking the same thing." I realized, "She's already looked at this, made an evaluation, and knew that she wanted poems. So, she wasn't jumping ahead.

She was still staying with me." I was again pleased that she was taking information from both sources, both verbal and in what she was seeing. I felt
pleased with her.

Her running mental model of her student had Frances engaged with the
lesson at this point and not racing ahead of the instruction. It also contained what all teachers feel, satisfaction when a student demonstrates an
understanding of what is required.

Prior experience with her discomfiture with time constraints while
teaching students to access information came back to affect Anne's thinking and actions. She did not want to allow time for Frances to make any
errors in taking them out of the software.

> I was thinking that . . . I was going to let her go ahead. But then I thought,
> "She might make the wrong decision and punch a wrong button," so I
> thought, "I had better halt her." I was kind of feeling a mixed thing of want-
> ing to give her a little independence and decision-making but also wanting
> to be sure that she didn't make any kind of mistake. . . . I was again feeling
> time constraints [and, adding a hindsight "here-and-now" reflective
> thought] that isn't because of the research project, the time constraint, that
> frustration would have been felt in a real-life situation too.

Anne wanted to take control of the session and the decision-making so
she could speed things up. Here, her mental model of errors being teachable moments was lost under the strain of her time constraint mental
model. Anne took control of the lesson direction. This action, which perhaps may be endemic given Anne's concerns about time, left no room for
her student to demonstrate any of her learning. A lack of confidence in
her student's ability to proceed without errors was also embedded in her
mental model of Frances.

Regardless of her persistent doubt about Frances's intent, Anne's mental model of working with Frances became increasingly positive after they
had actually accessed the public library's catalog menu. She said,

> I really did feel good about what was going on between the two of us. I was
> far less aware of the video equipment than I thought I would be and I think
> Frances was, too. I think for her, it was, "the computer and me." And I really
> felt good about that. So I think in addition to providing her with practical
> things that she will use for an assignment, it was building a relationship
> where she will look at me as a resource. . . . I do feel that relationship is
> almost more important than any skills and awareness. But I also feel good
> that now she knows that she can look up resources from someplace other
> than going to the [public] library.

The stimulated recall interview had shattered another supposition. Anne thought the lesson went well and that Frances would return to use the online public library's catalog. Perhaps she had underestimated the effect of her self-confidence with catalog information literacy that she consequently projected to Frances. Perhaps she also had underestimated Frances's catalog resource access skills. Anne reported that she valued success with finding a product only a little higher than the relationship with the student. Given what we know about the consistency of her mental models over the various sessions, we can be fairly confident that this emphasis on relationships with students was embedded in her mental model as one of the roles of an effective teacher-librarian. Students'—and Frances's—exploitation of her skills allowed her to maintain her self-image mental model as the useful and effective teacher-librarian.

Mental Model of Andrew

Anne told us that she knew Andrew was bright and capable. She knew him better than most students, because he called on her expertise regularly, and she respected his abilities.

> I don't know if it was at this exact moment [in the video] but, in this general area, I was thinking about knowing this young man and his capabilities and wanting to allow him to make some decisions as to where he would evaluate a proper source of information. I thought, "He will be able to rapidly go through accessing the information and that this would just be an experience of doing something with a modem that he was used to doing." So I envisioned at this point [pointing to the TV screen], this is going to be a very quick lesson. I actually thought, "This will go quickly!" [The remainder were hindsight "here-and-now" thoughts occurring during the interview.] You know, in retrospect, I would not have given him the choice, I would have directed. And I think this is a case where knowing the child, I made some assumptions about his decision-making that were incorrect.

She also was reviewing her espoused teaching strategy mental model of facilitating student learning rather than instructing student learning. Possibly, she was reverting to the instructional teaching model that she had experienced in her educational career. At the moment of these thoughts, however, she thought that her main problem was that Andrew was not ready for as much decision-making as she thought, "I hesitated to take control as much as I should have, thinking that his decision-making abilities and his assessment abilities were a little more advanced than they were. And I didn't want to insult him by telling him some things." She did not mention whether her mental model of Andrew included anything about his information literacy skills for evaluating resources. However, his decision-making would have revolved around his ability to discriminate among resources by their usefulness for his topic. She translated her perception of his inability into his not being ready to make decisions. Building conceptual mental models, however, is much messier than building procedural mental models, and can seem more unsuccessful. In the end, conceptual mental models have more endurance and value in unpredictable situations (Duff, 1992; Duke and Reimer, 2000). Perhaps her evaluation of Andrew's decision-making stemmed from her not realizing how awkward the process could be.

Anne told both students at the beginning of each lesson that she wanted to supervise their efforts when they next went online in the school library. Table 4.3 contrasts what Anne said during the lessons and what she reported thinking.

Anne's mental model did not allow her to trust her first student completely. She gave different reasons to her students for why they needed supervision when using the telephone to connect to the public library online catalog and databases. The reason offered to Frances diverged

Table 4.3.   Comparison In-Action Comments and Thoughts

Teacher-Librarian's Comments and Thoughts about Frances		Teacher-Librarian's Comments and Thoughts about Andrew	
In-Action Videoed Lesson Comments	*In-Action Stimulated Recall Thoughts*	*In-Action Videoed Lesson Comments*	*In-Action Stimulated Recall Thoughts*
"If you need to come in and do this at some other time, you need to let me come in and be with you while you're hooking up just in case you get into trouble. I don't want you to do it by yourself. I won't do it for you, but I need to be there."	I was thinking, "We have had a lot of problems in this lab recently that I'm not sure of the source of them. I want to be sure that this child doesn't come in here and wipe something out. So I want her to know that although she's having access to it, that it will be supervised access." [Interviewer: Did you think all that during the lesson?] Yes. I was thinking right there that I did not want her to think that I didn't trust her abilities or trust her.	"What we're actually doing is going on the phone out of [the school]. Any time we're doing that, I need to supervise, okay?"	No thoughts were reported.

from the mental model of other research teacher-librarians who kept reassuring their students that the students could not harm the computers. Two other fragments of Anne's novice mental models seemed to be running here. Anne's self-perception of herself working with online resources and her worry about having to retrieve lost ("wiped out") files or data made her anxious that Frances would somehow wipe files off the computer's hard drive. Research confirms the negative impact anxiety has on mental models and accomplishment (Ayersman, 1996; Wayment and Cordova, 2003). Anne knew that Andrew was Internet literate; she therefore articulated another reason than that used with Frances. Because she had had positive past experiences with Andrew, Anne seemed more concerned with following the standard school protocol for students using school telephones to call outside the building, regardless of the reason.

Aside from the matter of trust, a significant outcome from Anne's instruction would probably have resulted in both students embedding in their mental model of the online dial-up procedures, the notion that they could leave this knowledge out there in the world; that is, in the teacher-librarian's head. The literature (Halford, 1993; O'Malley and Draper, 1992) suggests that the mental model each student had started building would have been discarded in favor of the embedded decision. The decision to embed would have helped prevent working memory overload during the lesson. Also, as it is a common learning tactic (Cennamo, 1989, 1993; Norman, 1983, 1988; Salomon, 1983, 1990), the students would have been unconsciously trying to lessen the amount of mental effort they needed to expend to accomplish tasks and understandings. If teachers do not understand the role and functions of mental models in this regard, then teachers would have an imperfect understanding of what can or very likely could result from their instructions.

Summary

The discovery of Anne's mental models during the stimulated recall interview was revelatory for us. Anne responded in these lessons just as she would have if both students had approached her and asked for her help in finding a resource. Under those circumstances, her time and information needs mental models usually overwhelmed and competed with her mental model to help students develop conceptual understandings of the resource tool. Our stimulated recall interviews with Anne confirmed how deeply her mental model of the information specialist role dominated her thinking and actions. Her thoughts did not confirm strength in her espoused mental model that the teacher-librarian was a teacher whose focus was the student. Perhaps this dominance was a carryover from her teacher-librarian education training, when conceptual understandings of resources were subsumed to the need to place the actual information in the hands of teachers and students.

If this were the case, then the influence of her prior education, emphasizing the role of information specialist, would explain the priority order of Anne's mental models. As uncovered through the stimulated recall interviews, her thought processes demonstrated that she needed literally, above all, to place an information resource in the hands of her students. This mental model dominated her (Norman, 1988). When time became a factor, as it always did when she helped individual students use these resources, her thinking demonstrated that her time mental model controlled all but one of her other mental models. The time mental model ran in parallel with the product mental model to dominate her espoused mental model of herself as student-centered and her espoused mental model of her need to teach conceptually for the student to understand the database.

Anne's stimulated recall in-action mental models demonstrated that she believed that Frances did not need to get involved in making decisions about what type of database to use and how to use it. Rather, she needed only to make choices of actual resources and to observe and listen to Anne's directions and explanations while doing the actual keyboarding. Anne's stimulated recall in-action mental models also demonstrated that she believed she had given too much credit to Andrew's critical abilities to choose from the menu of online resources. Her in-action mental model of the need for her students to learn through hands-on control of the keyboard vacillated as her time mental model began to take control. Her stimulated recall mental model counteracted her verbalized mental model of hands-on control in her session with Frances. Her stimulated recall thoughts revealed her intention of using a show-and-tell strategy. However, her stimulated recall interview demonstrated, as she started her session with Frances, that Frances would benefit from hands-on control. Anne was spontaneously responding to her interpretation of Frances' non-verbal cues. This example was another stimulated recall in-action mental model of effective teaching strategies. Nevertheless, the "responding to non-verbal cues mental model" was superseded when time and product needs changed her planning in-action, as well as her mental models of appropriate teaching approaches, the lesson, and responding to her student. Her overriding mental model that Frances and, for that matter, any student, needed to leave a session with a hard copy product superseded these mental models.

Anne's espoused mental models also did not indicate the strength of her stimulated recall in-action mental model of the need to be the expert. Her recalled thoughts indicated that this "need to be the expert" mental model played an important part in her response to problem situations.

Her mental model of the student's computer abilities affected her response. Because she did not have an espoused mental model of Frances as a strong student with computer knowledge, she allowed herself the freedom of retrieving a mental model of using errors and problems as shared learning opportunities. Because she had given Andrew the status of having expertise with computers, her mental model of teacher-librarian as knowledge expert came under more challenge with the errors and mistakes, thereby foreclosing on any opportunities to use in-action mental models that delineated the problem situations as shared learning opportunities. Had she truly possessed mental models that contained an expert's knowledge of the database and its use, she probably could have allowed for the unpredictability of database behaviors. Her need to be the expert had prominence among her mental models in action during the database entry phase of each lesson but subsided when her confidence increased once they entered the catalog database. Then she did not need to be the expert; she was the expert and consciously could allow her time and product mental models to dominate the rest of the sessions.

With Anne's extremely recent acquisition of online access and database skills, Anne's espoused and in-action mental models of her status as knowledge expert was frequently challenged. Anne expressed considerable surprise when her procedural commands did not work, worrying considerably about her perceived loss of image as the knowledge expert, instead of couching her perception of herself in such a way that her self-concept mental model would have allowed the database to teach both her and her students. Anne could have retrieved from, if indeed it was ever incorporated in, her espoused constructivist mental model a joint problem-solving strategy by inviting Andrew to question why they were receiving inappropriate hits when their terms in the Boolean "and" search did not appear in the returned hits. She could have invoked, or more correctly, created an in-action mental model that utilized the prediction function (Gentner and Stevens, 1983; Halford, 1993) by asking each student to predict likely outcomes or join with her in predicting why the glitches occurred. Then they could have learned together what actually happened, a kind of discovery learning.

The pedagogical theory and method used to help students construct mental models seem to make a considerable difference to the image we have of ourselves as teachers and knowledge experts (Jonassen and Reeves, 1996). Facilitators do not have mental models that require them to be the knowledge expert. Such a mental model requires them to share the construction of mental models with their students or peers. Instructors need to maintain mental models that depict themselves as knowledge experts in order to feel like they are imparting material that their students would value. Had Anne's espoused, videoed, and stimulated recall in-action mental models subscribed to the difference in these perspectives, gravitating more toward the facilitator role in actuality, her impression of, and later reflection on, both sessions might have been very different than they were.

ENHANCED STIMULATED RECALL POST-INTERVIEW MENTAL MODELS

We purposely did not ask pre-interview questions that would draw on their mental models about planning for the lesson, what they knew about the selected students, and their pedagogy. We did not wish to skew the data by triggering thoughts and actions concerning these areas during the first teaching learning session. In effect, we did not wish to lead the participant by signaling our research agenda in the first interview. These questions were left to the post-interview. Obviously, the second lesson would be informed by their prior experiences from the research process. This was intentional. We were interested to see if the second lesson's mental models remained the same or changed as a consequence of their critical self-reflection.

First Impression of Lessons Mental Models

Anne's mental model of her lesson with Frances was generally positive at the end of the lesson. To say that she initially did not have a positive mental model of her second lesson at its conclusion would be an understatement. She noted,

> I'm still extremely frustrated and agitated. In retrospect, I wish I had made some decisions sooner. I wish I had cut my losses and gone to the online card catalog sooner. But then, the card catalog was a bomb, too! I mean there were just no materials [all were checked out or in the bindery]. It's a valuable lesson, that sometimes you use the tool and don't get what you want.

Nevertheless, Anne could see the learning function of this frustrating amalgam of problems. This, too, now became a part of her mental model of online literacy, as further comments below reveal.

Mental Model of Being "On Show"

She told us that she, and she believed Frances, became quickly unaware of the cameras as they searched the database catalog. This was not the case with Andrew's lesson. Anne reported that the cameras had an impact on her. She thought: "Had the cameras not been on, I would go, 'Andrew, this is not working. Can you come back another day?'" This strategy would give her time to puzzle out the problems. Although we were amazed when she voiced this thought during the stimulated recall interview, in retrospect, it should not have been that surprising. Embedded in all her mental models were her beliefs about herself and how others perceived her (Newton, 1996; Szabo and Fuchs, 1998). There was usually a cause-and-effect relationship. As we have mentioned throughout our case study analysis, technological glitches, mistakes, "unforgiving technology," and an inability to find worthwhile resources, particularly with Andrew, impacted her mental models of self-concept and status and how others—the researchers and the students—would interpret this. When the session was proceeding smoothly, her attention—and mental models—were rarely focused on herself.

Mental Models of the Databases

Her mental models of the public library online databases viewed "the primary limitation to be its inability to print. I really would have felt better if we could have printed a bibliography." Here was a further reinforcement of the tangible product mental model. Anne wished the database was icon-based because "anytime I turn a student loose at a DOS prompt, I'd be highly nervous so I think that's my main reservation about using this with students." Again she projected her own anxieties using DOS onto what she perceived would be reflected in her students' mental models.

Asked if the database presented her with any teaching problems, she smilingly replied: "Only my lack of memory of how to use it." The wry self-reflection revealed she could use humor on herself and was insightful. As a result of the second lesson, Anne changed her mental model of the online CD-ROM and online catalog database:

> I used to think it was user-friendly. I don't think it's as friendly today as I did previously! I did learn. I did not realize [pause] but surely I've made typos before because I'm not the world's best typist. [Pause] There were several things that I didn't understand: why it seemed to skip through screens, and at one point skip some steps, and at other times I thought I had done it right and it wouldn't allow me [voice trails off].

Although she was asking these questions now at the very end of the research sessions, she remained within her procedural steps and processes mental model. Her self-evaluation failed to challenge her mental model based on patterning of database entry online commands and a list of steps that occasionally took effort to recall. This resulted in high levels of anxiety because the mental model was inadequate for the task when either the patterning broke down or she was faced with unpredictable situations to troubleshoot.

Lesson Preparation Mental Model

Finding Out about the Student's Mental Model

Anne acknowledged that she did not know much about Frances, nor did she attempt to find out before their session, other than what teachers had mentioned. Frances had had talking problems in the library, but "she was really trying to focus in and cut down on her talking and it really was improving her workload. . . . In fact, one of the student teachers commented that she was one of their brighter students. But I really don't know any type of personal information." This comment was interesting on four counts. One, Anne interpreted our question about the student as limited to social and work behaviors, a global category of academic aptitude, and personal details. Two, because the teacher-librarian interacted with all students in the school, not trying to find out more about Frances was realistic. It provided us with a snapshot of what would be customary practice, and therefore helped maximize research credibility. Three, even with this understanding about Frances' improvement and intelligence, Frances admitting that she had done "nothing" toward her project kept the negative perceptions of Frances alive in Anne's mental model of the student. Four, what we knew from the pre-interview, videoed, and stimulated recall sessions was that Anne's mental model of herself as a knowledgeable information literacy expert meant that she did not have to inquire about her student's skills in this area. She felt she would be able to teach using her usual teaching strategies, one of which was allowing interpretation of the student's non-verbals to guide her teaching.

What the Students Had Learned Mental Model

We asked Anne what she thought each student had learned during the session with her. Anne thought she had been successful in getting Frances interested in, and comfortable with, using electronic databases, and that Frances "left with a desire to use this type of resource again." Anne did not verbalize this as one of her lesson goals prior to the session. Nevertheless, she seemed to emphasize the importance of effective aspects in the learning process with computers after the session. She felt that fear of using the technology would effectively sideline Frances in a world where information cyberspace was crucial. If Frances had embedded such positives in her mental model about using online databases and the usefulness of them, then Anne felt that she had achieved much. Anne stated that Andrew would have gained a new understanding of the problems that technology could present. The session with Andrew certainly demonstrated in various ways that "technology doesn't always work the way you think it's going to!" Anne hoped that "he understands that, just because it doesn't work the way you had hoped it would, that you don't give up on it and not use it again," and that "you don't quit when stumped with a technical problem. [Pause] I don't really think that this dawned on him as much as on me." These were the lessons Anne learned and hoped Andrew would have, too. By the time we reached this part of the interview, Anne was able to link her tenacity positively with overcoming technological glitches and what she perceived to be database inconsistencies.

Product-Oriented Goal Mental Model

Anne felt positive about her lesson with Frances because her product-oriented goal was achieved when Frances "did leave with the call number and titles of two books that are available for this particular project." Anne went on to tell us that, in between the videoed lesson and her stimulated recall interview, she had found some relevant books in the school library and had given them to Frances as she left her interview with us. This action demonstrated three of Anne's mental models. One mental model still contained a lack of confidence that Frances would actually go to the public library to find the materials they had identified. This mental model was linked to a second mental model that resulted in Anne's belief that Frances had to have a physical product from the session in order to "save Frances's assignment." This, too, was linked to a third mental model. To maintain the stability of her self-perception mental model, Anne had to be seen in Frances' eyes as the teacher-librarian who "came through for the student and delivered." Anne's action also reflected that the second mental model was embedded in a broader mental model. The strength of Anne's mental model, that the outcome of teacher-librarian and student interactions had to be a hard copy resource, was compelling.

Teaching Mental Model: Reaction or Conscious Process?

During the enhanced post-interview after the first student, Anne did not know how to explain how she taught or the kinds of strategies that she purposely used. She noted: "Most of what I did was in reaction to Frances but I don't know exactly how [pause] or the points at which I decided to do something a certain way. If I look back on it, it was because of some cue Frances gave me." This affirmed her mental model of using student non-verbal cues to direct her teaching. After her stimulated recall experiences with both students, she was able to summarize her teaching for us:

> The largest portion of teaching that I do is, I guess, what I would have thought of as more seat of the pants. Something arises and you deal with a learning situation right then. . . . Although I do formal instruction that is planned out with the classroom teacher, most of the instruction I do is when there is a question from a student or faculty and then we go with it without my actually having sat down with goals and objectives. I think what I found out from these sessions is that mentally I do those activities while in motion at somewhat more of a rapid pace but the process is still there, that during the course of instruction, goals are formulated. They may be changed because of student response, because of equipment not working as it is supposed to. So I think the components of instruction are still there, that there is a response to students. There is a focus at the beginning and ending of the lesson. There's a summation and then perhaps focus to go on. So although in the past . . . I've thought of the two activities [teaching in a classroom and teaching in the library] being different, I think they are very similar. They're done within a different time frame and [in the library] they're more done evolving [sic]. Evaluation is going on at the same time teaching is going on. Like, oh, my gosh, that didn't work, what can I do next? . . . The main thing I've learned, that most of my instruction is impromptu. It's in response to an immediate need. But those components of a lesson plan are still there.

The opportunity provided by the stimulated recall, which triggered her critical self-reflection in this enhanced post-interview, allowed Anne to retrieve older mental models from long-term memory and compare and contrast them with ones she often utilized. Now, she was able to articulate her teaching approach and strategies mental models and realized that many were embedded with tacit knowledge, revealed as lesson plan elements. Although she acknowledged the influential role in her teaching strategies mental model of how she was taught through school and teacher training and how she had learned, she also expressed her preference for using student-centered strategies because that was how learning was happening now. Her mental model as flexible was also present as she emphasized changes to emergent incidences and needs. Yet as we observed through the videotaped session and through her stimulated recall comments, habituation of a constructivist teaching mental model had not taken place enough for her to focus on teaching for conceptual understanding through her planning or in her in-action teaching strategies which reverted to the comfort level of teacher-centered strategies when problems presented themselves.

Critical Reflection Mental Model

Teaching Strategies Mental Model

Anne believed allowing Frances to control the keyboard was her most effective teaching strategy. She linked this to her contention that Frances left with a positive attitude to online resources. Anne only saw negatives with respect to her teaching strategies with Andrew because, at Anne's direction, Andrew could only note down call numbers of books that were out on loan. Further into this post-interview debriefing, she was able to see benefits for Andrew. He would (probably) have noted Anne's tenacity to continue until a resource was found in spite of the problems with the technology.

Role of Questions Mental Model

Anne saw her questions about their assignments as significant in the conduct of the lesson. It was because they directed her decision-making to provide relevant resources. Again, that interesting linkage between (at least) two mental models—questioning as a teaching strategy that provided direction to the lesson and the product-oriented goal—resurfaced. In the light of this, we found the following reflection revealing: "I think if I were disappointed with anything in these two lessons, in looking back, I don't think the students really asked questions. . . . I would have liked more. If I have something to react to and if I'm gauging the student, I'm doing much better." She placed the burden for her ability to meet students' resource needs onto her students. Thus, she presupposed that her students would know what questions to ask. Significantly, her post-reflection was not directed at her own questioning skills mental models.

Nonverbal Cues Mental Model

This mental model was run every lesson as she gave it a high priority in her armament of strategies. She reinforced and confirmed it in her mind during and after her lesson with Frances. Anne highlighted the importance of this mental model in her repetitive explanation about how she had reacted during the session with Andrew. It was

> more in terms of what was happening with the program rather than what was happening with the student. And I got so upset and frustrated that I realized I was really not in tune to his reactions. I did not pick up on a sense of frustration on his part. I have no idea if he picked up on my level of frustration, particularly because I have to admit I was not in tune with him.

In spite of the power of this particular mental model, Anne's knowledge expert mental model, embedded with a link to product outcome as a signifier of success mental model, was in a state of chaos and overwhelmed her attention to her second student's responses.

Self as Teacher-Librarian Mental Model

Anne's final mental model of herself as a teacher-librarian gave us much to discuss when we came to our data analysis. She commented,

> I see teaching to be my number-one role. I see myself as a facilitator. I see myself as a problem solver. I don't see myself as the lady with the answers but I see myself as a lady who will assist you in finding the answers. . . . I'm always troubled if I can't find an answer. I don't give up easily. I have a real hard time letting go and saying the search is over.

Anne's use of the concept "lady" rather than "teacher" or "facilitator," given the previous comment about the importance of teaching, was insightful as we debated Anne's definition of a "facilitator." It would seem to be different from ours if we judged it against her teaching. Ours connoted a more constructivist pedagogy with time spent on conceptual understandings through strategies such as questioning, predicting, and discussing the examples and non-examples.

Perhaps she viewed it in the light of what she next said about being the "lady" providing assistance rather than giving the answers. However, the lessons and her thoughts demonstrated that her product-oriented goal mental model meant that she provided Frances with resources and ensured that the lesson continued until there were some call numbers for Andrew to note down. This mental model of herself as a teacher-librarian explained why she had such a strong feeling of failure from Andrew's session. If her mental model delineated herself as a problem solver and she could not solve the procedural problems, then her problem-solving strategies must not be effective. If she did not give up easily yet wanted to quit Andrew's session so strongly, she therefore thought she had been more of a failure when compared with her mental model of herself as persistent.

Self as Learner Mental Model

"I think of myself as a learner. I think if I don't continue to be a learner, I can't be a good teacher." Anne claimed that she learned

> from both successes and failures. Failures are not failures, because I learn something. Ah, I learn, I think I learn best not under pressure, but I'm not certain. I actually probably learn more by doing and, until I actually make

my mistakes, and say, "Oops, next time I'll do this," I won't learn this by just reading. That's my perception.

These elements in her mental model as a learner were borne out by her thoughts, actions, and comments during the interviews. She was able to convert what she perceived as failures as learning events and embed this into her mental model. The pressure of the continuing technological problems caused frustration and anxiety. This did not allow her space to think through, and certainly not beyond, her weak procedural mental models.

Role of Change Mental Model

In response to a direct question about how she might have changed the session and how she might teach the same content to others in the future, Anne asserted that

> maybe one of the differences that I would do, and probably should have done, was to have found out how computer literate Frances was so far as keyboarding skills . . . and how familiar she was with the regional library program. I was assuming she wasn't. And after the whole thing was over, she might have been more familiar with it than I thought. But I think in working with other students, I'll be more aware to ascertain what level they're entering at.

From this, we realized that our assumption that her "how-to-begin-a-lesson" mental model with Andrew was influenced by her stimulated recall session of her lesson with Frances. Anne's focus with Andrew and future students still consisted of procedural skills of access and keyboarding. Ascertaining entry level skills would be important in terms of the strength of her mental model about time constraints dictating her lesson because it would help steer the focus of the lesson. If she discovered that her students had adequate entry-level skills, her emphasis on a product resource goal would most likely mean that she could devote more time during the lesson to finding more resources rather than providing experiences for conceptual understanding.

Summary

As Anne became more reflective and less emotional, the negativity that she felt toward her session with Andrew, and had embedded in her stimulated recall in-action mental model, dissipated to a certain extent. She actually used her experiences in both sessions, as well as the opportunity for self-evaluation, as a way of utilizing her reflection on her teaching methods mental models to explain her feelings and examine her strategies. During this process, she gave herself the opportunity to be introspective about her teaching and to comb her teaching for positive as well as negative outcomes embedded in the mental models. Unfortunately, at the time we concluded our interview with her, she had not had the chance to debrief with Andrew. She did mention that Frances had not returned to the library, but it was not in terms of asking Frances comments about the lesson, nor was it in terms of evaluating her positive comments about her lesson with Frances.

Anne revealed a self-concept mental model that allowed her to continue to feel comfortable with how Frances's lesson had gone and the end product. However, in her mental model of Andrew, she had no idea what, if anything, Andrew had learned from the experience. Anne linked this mental model with that of interpreting students' non-verbals and her self-reflective mental model. She had not observed his non-verbal reactions during the session, so consumed was she by the fiasco of events and her own disappointment in her performance. She reflected deeply about her experience with Andrew, exhibiting a sensitive teacher-librarian whose pride in her performance as a knowledge expert was considerably damaged by the technology problems, not to mention that, when she finally took them successfully into the public library automated catalog, it had nothing to offer to Andrew. Her mental model allowed her to assume a guaranteed source of material but the public library automated catalog had failed for Andrew's topic area. How this affected her mental models, with only several weeks of practice with the technology as her prior experience, was evident through the stimulated recall sessions as well as the enhanced post-interviews immediately after the stimulated recall where we probed her stimulated recall thoughts concerning the events of the sessions.

WRAPPING UP ANNE'S CASE STUDY

Stimulated recall allowed us insight into Anne's complex thinking during her two sessions. Outwardly, we could observe some frustration with the online technical access process but we could not tell how relaxed Anne was or was not about these problems in relation to her mental model of herself as information knowledge expert.

From her recalled thoughts during the lesson, we realized that Anne's mental model of Frances's lack of expertise with computer technology allowed her to admit her own errors and try to use them as learning situations with Frances. Although she was frustrated with the continued access problems, her thoughts indicated that she was reasonably certain of herself as knowledge expert, only being concerned about her loss of image as knowledge expert once. We further discovered how much influence finding out about Frances's lack of prior effort with the assignment prejudiced her mental model of Frances's ability to succeed with the assignment without having an immediate information product from this session. This mental model, combined with her always-present mental model of very little time available to accomplish what they needed to do, pushed the retrieval of a mental model of needing to give directives while Frances controlled the keyboard. Previously, she had thought she would demonstrate, followed by Frances demonstrating back to her, as was her own preferred way of learning. Her pre-interview-espoused mental model of herself as a teacher defined her as a facilitative guide more than a lecturer when, in fact, her thoughts elucidated during the stimulated recall session showed that the power of the time mental model controlled her teaching pedagogy choice. When time was short, Anne opted for the quickest way to reach her goal; that is, direct procedurally to attain the objective or information product.

Setting up the teaching environment for success is clearly important with a teacher of Anne's beliefs. She had a variety of variables against her during these two teaching-learning episodes. She professed that our presence and equipment did not bother her during her first session with Frances, but with Andrew, whom she described as computer savvy, she was very conscious of us and the cameras. Her inexperience with using the public library's online access software proved devastating to her confidence when she forgot the commands and not know where she made her mistakes. Her non-experience using the newspaper database during Andrew's session prevented her from managing her time and the session effectively. She did not have enough experience with online electronic databases to be able to call up effective problem-solving strategies or anticipate what would happen with specific keystrokes. We discovered through stimulated recall that she desperately wanted to halt the session and return to it later after she had regained her composure and practiced with the tools. While we could tell her frustration from our observation, we did not know that she had considered quitting, due to her espoused mental model of working until she achieved her goal and her self-description as a determined problem solver in the face of difficulties. We also would not have realized the extent of her lack of noticing Andrew's responses during the session because of her concern with the problems. Her espoused mental model was to draw upon student responses to govern her choice of teaching strategies and to tell her about their level of understanding.

Stimulated recall methodology clarified the differences, depth, and relationship among Anne's mental models in-action during her teaching compared to her espoused mental models. This methodology allowed us to determine whether her mental models controlled her or she controlled her mental models in response to events during her teaching-learning sessions.

5

Mental Models Facilitating Procedural and Conceptual Understanding

I don't see myself as a teacher, I probably see myself as a facilitator. Just someone to sort of nudge them forward and get them to find out the answer. I suppose it's just the connotation. I mean, a teacher in the old sense was someone who stood up and just talked and there's still too many of them around. That's useless. . . . Impart as little as possible and get them to discover the rest, hopefully. It's no good me saying, "Here it is." They've got to do it. Get them to use it for themselves. (enhanced post-interview)

Marie had been a teacher-librarian for fourteen years in various schools. The last three of these years were as a teacher-librarian in a large private day school that catered to students of various socio-economic and cultural backgrounds from pre-school through Grade 12. Before that, she had been a classroom teacher but admitted to escaping from the classroom because she did not "like standing up and teaching thirty kids." Marie liked the administrative role of the teacher-librarian and was proud of her leadership role in bringing computerized technology into the school's library. In addition to creating an automated catalog, she had overseen the installation of a computer classroom within the library and the addition of electronic databases for student research.

For this research project, Marie asked for a student from a Grade 4 class who recently had been working with the electronic *WorldBook* encyclopedia. After observing these students searching linearly through the automated text without using database search tools, Marie proposed to the teacher that she teach one of the students searching techniques for the database. Then he could teach his classmates as a peer tutor. Marie chose her other student through her observations of students who came to the library frequently but never accessed materials through the automated catalog. She knew this particular student loved to read but repetitively went to the same shelf location to borrow similar kinds of books. She never saw the student use the catalog or pay attention to other students using it. Marie suspected the student did not know how to use the catalog.

ESPOUSED PRE-INTERVIEW MENTAL MODELS

We identified and categorized the various mental models that Marie espoused from the pre-interview transcripts. The topic of the open-ended questions usually became the category. For example, the question "Please describe your role as teacher-librarian" resulted in an espoused overarching mental model titled "Role as Teacher-Librarian Mental Model." The sub-categories—that is, the embedded or fragmented mental models linked to the overarching mental model—emerged from the data. Some of the sub-categories of mental models identified from Marie's data differed from those identified from Anne's pre-interview transcript (see chapter 4), as did some of the content in the common major umbrella categories. This is because mental models are idiosyncratic (Fishbein et al., 1990; Johnson-Laird, 1983; Norman, 1983; Rogers, Rutherford, and Bibby, 1992).

Role as Teacher-Librarian Mental Model

Marie imbued her mental model of her roles as teacher-librarian with rich layers and love for the administrative variety of her responsibilities. She favored administration and public relations for the library and school as her two strongest teacher-librarian roles in her mental model as opposed to Anne who preferred her resource role. Co-planning with teachers to help them integrate computer technologies into curriculum units was an established role in Marie's mental model while Anne treated this role as an embryonic area in her leadership mental model. Marie's mental model of her teaching role as teacher-librarian acknowledged its diminished importance in relation to administration. In her words, teaching had decreased "just through the sheer weight of [student and staff] numbers and the amount of the work, and the things they've asked me to take on. . . . Once, I hope, things are fixed up and running well, I can step out of that more administrative role and back more into a teaching role." Nevertheless, she admitted that she enjoyed the administrative functions more than teaching and that she was "an escapee from the classroom." Both Marie's and Anne's mental models portrayed themselves as enjoying teaching one on one but not a whole class. Embedded in Marie's mental model was a depiction of her as a leader in the school, able to make suggestions and create change, and strong enough to fight for what she thought was right. Mental models contain representations of ourselves, our views and self-perceptions (Fischbein et al., 1999; Senge, 1997; Szabo, 1998; Williamson, 1999). Those embedded in Marie's espoused mental model of her roles as teacher-librarian were positive and contained preferences for various functions. Teaching was neither the favorite nor as important as organizing and computerizing the library.

Self-Concept Mental Models

Three of Marie's major mental models derived from the pre-interview are listed in table 5.1: herself as (a) a learner with computer databases, (b) a teacher with databases, and (c) a school change agent. Her interview comments are listed to exemplify each of the three mental models. In this way, our data coding is made obvious (see chapter 3) for readers as well as for researchers who wish to utilize our categorization.

Mental Model as a Learner with Computer Databases

Despite an initial steep learning curve with using and understanding how computers function, Marie's mental model of learning computer software

Table 5.1.   Marie's Espoused Self-Concept Mental Models

Learner with Computer Databases Mental Models	Teacher with Databases Mental Models	Change Agent Mental Models

• Explores hands on with guidance as needed
• Is enthusiastic
• Weighs costs and benefits of learning new technology to:
  ○ herself,
  ○ job,
  ○ school, and
  ○ students
	• Explores hands on with guidance as needed
	• Is positive about databases
	• Is probably not "a natural teacher"
	• Intuitively teaches with databases
	• Relies on prior experiences
	• Imparts information
	• Feels comfortable with technology
	• Helps students problem solve
		• Leads change with information technologies

prescribed a hands-on method (table 5.1). Before Marie invested the effort
to learn new software, however, she would examine its value: "If I can
see that it's got benefit to myself or the school or kids or whatever, I'll
grab it and learn about it. But, I don't want to do it [if] I don't really see
the benefit." Her espoused mental model of herself as a learner required
that she perceive benefits to the school's reputation and library needs, to
the resource's effectiveness and relevance to the students and her fellow
teachers, and to herself as teacher-librarian or for her personal use (table
5.1). After running these mental models in parallel by analyzing and jud-
ging the new resource through her priority criteria, she made the decision
whether or not to invest the effort. Her mental model as learner then
allowed her to feel comfortable and enthusiastic rather than resentful.
This facilitated her ability to create a new mental model of the resource
linking similarity and differences to other mental models (Gentner and
Forbus, 1996; Halford, 1993; Johnson-Laird, 1983) involving computer
resources.

Mental Model as a Teacher with Computer Databases

When she commented on teaching students to use electronic databases,
Marie's mental model supported a self-perception that she intuitively
knew how to teach the use of computer resources (see table 5.1). Also
embedded in her mental model was the justification that she had learned
enough about computers and automated databases to do so profitably.

> Oh, I think I do fairly well at that. . . . I'm not really a natural teacher but I
> think because it was something I got interested in personally and, because I
> sat down myself and learned a lot, by teaching myself and going to a few
> courses and things, I probably just am able to impart some information.

The mental model of herself as "not really a natural teacher" is a reflection of her perception that she had escaped to the library from the classroom. These espoused mental models of her roles as teacher-librarian and
her self-concept as a teacher confirm each other thereby strengthening the
applied research in mental models delineated in chapter 2.

Marie's mental model of how best to learn and teach with information
technologies held a commitment to hands-on practice in order to "learn
how to use the programs and all the pitfalls . . . [otherwise] you really
don't learn anything!" (see table 5.1). Marie's espoused teaching mental
model also contained a preference to provide some information to students (and teachers), leave them to explore, and guide them to problem
solve when they had difficulties. Two elements are relevant in Marie's
learning and teaching mental models.

First is the contrast with Anne's espoused, in-action, and reflective mental models. Anne often saw "pitfalls" as errors that she should have averted, particularly in the lesson with Andrew whom she credited as knowledgeable with computers. Marie viewed them as an integral component in her mental models of learning both how to use the software and how the software works (Dimitroff, 1992; Marchionini and Liebscher, 1991). In effect, this strategy allowed Marie and her students to embed examples and non-examples of procedures and functions in the software mental models they were creating. Incorporating correct and incorrect strategies and information in mental models allowed increasingly efficient troubleshooting, especially when under stress (Carroll, 1990; Evans, 1996). As people acquire procedural and conceptual knowledge, they run parallel mental models or fragments of mental models to sort, discard, or trial predictions (Haycock and Fowler, 1996; Holyoak, 1991; Schank and Cleary, 1995).

The second component indicates that Marie's espoused mental model of students posited that they could and would discover how to use electronic databases if, after some instruction, they had the freedom to explore with guidance when they "got stuck" (see table 5.1). Curiously, given that Marie believed she was not really a natural teacher (table 5.1) and preferred administration over teaching, her mental model of the best way to teach students appeared to reflect a social constructivist pedagogy. Marie scaffolded the learning tasks so that she acted as the guide who, in Vygotskian terms, was more capable and knowledgeable in the teaching learning partnership (Vygotsky, 1978). Her in-action mental models would later confirm or refute this supposition.

Her espoused mental models of teaching information literacy skills apparently contained a belief that no planning was required: "I suppose since I've learned it for a few years now, I just know how. . . . I suppose when a child asks me to help them, I just respond. I suppose as a gut response; you know, whatever their little problem is, I just help them to fix it up." In her stimulated recall and post-interviews, Anne had categorized a similar concept in her mental model as "teaching by the seat of her pants." The mental models of both teacher-librarians contained tacit knowledge based on prior experiences (table 5.1), and that this knowledge was adequate for teaching. Marie's espoused mental model also possessed a healthy self-concept toward teaching information literacy.

Change Agent Mental Model

Marie's mental model portrayed herself as a pioneer within the public and private school sectors in computerizing school libraries (table 5.1). When we attended a regional teacher-librarian meeting, her peers confirmed this profile unsolicited by us or other attendees. Marie noted, "I think eventually that some of the traditional skills may go. I think probably librarians will be electronic people more than book people." In comparison, Anne's mental model strongly sustained a duality of print and electronic resources; she saw it as a mission to ensure students and staff recognized the value of both. Marie's mental model of her change agent role affected the level of learning she invested in electronic technologies, her mental model of the value of electronic resource tools for students, and her mental model of how important this role was in the school.

Mental Model of Benefits of Electronic Databases to Students

Because of the successes her students at various academic levels had with electronic databases, Marie had a very positive mental model of them:

> They're wonderful for a whole gambit of kids. For the really bright child, they just love it . . . it really stimulates them even more. Then, at the other end of the scale, for the child who can't read or isn't achieving, as long as they can identify the key word and type that key word in, the computer goes and finds the answer for them. It puts the key word in lovely colored print—rather, it actually is [or acts like] a neon light that comes out and hits them on the nose! . . . So it's a success thing for those kids. You can see those kids who normally come here and have failure experiences with the books. [pause] You can just see it on their faces sometimes. You know, "I've found the answer, too!" when normally out here they can't always find the answer in the general library. I think it's great.

Marie's justifications strongly influenced her mental model, resulting in an unwavering endorsement of electronic databases, especially those that she had evaluated as worthwhile information resources for students.

We also identified one more characteristic embedded in her espoused mental models of electronic databases and their value to students. Computer databases had positively changed students' attitudes to information literacy research. Students' enthusiastically demanded to use computer resources in comparison with their half-hearted and quickly abandoned attempts to access book resources. Marie based this link in her mental model on her informal assessment, observations, and anecdotal evidence, particularly when teachers brought their class to the library to research a project.

Preparation for Lessons Mental Models

The two lessons Marie taught for our project matched mental model fragments of Marie's ideal teaching situations: one on one and problem solving. The first session involved solving the problem of using an encyclopedia database more effectively while the second undertook to solve the problem of getting a student to increase her understanding of how to find materials by using the automated catalog rather than looking on the same shelf for a storybook. The classroom teacher selected Nathan but Marie selected the second student, Alana. Both students were in Grade 4 but in different classes.

With her first student, Marie planned to continue a lesson she had taught in the library's computer classroom the previous week on using the *International World Book* encyclopedia database. Marie observed that students attempted to use the database as they would a book when finding answers to their teacher's worksheet. They did not use any of the special interactive multimedia tools for finding and using information. Her mental model of this event sparked her mental model of how the students should be using the search tools for more effective use of the database.

Her espoused mental model of her lesson with her second student was very different. She linked her lesson mental model to her mental model of the student. While Alana's class did not frequent the library, she often came by herself to get a book in her favorite series. Marie never saw her use the automated computer catalog and therefore thought that Alana probably did not know how to use it. She decided it was time for Alana to learn to do this. Thus, she designed a lesson that would build Alana's skills with the automated catalog, starting with finding books by author, title, and subject. Marie knew that the library contained books in the same vein as Alana's favorite author in other locations that Alana was missing. Marie wanted Alana to locate them by using the automated catalog and then find them on the shelves.

IN-ACTION VIDEOED TEACHING-LEARNING SESSION MENTAL MODELS

Explanations concerning the structure of this section reiterate comments in chapter 3 and those in the videoed mental model section of Anne's case study. We identified mental models from the transcripts of the videoed lessons and annotated these transcripts with relevant non-verbals displayed on the video. We made no attempt to list the categories identified from Anne's transcripts and find the data in Marie's transcripts pertaining to these a priori categories. Rather, we only identified categories that emerged from Marie's data. Nevertheless, given the nature of teaching electronic information literacy database skills, it was not a surprise that many of Marie's overarching mental models and their embedded fragment mental models (e.g., figure 4.1) have the same category title as those that emerged from Anne's video transcript.

This discussion did not presuppose access to subsequent data from Marie's stimulated recall or enhanced post-interview transcripts. In this way we could focus on the lesson interactions and their relationship with Marie's espoused mental models. We attempted to ignore explanations and justifications based on hindsight knowledge. However, we referred to any mental model in Marie's first lesson with Nathan that had relevant links to, or effects on, the series of interviews in the second lesson with Alana. Through this way of only utilizing what preceded each videoed lesson, we hoped to maximize credibility of our analysis.

Teaching Strategies Mental Models

Lesson Introduction Phase Mental Model

Marie's mental model of how to begin a lesson was to test her predictions about the students' procedural and conceptual entry-level understandings about the databases. Therefore, as soon as each session started, Marie ran her espoused mental models of the student and of what she needed to know to confirm or challenge her planning for that lesson. It soon became obvious that she activated another mental model, that of using questioning techniques to probe understanding and skill level. This "introduction phase of a lesson" mental model minimally echoed that of Anne's. Anne used questions to confirm her espoused database choices, to verify the assignments, and ran her espoused mental model of each student. Marie aimed her questions at ascertaining the students' procedural or conceptual skills with the databases.

Marie directed her first student, Nathan, to show her how he loaded the disk to find dinosaurs. As Nathan proceeded to go through the steps, Marie questioned him to find out his understanding of what he was doing. For example, when he was typing "dinosaurs" in the search field, Marie asked him how the computer would find his word for him and what it was doing. Marie was discovering Nathan's conceptual and procedural understandings of the database to add to her mental model of Nathan. When he gave a correct answer, Marie responded, "That's right; you're doing a search. That's very good." For both Anne and Marie, confirmatory praise was another component in their mental model of teaching with computer databases.

At the start of the second lesson, Marie questioned Alana about her knowledge of the automated catalog. Through her questions and responses to Alana's answers, Marie added to her mental model of Alana and started building Alana's conceptual mental model of the purpose of the automated computer catalog. Marie asked her, "Now, do you know exactly what the catalog helps you do?" When Alana replied that it helped her find books, Marie responded that the catalog helped Alana find out what was in the library and where she could find the book on the shelf. Notice Marie's mental model of responding positively while correcting and extending the student's understanding. She purposely stayed at an elementary level of providing conceptual knowledge, especially after discovering that Alana did not understand anything about the automated catalog other than she had seen the screen in the library and she knew that was where people looked up books.

Conclusion Phase Mental Model

This mental model of closing a lesson incorporated a brief review of what they had learned during the lesson, finishing with students demonstrating their understandings. These strategies seemed endemic as they occurred in both lessons.

The final step with Nathan was to reverse what had occurred as her first step in the lesson. This circular tying-off should have provided Nathan with a comfortable sense of closure. Marie requested, "You show me how we would go back to the menu, how we would close down our *World Book* now. [Waits for this to occur.] Now you've closed down the article but you haven't closed down the *World Book*. Now how will we put the screen back the way it was before? [Waits.] Excellent! Well done." Marie's second sequence of comments in this quote positively reinforced what Nathan had done and prompted for what he had forgotten to do by giving clues. It demonstrates the link between Marie's teaching techniques and closing routine to database procedures mental models. This routine required Nathan to demonstrate his mental model of database procedures for exiting the program. Marie enhanced her mental model of Nathan and his understandings with his success. These mental models were also apparent in the closure to Alana's lesson. Marie required Alana to demonstrate her procedural and conceptual understanding by using the automated catalog to find a book in a section of the library previously ignored by Alana before the lesson.

Hands-On Strategy Mental Model

Each student had hands-on control of the keyboard throughout the lesson, except for one brief section in Alana's lesson when the screen went blank. Marie took over to rectify the problem because of her knowledge of what had caused it. Unlike Anne, Marie neither mentioned her rationale for a hands-on strategy to her students nor kept control of the keyboard until the end of the lesson.

Questioning Strategies Mental Model

She used "how, when, and what" questions as part of her teaching strategy to obtain information to embed into her mental models of each student. This strategy also fed back into her mental model of effective questioning. Marie's mental model of effective questions to ask ranged from closed questions to open-ended questions, but the latter were more common. They often demanded higher-level thinking skills from the students.

Marie asked her first student, Nathan, to think about what he could have done differently to find the answers required by his worksheet: "All right, now you think back to the other day when you had your sheet. Now you said that you read the whole thing until you found the answers. What do you think you could have done instead?" Nathan had to run various mental models or fragments of mental models: what strategies he had used, his prior experiences with interactive software, the computer interface of the dinosaur page, and, perhaps, what he thought the teacher wanted. He had to predict a possible strategy based on these mental models. Marie had set up the learning conditions to allow Nathan to construct a hypothesis so that he could test its viability. Nathan's mental model of how to search encyclopedia CD-ROM databases changed through the process. Based on his answer, Marie added to or confirmed her mental model of Nathan.

When they found the main database page for dinosaurs, Marie utilized her own mental model of the multi-literacies required when using the interactive multimedia databases. She used her questioning strategies mental model to guide Nathan to build a mental model that incorporated conceptual understanding about how to read the interface for search aids. She wanted to show him these aids and their function but she did so through questioning. Marie invited him to look for particular aids and then asked him what those aids meant. By doing this, she led Nathan to form a much broader mental model of the type of searching tools he could use within this database. She included shortcuts and tricks that would help him: "Now scroll this little screen for a minute. Stop anywhere. It doesn't matter where you stop. All right, I want you to click on another one of these and see what happens. What just happened?" When he answered these types of questions with a literal response about what action had taken place, Marie would reflect about what had happened, extending his answer a little. Then she probed for deeper understanding. For example, Marie asked, "I wonder why that one might be different but when we clicked on this one, they were the same?" Marie let him reason, thereby contributing to his conceptual understanding of whatever step she was having him take.

Marie's questioning strategy mental model and her Alana mental model were also obvious when Marie asked her second student, Alana, to predict outcomes. However, based on Alana's verbal intonation (as noted in the transcript), many of Alana's responses appeared to be guesses and, hence, she would probably not have used metacognition because she was not sure whether she knew or did not know the correct answer. Nevertheless, Alana's mental model of Marie would have incorporated an acknowledgment that Marie's questioning techniques did not allow her to give an answer without Marie probing for clarification. The following provides an example of this.

Notice how Marie's questioning strategy is cognizant of Alana's answers. Her questioning strategy mental model sorted through how to word an appropriate second question and thereby demonstrated that Marie linked this mental model to her mental model of Alana's level of understanding. Tying off this questioning segment involved Marie's affirmation of the student mental model in conjunction with Marie's mental model of "imparting" a more comprehensively correct answer. Marie commonly used this strategy in her teaching in both lessons, thereby reinforcing our claims that these mental models were deep-rooted in long-term memory.

Marie: Do you know exactly what the catalog helps you do?
Alana: Not exactly.
Marie: Not exactly [repeats Alana's words; slight pause]. Can you give, can you tell me one thing that you know that the catalog helps you do?
Alana: Helps you find books.
Marie: That's right. But it does two things actually. It helps you find out what's in the library and then it helps you find where they are on the shelf.

Marie realized that "not exactly" implied that Alana knew something so she asked another question to test that assumption. Marie could have given the answer to Alana, but that was not part of her mental model of effective teaching. The re-worded question required one example, thereby limiting the mental effort required by Alana and maximizing her success. When confirming the correct answer, Marie provided further information to allow Alana to build a more robust conceptual mental model of the role of a catalog. We saw how Marie activated her mental models of past experiences, decisions concerning effective teaching strategies, and questions that check for student understanding, praise, and full explanations. By doing this, Marie ensured that Alana was cognitively active rather than listening to information from the expert.

Reflecting Back to Student Mental Model

When Marie asked how Nathan found the answers to the dinosaur questions, Nathan said, "I read all of it [pause]. So it was really easy and I just had to look through to look for the sentences." Marie reflected back to him about what he had done, "Okay, so what you actually did is, you just read through all the information until you found the answers, nearly the same way as you would when you use a book. Is that what you did?" Nathan verified that he had used the computer database as if it had been a book. That is, he read the text without using the keyword searching tools or section headings and sub-headings. This is but one example of Marie's reflecting-back-to-the-student mental model in action.

Cross Checking for Proof of Student Understanding

Marie did not just accept Nathan's verification that he searched the database like a book. Marie checked his actual procedure for doing so. While he was showing her, Marie asked him to watch how the computer was responding to his actions. Marie crossed-checked that the student had not been "giving the teacher the answer he thought she wanted" and that he really had skimmed the text looking for the actual words or phrases to find the answer to the worksheet question. This strategy seemed embedded in her mental model, as it was a repetition of her asking Nathan to load the dinosaur section of the encyclopedia, and then watching and questioning him. To check Alana's understanding of how the computer catalog could help her, Marie asked her to choose a second favorite title and to demonstrate how to find the title in the catalog. As with Nathan, Marie activated her "closing the lesson" mental model when she invited Alana to demonstrate her understanding by searching for an unfamiliar author and identifying where his books were physically located in the library.

Marie's cross-checking mental model provided an example of the generalizable function of mental models (Halford, 1993). She utilized this mental model on numerous occasions in different sections of each lesson, and for different activities and different types of software.

Capitalizing on Motivation Mental Model

The following example is sufficient to demonstrate this mental model. Marie's mental model capitalized on Alana's motivation. She guided

Alana through tasks deliberately associated with Alana's favorite authors and book titles until just before the closing phase of the lesson. Partly, as a final verification of Alana's understandings, she had her try one more book by herself, this time giving Alana the author's name for a book in a completely different category and, therefore, place in the library. The other objective for doing this interconnected with Marie's mental model of one of the lesson's goals. Alana had only gone to one place in the library where she could locate her favorite author's novels. Based on the video, we could claim that Marie demonstrated that she facilitated Alana's understanding of using the catalog. That is, her (videoed) in-action teaching mental model fulfilled her espoused lesson plan mental model and, in so doing, utilized her "student motivation mental model" as a tool to promote Alana's learning.

Facilitating Conceptual Understanding Mental Model

You will have noted the previous examples in which Marie activated a teaching strategy mental model with the goal of enhancing and verifying the students' conceptual understandings. Here are two further examples, one each from Nathan and Alana's lessons that helped strengthen the students' "how it works" mental models.

Marie ran her questioning mental model, which included a scenario plus explanation to set the context for her question: " 'Dinosaur' is like a very general article about all dinosaurs. Sometimes, your teacher wants you to do a project on a Brontosaurus or one of the other ones. How could you find out which ones [dinosaurs] are actually in the encyclopedia?" It was a ploy for illustrating the concept of "related articles." In her mental model of her aims for the lesson, this was the second of her two goals. She wanted him to figure out what related articles were and how the link lists the dinosaurs contained in the database. She inquired, "Now, what do you think 'related articles' is? Have a little read of that and see if you can figure out what that might be." Again, Marie immediately retrieved her questioning mental model and, given the time it would take to read, actioned a "wait for the answer" link in her questioning mental model. When he replied, "Tells you what is in it, in the encyclopedia on dinosaurs," Marie ran her "check for understanding" mental model and asked him if he could find "dinosaurs that he recognized" and, after he rattled off five, she asked "if I, for example, wanted to do Brontosaurus, would I be able to find Brontosaurus in there?" Marie summarized his answer as an aid to fortify his understanding, that is, mental model (Johnson-Laird, 1983), "So you can see, when I'm in my general article, I can use the related articles to help me to see if there's any information about other things in it." Marie scaffolded Nathan's experiences to discover not just that the database gave him a related list of what was in the encyclopedia on dinosaurs but also the function of a related article. In addition, Marie was reinforcing the links among the computer database interface mental model, the procedural information literacy mental model, and conceptual information literacy mental model held by Nathan as well as by her.

With some coaching from Marie, Alana "discovered" Marie's mental model, that there was no need to type all the letters in a long title because the catalog accepted truncations of words. Marie helped Alana develop a mental model of the computer catalog as a tool that could respond to incomplete commands. Alana also could have created a new conceptual mental model about the concept of truncation and linked it to the catalog database. Alana's mental model of the computer catalog could have embedded the notion that she did not have to have perfect spelling or the complete title to find what she wanted. What this meant was that she could leave some "knowledge-out-in-the-world" (Norman, 1988; O'Malley and Draper, 1992) as she could still obtain the correct result from the user-friendly database until she learned the correct spelling for book titles or the correct complete title.

Summary

From the video transcript, we identified a number of mental models in action during both sessions. We could assume their connected links but could not know positively without knowing Marie's thoughts during her actions. Her thoughts would answer why she activated these mental models and how she connected them together. Her use of questioning at the level of the student's understandings and her reflection back to the student's responses provided us with a demonstration of constructivist teaching that confirmed her mental model of herself as a learning facilitator. At this point, we could have adopted the product-process paradigm (see chapter 3) and provided our own explanations of her actions but our explanations would not necessarily be correct. Only her thoughts could give us the answer to what she was thinking as she ran these mental models.

IN-ACTION STIMULATED
RECALL MENTAL MODELS

We conducted the stimulated recall interview according to the strict protocols delineated in chapter 3. When either of us, or Marie, stopped the replay video of the lesson, our questions were non-directive, such as "You were frowning. Can you remember what you were thinking?" In this way, we did not skew the interview data by asking a priori research questions. Depending on the wording of her answer, we checked the reliability of her recall by asking Marie if her thoughts had occurred during the lesson or just now during the interview. When coding and categorizing the data, we did not exclude the latter category but relegated any hindsight thoughts and justifications to the reflective mental model category for coding. An assumption that we could obtain the same data through our post-interview based on using probe questions from the previous interviews and lesson video is inherently problematic. Such questions, even if open ended, such as, "Tell us about your strengths in this lesson?" would skew the data toward our a priori objectives. We would have accidentally cued the participant to run mental models that had this information embedded in them. We constructed the post-interviews as enhanced post-interviews to elicit reflective mental models resulting from reliving their experiences through the video and, crucially, the stimulated recall interview (see figure 3.2 and table 3.2).

Lesson Planning Mental Model

Neither Marie nor Anne or, for that matter, any of the other eight teacher-librarians developed a written lesson plan for their sessions with the students. This included those teacher-librarians who had not taught or only minimally taught online database literacy skills. This lack of formal planning followed the pattern that usually happened to teacher-librarians engaged in one-on-one teaching learning episodes. The pattern appeared to be a generic mental model held by teacher-librarians for these situations. The one-on-one or small group episodes usually resulted from on-the-spot student requests for information-finding assistance. The teacher-librarian would usually evaluate the situation according to the student's information need, time available, and complexity of the request. This was not necessarily according to any perceived need for enhancing the student's conceptual understandings. Opportunities for devoting teaching to expanding conceptual understandings typically came from classroom teacher requests for information literacy lessons in conjunction with content units requiring student skills with these tools for their learning success. Whether teacher-librarians taught one on one for conceptual understandings depended on their assessment of the need for concept knowledge in order to understand and integrate procedural knowledge.

Although we asked that their teaching learning episodes be as authentic as possible, both Marie and Anne (and the other eight teacher-librarians) had the opportunity to plan the lesson content and teaching strategies based on what they could find out about the student's prior knowledge from the classroom teacher. Marie invited Nathan to the library to chat with him about the research project and make him more comfortable with her. She knew Alana from her many trips to the library. She also knew that Alana's class had never come to the library's computer lab so she thought she could assume that Alana did not understand the automated catalog tool. Anne knew Andrew well and Frances somewhat. That both did not create a formal lesson plan for these sessions would be typical of their mental models for this type of teaching.

At the beginning of the lesson with Nathan, Marie recalled that she was considering what she had mentally planned yesterday.

> I didn't know whether I was going to do something entirely different with him or take something that we'd already done, so I decided to take something we'd already done [hindsight thought]. So [at the start to the lesson] I thought about what I was going to do in my head . . . [Interviewer: Were you thinking that during the beginning of the actual lesson or just now?] Yes, I did. I was thinking about what I'd thought about yesterday.

Marie's planning mental model held an "in the head" decision about what database to use and the database functions that she wanted Nathan to use. Her mental model was not a detailed plan of procedures, such as when to do what or what extra functions to explore. Nor did she have a plan of what concepts to teach about the database functions, beyond the goals (see below). Marie was confident with this level of planning, and that she could utilize various mental models to ensure a successful lesson that led to procedural and conceptual understanding.

Notice that in the above recall of what she had been thinking, Marie did not say, "teach Nathan." Coupled with this omission were words that had an embedded concept of learning *"with* him" (cf. Jonassen, Campbell, and Davidson, 1994) in order to choose "something *we'd* already done" (our italics). These three pointers support our contention that her espoused mental model held a social constructivist view of teaching.

Goal for Lessons Mental Models

The stimulated recall interview highlighted that Marie's mental model goals for both lessons were concept-oriented, not product-oriented. For instance, Marie told us that, when she had taken the opportunity presented by something that occurred during the lesson, it (i.e., the mental model) became a checking mechanism. She noted,

> I was thinking that the main things I had wanted to do in this lesson were to introduce him to the fact that you can use the small screen to go [to] for your information rather than reading the whole thing [article] and to introduce

him to the fact that the related articles will help him find other bits in the encyclopedia.

By retrieving her thoughts through stimulated recall, Marie told us her specific goals were to develop Nathan's conceptual understandings of important database searching tools. We could now identify that her mental model of critical database searching skills included using the small screen to avoid reading the whole article and using related articles to find additional information. This was the first time that we could see the specificity of this mental model. Because she did not focus exclusively on retrieving an information product, Marie was able to run two lesson goal mental models oriented more toward conceptual understanding of the tool and the student's use of the tool. Her strategies to achieve these goals demonstrated mental models that were student-centered and tool-centered rather than information product-centered.

Toward the end of the stimulated recall interview, Marie offered her thoughts about the lesson with Alana. She said, "I remember thinking, 'I didn't achieve my objective. I doubt she'd be able to go to the catalog next time and find what she is looking for.' I thought, 'She probably needs a bit more practice, more help, a bit more understanding on how computers work.'" This in-action stimulated recall reflective evaluation confirms other research findings concerning the outcomes of teaching for procedural or conceptual understanding (e.g., Duff, 1992; Rogers, 1992). Marie's mental model incorporated the messiness and incomplete understandings left by her conceptual approach with Alana. Yet, she prefaced her remarks with "probably" and "a bit more understanding," which indicated Marie saw growing understanding in Alana that was neither unfailingly functional nor fully conceptual. If Marie had used procedural teaching to give Alana an ordered set of steps to follow in order to carry out a specific task, she might have left the session confident that Alana could find an author in the catalog. Instead, Marie wanted to help Alana understand all the ways the catalog could help her locate materials, not just her favorite author. Teaching conceptual understandings took Marie longer than the "do what I tell you" procedural approach. It also left Marie doubting whether her student really understood the concept of how the computer catalog worked.

These findings confirmed those of Rogers (1992). Marie thought she might have to help Alana again in order for her student to habituate the procedures and understandings in her mental model. In contrast, procedural teaching would have been clean, directive, and would have taken care of the student's immediate product needs but would only be applicable to the immediate information need (Renkl, Mandl, and Gruber, 1996). By opting to teach both procedural and conceptual understandings,

Marie would eventually make the catalog more useful to Alana (cf. Duke and Reimer, 2000; Seel, 1995).

Teaching Strategies Mental Models

Introductory Lesson Phase Mental Model

We confirmed some of our assumptions about the espoused and "video in action" mental models that Marie utilized through our analysis of the stimulated recall interview. Marie ran her introduction lesson phase in-action mental model as a device to accomplish at least three objectives. One objective was to check each student's entry-level understandings and match them with fragments of her espoused mental models of her students' knowledge. The second was to match this objective with her lesson goals mental models. The third objective was to activate her questioning mental models as her strategy to accomplish these objectives. The literature (e.g., Schoenfeld, 1987; Williamson, 1999) on mental models revealed that comparing for similarities helps chunk the fragments thereby reducing working memory overload (see chapter 1).

Marie's thoughts also corroborated the assumptions we made earlier about what mental models the students could have activated. Marie explained, "It suddenly dawned on me there at that point [indicating the image on the TV monitor where we had stopped the video], a lot of children can't come in here independently and choose and load the program." She therefore asked Nathan to "show me how you loaded the dinosaurs and how you found dinosaurs. Show me all the steps." Nathan demonstrated he could select and load the *World Book* encyclopedia from the computer CD-ROM server menu and choose "dinosaurs." This verified Marie's video in-action mental model of the value of checking as well as her espoused mental model of Nathan's procedural computer literacy.

When asked for her thoughts at the beginning of Alana's session, Marie recalled thinking, "Well, exactly where I was going to start her, actually, because I was wondering, 'Will I have to go back to exactly explain what a catalog was . . . or had she had an experience even with a card catalog, never mind an automated one?'" Marie asserted that her thoughts had been centered on "trying to get her to tell me that (a) it was a database of what's in the library and (b) that it tells you where to find those things." Marie confirmed that these thoughts were "there and then" as they had occurred at that point during the lesson. These thoughts also established that Marie was running a number of linked fragments of mental models in parallel or, perhaps, was accessing them in a hypermedia mode (Haycock and Fowler, 1996; see chapters 1 and 2). The mental model fragments included her Alana mental model linked to why she had chosen Alana as the second research participant, and various teaching strategy fragments, such as "how to start the lesson," questioning to obtain Alana's conceptual understanding of a catalog, and how to explain the function of a catalog in language that Alana would understand.

Marie's actions and language (videoed discourse) simultaneously mirrored her thoughts (stimulated recall interviews) and substantiated Cohen et al.'s (1995) conclusion that as a task was evolving (in our study, starting the lesson), the plan (what to do) and action (how to accomplish) mental models were run in parallel rather than having to think through the plan in its entirety before implementing it. This conclusion would explain why Marie did not create a written lesson plan before teaching her two students. She felt confident that she would know what to do as her lessons were evolving; that is, both her plan and action mental models would run in parallel with her lesson goal mental model.

Hands-On Control Mental Model

On one occasion, Marie took over the keyboard because the screen had gone blank and she needed to rectify this promptly.

> Marie: See, I shouldn't have done that [kept the keyboard a little longer], I should have just handed it back.
> Interviewer: Did you think that then?
> Marie: Yes. "I should keep my little hands to myself off the keyboard and let her do the keyboarding, and me do the pointing." [Watching the replay of herself handing back the keyboard, she commented with a hindsight thought], "pushing temptation away!"

From Marie's experience, taking control of the keyboard was definitely a seductive temptation. Marie's thoughts confirmed her espoused and demonstrated mental model during the video session. She revealed a mental model where her preferred strategy when teaching computer skills was for students to have hands-on control of the keyboard. Marie demonstrated she utilized her critical self-reflection mental model here too.

Nonverbal Cues Mental Model

Table 5.2 identifies Marie's thoughts vocalized during the stimulated recall interview, whether the thought was an introspective "there-and-then" thought that occurred during the actual lesson or a hindsight observation, and the in-action mental models categorized from the stimulated

Table 5.2.   Identifying In-Action Mental Models from Stimulated Recall Thoughts

Stimulated Recall Thoughts	Type of Stimulated Recall Thought	Stimulated Recall In-Action Mental Models (MMs)
I noted to myself, "Her eyes are *focusing at the top of the screen all the time."*	Introspective there-and-then thought	*Alana MM* • keyboarding skills • beginner not novice
I then noted she *didn't look over the screen* to find anything.	Explanatory in-action thought	*Teaching Strategies MMs* • Non-verbal cues ○ Alana's eye focus
I was thinking, "I'll *let it go for 30 seconds* and then I'm going to *have to prompt her,* focus her attention onto the screen. She's *not getting the clues* because she's obviously *not familiar with the buttons matching with the keyboard."*	Introspective there-and-then thoughts	• Wait time • Guiding through prompts *Keyboard (physical and spatial aspects) MM*
Now here, I thought straight away, *"She's got no familiarity with the keyboard at all."*	Introspective there-and-then thought	*Alana MM* • keyboarding skills • beginner not novice
I was *watching her eyes* and I thought, "She *doesn't have a clue where even to look for some of the letters. She's got the S and the T all right"* and	Introspective there-and-then during the lesson thought Explanatory in-action thought	*Teaching Strategies MM* • Non-verbal cues ○ Alana's eye focus *Keyboard MM*
then I *noticed that her eyes were not even going across the keyboard to find the "I."*	Explanatory in-action thought	
I would very much doubt whether she's got a computer at home because she hasn't got very much experience at all.	Hindsight justification just occurred in the interview	This is not a stimulated recall in-action MM. It is a hindsight reflective MM.

recall "there-and-then" thoughts. The italicized words indicate our coding strategy. The italicized statements in the Stimulated Recall Thoughts (column 1) are causally linked to the italicized headings in column 3. These headings demarcate Marie's stimulated recall in-action mental models, of Alana and of her own teaching strategies. The dot points under each of these mental models delineate either descriptive content in the mental model (e.g., Alana is a beginner with very weak keyboarding skills) or the type of teaching strategy mental model (e.g., using non-verbal cues to ascertain Alana's eye focus).

Unlike Anne, Marie had not reported in her pre-interview that paying attention to non-verbal cues was an espoused mental model. The videos revealed that Marie's mental model of where to sit in relation to a student to teach computer literacy mirrored Anne's strategy. Both positioned themselves so that they could see each student's non-verbal reactions, the keyboard, and the computer screen. The videos did not reveal that Marie ensured she also noted Alana's eye movements. We obtained this ingredient in Marie's mental model from the stimulated recall interview. First, Marie realized that Alana was a beginner rather than a novice because Alana only focused on the top part of the screen (table 5.2). Second, Alana did not associate the F7 button icon with the keyboard F7 key. Third, when Marie added the "at all" to her comment, "She's got no familiarity with the keyboard *at all*" [our italics; table 5.2], it confirmed our designation of Marie's "beginner" mental model of Alana. Marie validated Alana's "beginner" status when she realized that Alana was only looking at the top left part of the keyboard (second-row sequence of comments, table 5.2). Previously, she thought that Alana was searching the whole top of the keyboard. Now she realized that Alana did not look at the right part of the keyboard to find the "I" in order to continue typing the author's name, "Stine." Stimulated recall brought into the open that Marie had deliberately positioned herself to see Alana's eye movements, and that her non-verbal cues mental model was critical in this lesson.

We included Marie's mental model of the physical-spatial layout of the keyboard in table 5.2. We concluded that Marie would have been drawing on what would be a habituated mental model because she was looking at Alana's eye movements and not the keyboard to understand Alana's difficulties. For example, she did not need to view the keyboard to prompt her memory for the location of the "I" and "N" keys. This suggested that Marie was not using distributed mental models (O'Malley and Draper, 1992; Payne, 1990).

Wait Time Mental Model

In order to confirm or disprove the label she had embedded in her mental model of Alana, Marie allowed Alana time to demonstrate her skills (table 5.2). Research (Atwood and Wilen, 1991; Rowe, 1980; Tobin, 1980) revealed that teachers often did not allow students, whom they had identified as "weak" in a particular area, time to answer questions or demonstrate their understanding. Marie's thoughts exposed an effective in-action teacher strategy mental model that contradicted her espoused mental model that she was not "a natural teacher." She highlighted this contradiction when her thoughts revealed that she linked her "wait time" teaching strategy mental model to her "guiding through prompts" mental model teaching strategy. For instance, when Alana was trying to type "Stine," Marie did not direct Alana by pointing out the "I" key and telling her to type it. Marie would have used her "leaving knowledge out there in the world" and checked the keyboard or have unconsciously run her habituated physical and spatial layout of the keyboard mental model. This last would have been a fragmented mental model as she would not have had the short-term memory space to run all the key functions along with dynamic linkages to the other fragmented mental models being run in parallel. In these ways, Marie ran multiple mental models (Haycock and Fowler, 1996) to adjust her teaching methods to meet and enhance Alana's computer skills.

Waiting for Nathan's responses demonstrated that this tactic was customary and deeply embedded in her teaching strategy mental model. We provide two examples from the numerous occasions Marie allowed Nathan time to demonstrate his understanding to validate this contention. One occurred during the introduction and conclusion phases of the lesson. Marie waited while Nathan demonstrated what he had done to find information from the teacher's worksheet during the previous lesson with his class. Second, she gave Nathan and, for that matter, Alana, ample time to answer her questions. She never jumped in to answer her own questions but would occasionally rephrase them when she thought, as we later found out through stimulated recall, that she had asked them ineffectively. Marie's videoed lesson and stimulated recall thoughts highlighted that she implemented this wait time mental model without any overt verbal or non-verbal sign of impatience.

Repetition Mental Model

As the lesson with Alana progressed, Marie ran her "repetition for clarification" mental model. Alana did not know about the F7 key or its function. After some unsuccessful prompting about where to find the F7 key on the keyboard, Marie had Alana use the F7 key to toggle between title, author, and subject until Alana could understand what was occurring and why she would want to use the F7 key. Table 5.3 delineates the lesson's discourse and Marie's thoughts during the stimulated recall interview when this toggling was occurring during the session.

Table 5.3 provides an exemplar of how the interviewers were constantly assessing participants' recalled thoughts during the stimulated recall interview and double checking when they judged the thought to be a dubious "there-and-then" thought. Pressley and Afflerbach (1995) contended that verbal data can be distorted by a participant's interpretation rather than containing pure content from memory. Marie's thoughts were worded in a way that did not demonstrate clearly that they were intro-

Table 5.3.   Comparison of Video Discourse and Stimulated Recall Discourse

Videoed Discourse	*Stimulated Recall Discourse*
Marie: You press the F7 key and see what happens. [Waits.] Now what does it say? **Alana:** Search by author. **Marie:** Do the F7, just do the F7 key a few times and just see what happens. [Waits.] What happens every time you press F7? **Alana:** It changes. **Marie:** It changes, and what's it changing? [Waits for quite a while as Alana does it again.] Can you tell me the three things it is changing to? **Alana:** Title, author, and subjects. **Marie:** OK, all right. So, what's the one we need? **Alana:** Author.	**Interviewer:** Can you tell us what you were thinking then in the lesson? **Marie:** Yes. If she'd have been more familiar, I would have skipped this and gone straight to what I was going to do, but I just wanted her to keep pressing the F7 key and find out if she could see the screen changing at the same time. **Interviewer:** And you thought those things then, during the actual lesson? **Marie:** Yes, yes.

spective (see table 3.2). She said, "I would have . . . ," "I was going to do . . . ," and "I just wanted her to. . . ." These statements indicated to us that they might be an explanation just occurring to her during the interview about what she wanted Alana to do. However, when asked if she had "thought *those things*" during the lesson, Marie replied, "Yes, yes." Her answer confirms that she had thought about the *substance* (i.e., *those things* she mentioned; our italics) rather than the actual words. This meant that Marie's actual thoughts had been something like this: "She's not familiar with F7. I won't skip this and go straight to what I was going to do. I want her (or she needs) to keep pressing the F7 key and I need to find out if she sees the screen changing at the same time." It was important to determine that there was recall as opposed to a verbal report (Gass and Mackey, 2000). Double-checking immediately following the vocalized thought helped maximize reliability of the participant's memory and credibility of the researchers' categorization (Marland, et al., 1992; Vermersch, 1999).

Marie ran her "repetition for understanding" mental model twice during the part of the lesson that followed her scaffolded guidance of Alana's search for an author. Marie explained the call number because Alana had no idea that this was what she should call the numbers and letters on the spine of a book. First, Marie asked Alana to search for a book title of her choice and to explain her comprehension of the role of the call number.

Second, Marie asked Alana to find an author suggested by Marie and to explain how to find out more information about the book. Demonstrated in many of the examples already given in this in-action stimulated recall mental model section was the running of the same mental model in Nathan's lesson when she had him repeat various activities in order to promote his procedural and, particularly, conceptual understanding.

Stretching the Student's Understandings Mental Model

When Alana retrieved the details from her search for a favorite book title, Marie then linked to her mental model of "stretching the student's procedural and conceptual understandings." She asked Alana to explain how she could find the book's reading level suitability (P-Grade 3; junior, middle, or senior) from the information on the screen. Asking Nathan to repeat the opening sequence in reverse in the closing phase of the lesson required him to demonstrate a higher level of understanding in his use of the "if . . . then . . ." function when recalling his mental model (Gentner and Stevens, 1983; Halford, 1993).

Teaching for Conceptual Understanding Mental Model

Table 5.4 provides an example of Marie's mental models of teaching for conceptual understanding through disclosing Marie and Alana's discourse, recalled thoughts, and their in-action mental models as evident from both the videoed lesson and the stimulated recall interview.

In table 5.4, the comments in the mental model column allow there-and-then clarification when reading the table. Alana's thoughts are included. In this way, we demonstrate the interwoven relationship among the teacher-student talk during the lesson, their respective thoughts from the stimulated recall interview triggered by the videoed lesson and our questions, and the mental models that were in operation as identified from the data. What is again striking is the volume of thoughts from the teacher-librarian and the number of mental models running during this small segment of a lesson (table 5.4). The fact that Alana recalled few thoughts in this section (table 5.4) could be a reflection of her introspective recall abilities as a Grade 4 student.

If we had used the process-product paradigm (see chapter 3) based on the video discourse, we could merely surmise that, as Alana's last answer (table 5.4) was the first that was informative and confident, it suggested she used metacognition, "I know that I know," when using this mental model (Haycock and Fowler, 1996). Utilizing the mediating processes paradigm through the stimulated recall interview (see chapter 3), our coding

Table 5.4. Lesson Discourse, Stimulated Recall Thoughts, and Mental Models

Marie	Alana	Stimulated Recall Thoughts	Mental Models (MM)
All right, just before you press anything else, that's in small letters. Do you think that will make a difference?	Yes. Put a capital letter.	**Marie:** Well, I was thinking, "A lot of kids get really funny about capitals and not capitals because the class teacher would be harping on the fact that you start the name with a capital." Here, it doesn't matter, the computer doesn't care whether it's capitals or not so there's no need to worry about capital keys.	**Marie** ran her *higher-order thinking skill question-type MM*; it demanded prediction skills. She also ran her *prior experiences with teachers and students MM* linked to her *capitalization MM*. **Alana** utilized the *"if we've learned that names begin with capitals then it needs a capital" propositional function* in her *catalog MM*.
Well, let's test it out if you think that because, yes, we normally do put a capital with someone's name. OK, did it make a difference? What sort of letters are they on this screen?	[presses enter key] No! Capitals.	**Marie:** I thought, "I want her to point out that she'd typed it in small letters but on our catalog it was all capitals and I want her to tell me it didn't make any difference in the catalog whether she had the S with a capital or not." **Alana:** No thoughts recalled.	**Marie**'s *teaching strategy MM* required Alana to: • test her [Alana's] prediction • give one-word answers to Marie's closed-answer questions (*question type MM*) • tell Marie the results **Alana:** embedded the difference into her *MM of the school's computer catalog*.
OK, so does the computer care whether it . . . ?	No! It doesn't care at all, so you don't have to worry about capitals and small letters.	**Alana:** I remember thinking, "I hadn't known this before." Nil from **Marie**.	**Marie** added Alana's successful understanding into her *MM of Alana*. She again chose a closed-answer question from her *questioning type MM*. **Alana:** Embedded in her *computer catalog MM* are the: • difference between capitals for names in the catalog compared with elsewhere • user-friendly nature of the school's catalog Embedded in her *rules of capitals MM* is a link to the exception of the rule when using the school's catalog.
Great answer.	[smiles]		**Marie:** activated her praise and Alana MMs. **Alana**'s self-concept MM became more positive.

enjoyed a high degree of reliability that Alana had employed her meta-cognitive thinking skills.

Marie continued to run her teaching for conceptualization mental model. She had Alana test various ways to enter the author's name to make certain that the catalog did not require strict capitalization of the given name. Alana also discovered that the computer catalog accepted initials followed by the author's family name and visa versa (table 5.4). In comparison, Anne allowed her student to proceed without a capital on the poet's name rather than correcting her so that Frances would learn from her own decision. Anne and Frances found that the public library's catalog was more flexible than the school's because the latter required capitalization. However, Anne did not suggest that Frances try various versions of the name to reinforce what was and what was not acceptable. One reason for this may have been Anne's focus on time constraints and product instead of understanding. Marie did not articulate time constraints as being an active mental model.

Seizing the Teaching Moment Mental Model

Like Anne, Marie used her errors as teaching opportunities. We provide one extended example to demonstrate the quick running of fragments of mental models in parallel. Marie recalled thinking,

> "Oh, yes, I bungled this one. He's clicked on the one that wasn't a heading." It was a film clip and it didn't match [hindsight explanation]. I thought, "Oh, no! I wasn't paying enough attention to what was actually on the screen" [there-and-then thought]. This was because I was just expecting it to come up [hindsight explanation]. When he said, "No, it doesn't match," I thought, "Oops, you're right! It doesn't match." Then I realized what he'd done. So then I was thinking, "Do I digress or do I try and get him back on track? If I don't go back to it perhaps he may be confused or that I've missed a step with him. But if I go back to it, at least I'll clear up the reason why those two didn't match." Then I thought, "I wasn't going to do this [lesson plan and goal] but since we have a little slip-up here, I might as well show him some of the other levels, icons they use to indicate the photographs and things that don't match headings." So I've slipped a bit in there that I didn't really intend to do [hindsight explanation]. I'm flexible [hindsight explanation].

The delineated mental model fragments utilized and linked in this part of the lesson included her: evaluation of her teaching, assuming rather than paying attention, lesson goal, lesson plan, grasping the teaching moment strategy mental model, what is best for the student's understanding, function of headings in the database, functions of database icons, and self-concept mental models.

From Marie's recalled thoughts, most of her mental models or "pieces" of mental models (Di Sessa, 1988) were being run simultaneously, probably in hypermedia mode (see chapter 2). She utilized the prediction function of mental models to analyze her decision-making about which path to follow. Then the planned lesson goal mental model and her newly decided subgoal were compared for similarities. Marie confirmed her new sub-goal and strategy mental models after a little more analysis of, and "if . . . then" propositional thinking about, the possibilities they afforded.

Questioning Mental Models

Setting the Scene Role of Questioning Mental Model

Marie told us she used initial questions "to set the scene" for the lesson. We discovered through stimulated recall that Marie had not developed a mental model of a detailed plan of what to do but was going to use questioning to guide her teaching, which we now realized was what she meant by teaching intuitively.

Her objective in her first lesson was to show Nathan how to find information using database search strategies (table 5.5). By asking questions to find out his information literacy research skill process, she could then use his research process as a basis for helping him choose more effective searching tools than the one he used with books (table 5.5). Thus, she included Nathan's prior knowledge in her teaching mental model. She was establishing how she would structure this part of the lesson to give him opportunities to run his prior experience mental model, use prediction based on this, and add similarity and difference links. This confirmed our assumptions made from the videoed in-action mental models.

Interconnecting Questioning, Imparting Information, and Checking Mental Models

One clear example will suffice for demonstrating this in-action stimulated recall mental model. Marie realized that Alana had less understanding than the entry level that her lesson had targeted. Therefore, demonstrating some of the flexibility shown by Anne, Marie switched her intended strategy to a mental model that incorporated an interactive blend of questions, information, and verification in order to facilitate Alana's understanding.

> Well, I just thought, "She doesn't know how to use a print, let alone an automated, catalog or what their functions are, so I won't carry on the technique

Table 5.5. Comparison between Videoed Discourse and Marie's Stimulated Recall Thoughts Concerning Student's Research Strategy

Videoed Discourse	Marie's Stimulated Recall Thoughts
Marie: We came here the other day and you had this sheet and you found the answers. Can you tell me, how did you find the answers? How did you go about finding all the answers to that sheet?	I thought, "I need to get him to think about what he did . . . and ask him to think about what process he used to answer those questions on the sheet." I also thought, "If Nathan knew the strategies then I probably would need to change what I was going to do with him." I was thinking about that, the steps I'd thought that I was going to try and take him through. I realized then that I hadn't exactly thought where we were going to get to or exactly which features I was going to teach him. I remembered that I'd thought [before the lesson] that I was going to just try and show him some things that I knew that they hadn't done the other day.
Nathan: I read all of it, and I was just, like, the sentences I was looking for was [sic] written down on the sheet so it was really easy, and I just had to look through to look for the sentences.	The other thing I thought then, too, when he said to me that he looked for the sentences on the sheet, I thought, "Oh, great, he obviously knows something about key words and matching what's in the questions on the sheet with what's in the information [in the database] so he obviously has that step."

of explaining and getting her to tell me what she knows and tell me the answers. I'll use the questioning technique to get what she knows, but impart some information to her as well." I then thought, "I'm going to have to tell her some things that I wouldn't have to tell a child who could honestly give me the right answer." Some times the kids know the right answers [but] it's not conscious knowledge that they have.

We confirmed with her that these were "there-and-then" thoughts she had had during the actual lesson. They were, except for the last reported thought that was a reflective "here-and-now" thought. This last thought only occurred to her in our stimulated recall interview. She used it to justify her rationale and demonstrate her awareness of the difference between regurgitated inert knowledge and understanding (Renkl, Mandl, and Gruber, 1996). What we identified was Marie's use of one of the planks of transformational teaching. Transformational teaching is learner centered. It commences with tasks that start with, and capitalize on, what the learner knows that involves their prior experience mental model. It then proceeds to develop new understandings—that is, in-action mental models—while the student works on a meaningful activity (Pea, 1992).

Evaluation of Questioning Skills Mental Model

Marie provided thoughts, both introspective and in hindsight, that evaluated her questioning skills (table 5.6) during the stimulated recall interview.

Marie realized when she was teaching that she was having trouble with the clarity of her questioning. Marie had imbedded a description of her questioning strategy as "lousy" and inappropriate in her mental model (table 5.6). Besides those given in table 5.6, there were more instances throughout Marie's case study of this technique of asking one question (or a truncated question), followed by a rewording of the question based on thinking that the first question was inadequate to obtain a thoughtful answer from the student (for instance, table 5.5). Nathan generally coped with this questioning technique. Marie taught her lesson with Alana one week after her lesson with Nathan. The same pattern of questions occurred during the lesson with Alana, but less frequently. This suggests that it is quite difficult to change an entrenched mental model spontaneously, first, during a teaching-learning lesson and, second, during another lesson that followed a decent critical review period resulting in a self-evaluative commitment for improvement. The research literature (Norman, 1983; Senge, 1992; Williamson, 1999) spoke of the inability or refusal, even if the latter were unconscious, to change a mental model because of the mental effort that was involved, particularly if it related to the participant's beliefs or values, even if they were erroneous.

Types of Questions Mental Model

Marie's first stimulated recall thought under "First Example," table 5.6, indicated without a doubt that Marie deliberately wanted "the one right answer" to her question, thereby indicating a closed-answer-type question from her questioning strategies mental model. She wanted Nathan's mental model to match her own by telling him the term "search" (table 5.6). Perhaps she wanted to ensure that Nathan knew the appropriate terminology. However, her second question in the "First Example," table 5.6, demanded a more complex thinking strategy than recalling a label, even though this was what she wanted. Nathan revealed that he comprehended the "lousy" question, "It computes. It's going to search through all the words and find it." In fact, in both her comments and thoughts, Marie ignored his wider conceptual understanding of the term "computes" that was linked in his mental model to a process called "search." She focused on obtaining the answer she wanted.

Marie ran her mental model repertoire of questioning strategies when

Table 5.6.   Comparison between Videoed Discourse and Stimulated Recall Thoughts Concerning Questioning Strategy on Two Occasions

Videoed Discourse	*Marie's Stimulated Recall Thoughts*
First Example:	
Marie: Do you know what this is called? What are you doing?	I thought, "Well, I'd better check to see if he knows what it's called."
Marie: Right [confirming his comment that he was "writing in the topic"]. How is the computer, [tiniest of pauses] how is the encyclopedia going to find this word for you? What's it doing?	I wanted him to actually tell me that word, "search." [Marie confirmed that the latter was a there-and-then thought.] I was thinking, "I didn't word it enough for him to get what I was meaning [there-and-then thought]," so that was really not a very good questioning technique at all [hindsight thought]. I thought, "It's such a lousy question" because as soon as I said it, I knew, "He's not going to understand what I'm asking him" [there-and-then retrospective thoughts].
Second Example:	
Marie: I want you to keep scrolling down there but, while you're watching that, I want you to have a little look and watch what this is doing at the same time. [pause] Keep scrolling. [pause] Now what's happening over here? **Nathan:** Still in the different sort of thing. **Marie:** Do you think you know what's happening here? Do you think you can explain it to me? **Nathan:** Yes. It's changing to different from different information. **Marie:** Right, so what do you think [tiny pause] What connection do you think this little screen here has got with this big screen here? **Nathan:** That's the sort of thing it's telling you about. **Marie:** All right. OK, that's pretty good.	In a convoluted way, I was trying to get him to tell me that the little screen is connected with the headings [hindsight explanation]. Well, I was thinking, "I'm not getting through to him. He's not getting what I'm getting at. So I'll have to keep getting him to click something 'til obviously we come across one where the match is very clear."

she asked the question in table 5.5 that required higher-level thinking strategies: "Can you tell me, how did you find the answers? How did you go about finding all the answers to that sheet?" This did not just demand recall. Nathan needed to have had a conceptual understanding of his information literacy strategy and the role that the strategy played for his comprehension (table 5.5).

In the following example, Marie's question also required that Alana activate higher-level thinking skills because the catalog was new to her. Alana could not rely on a prior experience procedural mental model. It could seem an unfair strategy given Alana's beginner status, and therefore argued that Marie should have told Alana what to do. Firstly, Marie did not initially realize that her student was not looking in the correct area of the computer screen (see quote below). Secondly, not allowing Alana to try to "figure out how" (see quote below), by looking closely over the whole screen for graphic clues, would have been an inadequate way for rectifying her understanding of how to read the database interface. Simply telling Alana would have ensured a continued deficit in Alana's conceptual understanding of the multi-literacies involved with computer interactive software and databases.

> All right, you have a look on the screen and see whether you can *figure out how* we might change the screen so that we can search by the author? [Italics are our emphasis. Long wait while Alana looks at the screen, during which Marie prompted.] You have a good look at the screen. There's a little clue on the screen that tells you how to do it. [Marie realized that Alana was only looking at the top of the screen. She again prompts.] Look down towards the bottom.

Alana would have searched for "out in the world clues" from the computer interface and run a mental model when she had singled out a possible icon to test her hypothesis, or she may have been so overwhelmed that she aborted the process before she carried it out. Alana's inadequate prior experience mental model thwarted Marie's prompts to help Alana distribute her cognition between her mental models and that from the catalog interface. She also intended the prompts to help Alana embed in her mental model that she needed to examine all parts of the computer screen and not just focus in one area. When Alana realized that the F7 button linked to the clue on the computer screen, Marie ran a mental model that invited Alana to practice and verbalize what was happening. In this way, Alana was using kinesthetic, visual, and oral learning strategies.

Mental Model of Students' Computer Illiteracy

Marie's mental model contained her dismay with Alana's lack of computer experiences. Marie recalled that she had had these thoughts during the lesson, "It's terrible, isn't it, a child in Grade 4 doesn't know [how to use the computer catalog] or been given opportunities for computer experiences." She did not blame Alana for this situation. Rather, she put it down to the fact that Alana's classroom teacher had not brought the children to the lab. When they did come to the library to borrow, very few of them used the automated catalog. By the end of the lesson, Marie had strengthened the consternation in her mental model. Marie pointed to the paused video, "Yes, this is where she hesitated." Marie recalled thinking, "She's sitting there; doesn't know to go to the next level or to press the enter key—obviously not understanding what I was talking about before." Drawing comparisons between her mental model of Alana with her mental model of a student who is computer literate, Marie commented, "A child who is fairly au fait with computers, they [*sic*] understand that concept of windows, levels, you know, or things on top of each other." On both occasions, Marie had run her mental models of Alana, Alana's teacher, and the consequences for Alana, and perhaps the remainder of the students in Alana's class, of not having had the opportunities to develop keyboarding and procedural skills, let alone conceptual skills and understandings. Thus, children are relegated to the information poor in a society and education system that increasingly demands computer literacy, even in a school that prides itself on its strengths in computer information technologies.

Marie had not attempted to find out anything about the students beforehand in terms of their computer literacy skills beyond her earlier comments. She knew Nathan would have had prior experiences with the database (and that Alana studiously ignored using the computer catalog in the library). Anne had not done this with her students either. Both believed their competency with computer databases would allow them to teach by drawing on their prior experiences mental models and teaching strategies mental models. This far into the research, Marie had not reported to us that she had inquired about their general academic levels. She confirmed her lack of previous knowledge of Nathan's academic level when Nathan found a related article and she noted, "Well, now I was sort of thinking, 'We're going to get to the end now and I don't know whether he's going to understand what that [the text on dinosaurs] was either.' But he did." Marie structured links between her critical self-evaluation mental model to the following faults in her pre-planning mental model. She admitted that she had not attempted to find out about his reading, comprehension, and spelling abilities. Fortunately, he demonstrated that "he's obviously quite a good reader and speller." Marie also confessed that, if he hadn't been, the paucity of her mental model of Nathan in these areas would have been disastrous for the lesson.

Learning from Students Mental Model

While Nathan was demonstrating that he was constructing a new mental model of searching tools, she had him figure out the backspace button by asking him a series of questions about what it would do. Interspersing her questions with critical bits of information, she facilitated Nathan's ability to piece the concepts together. In the process, Nathan surprised her by suggesting a further use of the backspace key that Marie had not recognized. Marie appreciated being taught by students, "I thought, 'So that's something that I've learned today. So he's taught me something as well.' I thought, 'It's great. I love when these kids discover things for themselves.' It's really good."

Like Anne, Marie shared this new learning with her student, "I didn't know that one. That's a new thing I have learned. Very good!" When Marie told us that she was going to use this with her next student, it confirmed that she had embedded this function in her mental model.

By telling Nathan and praising him, she was providing Nathan the opportunity to embed another item into his self-concept mental model. Nathan took the opportunity. In his stimulated recall interview, he recalled thinking, "I felt surprised [and] smart that I found it and she hadn't." Probably more important, Marie's strategy would have allowed Nathan to add four important concepts into his mental model of "Marie, the teacher-librarian." One was the realization that this teacher learned from students. Two, she was willing to admit this. Three, there could be a genuine sharing between student and teacher. Four, we argue that Nathan would have embedded a comparative link to his mental model of his current teacher. This seemingly small episode in the lesson provided all of us a glimpse of the pleasure afforded by a shared mental model. The episode also influenced our judgment that Marie's mental model of herself as a teacher within her role as teacher-librarian was more aligned with social constructivism than behaviorism as she took the role of the "guide on the side" rather than the "sage on the stage."

Perseverance, Patience, and Flexibility

Even though Marie did not label these mental model characteristics, it was obvious from the video and now supported by the stimulated recall interview that Marie's mental model of teaching included personal attributes of patience, perseverance, and flexibility. (Marie's comment about being flexible in an earlier section of her case study was not a thought she had had during the lesson; it was a reflective mental model.) Anne had equated perseverance with tenacity. What we learned from the stimulated recall interview was that, although Marie mentioned thinking that "it's taking her [Alana] an awful long time just to find each of the keys" at the beginning of the lesson, she exhibited a hint of internal impatience on only one occasion. About two-thirds of the way through the lesson, she commented, "I thought, 'Good Lord, we'll be here all day if she's got to type *Grandfather's Garden.*'" Marie never took over the typing from Alana to prevent having to wait for Alana to find the keys and fix mistakes. She persevered. (She had only taken over the keyboard when the screen went blank because of problems with the server, and gave it back shortly afterward.)

Marie also followed the previous thought, with "Oh, well, we'll do the shortened version then she can see that you don't have to type the whole thing." Marie's problem-solving mental model linked to her mental model of being flexible allowed her to turn the situation into a positive by encouraging Alana to find out for herself that the computer would offer suggestions based on keying in a word or part of a word of a title. Though not part of her initial pre-plan or her "beginning of the lesson plan" goal, Marie capitalized on Alana's weak keyboarding skills rather than sink into frustrated impatience or take over the typing. Marie's mental model of herself included implementing positive solutions, such as teaching the concept of truncation, in her teacher actions.

Critical Evaluation of her Teaching Mental Model

Marie's thoughts as she watched the video sometimes revealed disappointment with her teaching. About two-thirds the way through the replay of the lesson with Alana, Marie remembered thinking (there-and-then thoughts), "It's not going very well actually" followed by, "The other one [with Nathan] I did was better." Here, she ran her teaching performance mental models of both lessons in parallel to make these self-evaluations. However, during her lesson with Nathan, Marie had also been less admiring of some of her techniques during her stimulated recall interview.

Marie's critical evaluation tended toward the negative perspective. We provide three examples. In the earlier section on questioning, we mentioned that Marie's questioning techniques mental model contained a negative evaluation of her questioning strategy, where she asked a question and then reworded the question virtually straight away, because the original question was "lousy" and "confusing for the student." A second example embedded in her critical evaluation of her teaching mental model occurred when Marie chastised herself for exploring the tables function in the database. She knew Nathan would not have had adequate prior experiences to draw upon. Marie admitted, "As soon as I asked him I thought, 'Oh, I made a mistake. I took it too far. Grade 4's haven't done things like that. That's pretty silly.' However, I thought, 'I shouldn't have done that but, now I've started, I'd better keep going.'"" Drawing on her previous experiences and her "what was best for the student" mental model, Marie believed that to abort an exploration of the tables function would confuse Nathan. Perhaps outside the classroom, Nathan would very likely have seen complex tables, perhaps in the sports section of the newspaper, and maybe made links to that mental model. Nathan could also have embedded, even if incompletely, the notion that there was a table section into his mental model of the database and that this could be retrieved and explored on a subsequent visit to the database. On a third occasion, Marie worried about the errors in directives that she gave, "Yes, I did think, 'Oh, I could have come a cropper [i.e., unstuck] here.' If it had been a child who wasn't obviously as literate as he is, the lesson could have gone straight down the tube, as they wouldn't have been able to read a word." She recalled thinking that his brightness and reading abilities had prevented her misdirection from spoiling the session.

Distributed Mental Models

From the examples we have provided, we noticed that Marie had distributed her mental models between teacher-librarian, student, and the computer databases and their interfaces (Banks and Millward, 2000; chapter 2). This also occurred in Anne's lessons. When both teacher-librarians and the four students were running their mental models in their particular community of practice, they were constructing individual mental models as well as utilizing distributed or shared mental models among themselves and artifacts (Banks and Millward, 2000; Bibby, 1992a; Cohen et al., 1995; Rogers and Rutherford, 1992). The teacher-librarians and their students were certainly not learning in isolation.

When Marie, Anne, and their students used their respective computer database artifacts, they each retrieved or created two mental representations: one of the artifact and one of the world represented by the artifact (Payne, 1992). This meant that their mental model of the artifact would have contained factual knowledge, such as the encyclopedia's computer database has a search function; procedural understanding, for example, how to load and navigate through the choices offered; and, definitely more so with Marie's rather than Anne's students, an understanding of the role of these features to support conceptual information literacy. By the end of the lessons, the second mental model, that of the world represented by the artifact, would have contained understanding about, for example, dinosaurs and how they became extinct, and the credibility and currency of the information needed to support the project. Alana would have had a clearer conceptual understanding of how the library "worked" with respect to the role of the call number and automated catalog as well as their relationship to how books are shelved according to categories in different locations in the library.

The literature discussed the distribution of mental models between the artifact and the person (Banks and Millward, 2000; O'Malley and Draper, 1992; chapter 1). This would mean that as the teacher-librarian and the student interacted and used the artifact, both their mental models drew on the "knowledge left out in the world" as contained in the artifact as a prompting aid to their current mental models of the database (Bibby, 1992a). However, based on the data, Marie appeared to have internalized both the *World Book* database and the catalog database. For instance, Marie had absorbed the catalog's features, functions, and idiosyncrasies and was not relying on help from the computer's interface as prompts. This is not surprising given the amount of time she had spent evaluating and using the *World Book* database, and creating and then rectifying all the typing errors caused by helpers incorrectly entering the data in the computer catalog, as well as teaching staff and students to use both. There was an exception to our claim. Nathan taught her new things about the functions of certain keys within the dinosaur's database. Until she had habituated these new bits of knowledge, it was probable that she utilized the distributed mental model residing in the artifact's interface. In comparison, Anne still distributed her mental models between herself and the online dial-up connection to the public library's catalog and the newspaper section of that catalog. However, she appeared to have internalized the workings of the public library's book catalog, which we could expect from a teacher-librarian used to accessing the public library for extra resources for teachers and students.

Cognitive Apprenticeship Mental Model

Cognitive apprenticeship and transformative teaching embrace the theory that learners socially construct knowledge through active learning (Collins, Brown, and Holum, 1991; Collins, Brown, and Newman, 1989; Pea, 1992). Both lessons demonstrated that Marie's teaching philosophy and pedagogy mental models exemplified this epistemology. Her strategies belonged more in the social constructivist than behaviorist category. She was the "more capable other" in Vygotsky's definition of the Zone of Proximal Development (Vygotsky, 1978). Vygotsky defined this zone as the difference between what we can cognitively do by ourselves and what we can cognitively accomplish with the scaffolded support from a more capable other (Vygotsky, 1978). Neo-Vygotskians (e.g., Newman, Griffin, and Cole, 1989; Wertsch, 1991) contend that teachers need to work within this zone in order to guide students to achieve what is possible at that point in time.

In effect, the students became cognitive apprentices to Marie, who scaffolded the learning tasks. Scaffolding is a critical strategy within such an apprenticeship. It is a metaphor adopted from the building industry that erects a scaffolded grid of bars that grows as the building rises in height and thereby provides safety for the builders. In education, teachers provide students with a structured process of supported guidance that is scaffolded to provide security as the tasks become more complex once previous understandings, or mental models, have been achieved and demonstrated. The cognitive support is gradually dismantled, that is, withdrawn from the apprentice as, in this case study, Nathan's and Alana's procedural and conceptual mastery was accomplished. Marie's scaffolding mental models contained various characteristics to support her apprentices' mastery (see table 5.7).

We have delineated the strategies that Marie used to scaffold the students' understanding in table 5.7. Marie implemented these types of scaffolding strategies throughout both lessons, thereby indicating that she had entrenched them in her mental models. Marie's scaffolding mental models revealed that they met the criteria established by Greenfield (1984). From the previous examples provided in this case study (and those in table 5.7), it is clear that Marie commenced with the students' level of skill and understanding, then proceeded to enhance that knowledge by building incrementally on each step until she had met her goals for the lesson. She extended the students' understanding to allow the accomplishment of tasks not otherwise possible by selectively utilizing the various strategies to provide support when needed (Greenfield, 1984). As the second to last strategy mental model and example in table 5.7 shows, fading the scaffolding buttressed the students' efforts to "grow out of" dependence on the expert (Scardamalia and Bereiter, 1991, p. 50). Scaffolding could also involve engaging students, as Marie did, in "legitimate peripheral participation" (Lave and Wenger, 1991). In practice, this meant the students participated alongside Marie within her area of expertise, "but only to the extent that they could handle the task and with the amount of responsibility that they were capable of assuming" (Chee, 1996, p. 139; the one clear exception here would have been the table episode in her lesson with Nathan). These last two scaffolding strategies, fading and legitimate peripheral participation, would have drawn on Marie's mental models of the students. Marie's mental models certainly contained these various strategies, even if she did not conceptualize them as scaffolding strategies within a cognitive apprenticeship paradigm.

It surprised us that Marie activated nearly all the spectrum of cognitive apprenticeship technique mental models during her two short lessons.

Table 5.7. Cognitive Apprenticeship Mental Models and Lesson Examples

Scaffolding Strategy Mental Models	Examples from Lessons
Asked questions to ascertain students' entry level for various skills.	Nathan's strategy of finding information in the encyclopedia database and obtaining Alana's understanding of, and experience with, the computer catalog.
Required proof of understanding.	Nathan demonstrated that he knew how to load the CD encyclopedia and search for dinosaurs.
Probed for current and subsequent level of understanding and promoted higher-level thinking activity.	"Why do you think that happened?"
Used repetition to embed the correct procedures and concepts within the students' mental models.	Alana used the F7 function key to toggle between categories a number of times.
Required further proof of understanding by asking students to replicate the procedure but with one different element.	Teacher-librarian and student worked together on the first search by author; then asked Alana to search using a book title.
Incrementally imparted additional information and added new procedures and concepts.	When using the book title search, Marie and Alana explored the concept of truncation.
Commenced the process of "fading" out her expert support to allow the students to manage more of the task on their own.	Alana was required to manage the last search using an author selected by Marie because the book was shelved in an area not frequented by Alana.
Engaged students in legitimate peripheral participation in the area of expertise for a teacher-librarian.	Nathan and Alana were inducted into the world of computer information literacy with activities and responsibilities appropriate to their levels.

These are modeling, coaching, scaffolding, articulation, reflection, and exploration (Collins et al., 1989). Marie used her modeling mental model through questioning and prompts rather than demonstrating how to do it. This proved an effective strategy with Nathan and Alana, at least according to their accomplishments during the lesson and their assessment of their own procedural and conceptual literacy (as recalled during their in-action stimulated recall interview and reported during the enhanced post-interview session). They were kinesthetically and cognitively active in their learning. Marie displayed her coaching mental model through prompts as well as affirmation of the students' answer in combination with imparting more information. Occasionally Marie required the students to articulate their understanding (e.g., "So what's some of the quick ways that you can look to find your answers in a much quicker way than reading the whole article?"). There were a few minor instances of exploration; for example, when Marie allowed Alana to find out about truncation rather than telling her. However, Marie did not activate her cognitive apprenticeship "exploration by self-initiated investigation" mental model. Nevertheless, as we found out during the enhanced post-interview, it was a significant part of her mental model of teaching computer information literacy.

Cognitive apprenticeship can include teaching for procedural and conceptual understanding as long as the teacher situated the tasks in applicable contexts or in the context in which they applied (Chee, 1996). This occurred in Marie's case study. It resulted in the students generating hyperlinks (Haycock and Fowler, 1996) to move easily between the associations created in their procedural and conceptual mental models (students' data). This should have lessened the possibility of "brittle" links between conceptual and procedural mental models (Collins et al., 1989, p. 4) or the maintenance of inadequate and incomplete mental models (Norman, 1983; Szabo, 1998).

Summary

Through her active use of cognitive apprenticeship mental models in her teaching, Marie demonstrated the most social constructivist pedagogy of any of our ten participants. Her use of questioning strategies to take her students to higher levels of thinking in constructing their knowledge helped provide her students with a richer understanding of the databases they were learning to use. She was able to scaffold their answers when they stumbled or extend them where they could profit from a broader or more in-depth explanation. Interestingly, Marie probed her students to give herself an understanding of the level of expertise her students had. She did so only for as long as her probes brought increased knowledge of what her students knew or did not know. Once she had decided how much they had in conceptual understanding, she solidified her lesson goals and approach for each student. Up until that point, she remained flexible about her ultimate lesson goals.

Marie's teaching was a classic example of how to use cognitive apprenticeship as a strategy in one-on-one teaching episodes. She created an active learning environment for her students, in contrast to several other teacher-librarians who commented on their students' passivity. Marie did not question how much or how little her students were absorbing because her cognitive apprenticeship methods informed her of what they were learning. She knew what both students had learned through asking them to demonstrate actively their new learning. As researchers, we could see Marie's student-centered teaching beliefs. Because Marie did not have to rely on "knowledge out there in the world," she appeared to have the catalog, the interface, and the functions embedded in her mental model of the automated computer catalog. Her confidence in using these tools reflected the teacher-librarian as expert with these databases. The question that her example sparked in us concerned whether teachers who used the cognitive apprenticeship model had to be the expert or whether joint discovery learning could use this model, even though both student and teacher might trade the "more knowledgeable other" status throughout the teaching/learning episode.

REFLECTION MENTAL MODELS FROM ENHANCED STIMULATED RECALL POST-INTERVIEW

Lesson Preparation

Finding Out about the Students' Mental Models

As we mentioned in Anne's case study, we purposely did not ask any teacher-librarian a pre-interview question about what they knew about the students or lesson planning because we wished to see if the teacher-librarians voiced comments about these teacher tasks unprompted. We wanted to understand our teacher-librarians' habits of mind; that is, their mental models. We also wished to see if the first session influenced the second session.

Marie reported that she did not know much about Nathan at the beginning of the lesson. The Grade 4 teacher recommended Nathan. Marie noted, "She brought him to the library to introduce him to me so that we actually knew each other, and we had a little social chat." His teacher told her that Nathan was new to the school and having trouble adjusting but she thought this experience would give him a morale boost. Marie also knew from the teacher that Nathan was "a fairly good student and fairly outgoing, and liked computers." She had not asked about his academic or computer abilities beyond this, "No. I could have come a big disaster, couldn't I, if he couldn't have read. But in past experiences, most kids are motivated by the subject of dinosaurs and read about them." Marie said she knew a little more about Alana than she had known about Nathan, "She comes to the library a fair bit by herself. She's a fairly good reader, I suspect. I think she borrows books probably a little bit too easy for her. She borrows them copiously. She never uses the catalog." Marie thought that, regardless of the amount of reading she does, "she's only fairly average academically." When we asked Marie what she had known about Alana's computer background, Marie replied, "I knew she didn't have any here at school." Anne had not asked about her students' academic or specific computer skills, either. Both teacher-librarians held mental models that their expertise would allow them to teach without this knowledge.

The selection of the students for the research sessions differed in the two case studies. The teachers in Anne's schools had recommended two students. Marie expressly wanted someone from Nathan's class, not specifically Nathan, but she targeted Alana for the second student. Marie's mental models with respect to her motives for the selection were similar. Observation of Nathan's class and their inefficient research strategy mental models using the computer *World Book* encyclopedia dictated that she do something about this. The motivation to rectify negligible computer information skills in a student she had observed over time was persuasive. This was precisely why Marie had specifically wanted Alana to participate in the research. The research project triggered a "missionary" zeal mental model to improve two students' computer literacy skills.

Critical Self-Reflection Mental Models

What the Students Learned Mental Model

We asked Marie what she thought Nathan had learned from her teaching. She replied that the next week, when the class came to the library computer lab "with their sheets or questions or information to find, I will make sure I have a look to see if he is just reading the whole text or trying to look at headings and maybe trying to just not stay in the dinosaurs but maybe go and have a look in some other areas as well in the related information part." These were her two initial aims for the session. She ran her mental model of her lesson goals either to embed in it, or create a link to, an assessment that evaluated the success of the lesson on Nathan's information literacy actions in a week's time. This self-notation to monitor Nathan's progress demonstrated another link in Marie's mental models of cognitive apprenticeship, that of individualizing learning and teaching. Marie would then discover whether Nathan had internalized the strategies to execute her lesson goals. Her mental model contained an element of confidence in her student's procedural and conceptual knowledge. This was not misplaced. Nathan told us he believed he had coped and felt confident of his new learning (Nathan's stimulated recall and enhanced post-interviews).

Marie thought that Alana had "probably grasped some of the rudimentary bits. I think she'd probably go over there and be able to use the F7 key and probably type in the author or title." She compared her mental model of Alana with that of other students who did not know how to change the default "subject" setting: "So she might be able to, at least, know how to move that bit around. She'd probably get up the next two levels of the screen, but I doubt whether she'd be able to go right down to the bottom level where it actually shows the individual record of the book."

Marie's mental model of Alana's computer database procedural and conceptual skills was discriminatory. Alana was not as hesitant. She was adamant about her skills, "Yes. Now I can [use the automated catalog]." Her mental model had an embedded self-confidence. In answer to the enhanced post-interview question, "If a new student came to the school, what would you tell her about using the school's computer catalog?" Alana listed procedural steps and conceptual clarification of the roles of various functions and screens, including how to access the individual record of a book and the implications of the details in each of the columns displayed on the computer screen's interface. Marie's judgment could prove correct given the need to practice procedural steps to ensure habituation in a mental model. On the other hand, providing Alana with conceptual understandings could have provided Alana with the confidence to troubleshoot any procedural mistakes.

What I Did Not Like about My Teaching Mental Model

The following are but two of the comments Marie made. She reflected, "I missed a bit out there. I should have actually said to her, 'These with the arrows on them are called arrow keys.' I didn't do that." She was also thinking in hindsight that "I didn't handle this escape key well the whole time. I think eventually she got the idea, but I didn't explain to her enough how it takes you out all the time." Marie was strict with herself, calling herself on a number of self-proclaimed teaching errors.

Marie felt that the lesson with Nathan was not "a perfect lesson and it didn't go exactly the way I wanted it. I hopefully got my message across to him. But what I thought was, 'Good, he's got it, yet there's no guarantee that he'll keep it. But he's got it for now.'" As had occurred with Alana, Marie was implementing that fragment in her mental model that recognized that repetition of both procedural and conceptual understandings was important for implementation and confidence.

What I Did Like about My Teaching Mental Model

Both teacher-librarians had some difficulty in exposing this mental model, probably influenced by a reticence to praise themselves.

Marie thought her most effective teaching strategies with Alana were in the basic areas of Alana's computer skills. She singled out two areas.

> I directed her to look at specific areas of the screen because she didn't have any idea herself and try and get [her] comfortable with the keyboard, too. I think probably because, otherwise, she would have been far too lost. She didn't have enough experience herself. I helped her to actually make sure she knew where she was going.

To be able to know where to look on a computer screen, Alana needed to have possessed a conceptual understanding of the role of the screen's interface and the visible features of the programming behind the catalog. For instance, when the screen reflected search attributes of an automated catalog, not only was an understanding of the features of a catalog important but knowing the relevance of the arrow keys to navigate between those features was also required. In effect, Marie was not merely teaching her procedural skills and a sequence of steps but she was helping ensure that Alana would make use of the mental models embedded in the computer's interface (Cole and Leide, 2003; Hammond, Morton, Maclean, Barnard, and Long, 1992; Rogers, Rutherford, and Bibby, 1992) to prompt Alana's thoughts and actions. In this way, Alana would embed in her mental model, maybe hesitantly, the notion that we can leave such "knowledge out in the world" (Payne, 1990).

A further mental model revealed Marie's appreciation of a mental model that drew on her ability to turn possible glitches and disasters into valuable teaching moments.

> Um, I suppose I can make gaffes along the way, but I've got the experience now to be sort of quick enough off my feet to, you know, jump in and maybe do something about them. In comparison, a lot of the younger teachers can't do that. [small pause] And eventually, too, I suppose, when something doesn't go right, you can take that and use it to some advantage [so] it's not a complete disaster.

Marie did just this in both lessons. She acknowledged, possibly for the first time articulating it, that she was flexible enough as a teacher to overcome problems and mistakes. In order for Marie to have been able to overturn the negatives so effortlessly, her mental models had to have contained a positive self-concept of her expertise with computer database information literacy, her ability to be a facilitator of learning, and her flexibility to cope.

Again comparing her teaching over both lessons, Marie commented, "I probably learned that the approach that I try to take is probably a good approach. . . . For it to be a good learning experience, they've got to do it themselves and discover the answers. They remember it better if they discover it for themselves than if you just tell them. It's just like Mum speaking, you mightn't hear it!'' Her mental model of her teaching the use of the computer had taken on a more positive note as she analyzed how she had taught. She had lost the negative mental model she had had during and right after Alana's session. This happened with Anne, too. Critical reflection allowed the teacher librarians to focus on both weaknesses and strengths in their teaching.

Facilitator, Not a Teacher Mental Model

Our conclusion at the end of the in-action mental models section was that Marie was more aligned with constructivist pedagogy and epistemology. Her summation of the session confirmed this. In Marie's mental model, the teacher part of being a teacher-librarian contained the following characteristics. She explained,

> I don't see myself as a teacher. I do not like the image of the teacher as the knowledge figure. I see myself as a facilitator, to sort of nudge them forward and get them to find out the answer. I don't want to stand up and impart information. That's useless. I know that at some stage you've got to impart some information but impart as little as possible and help them to discover the rest, and get them to do it themselves. Get them to use it for themselves.

She was describing some of the tenets of constructivism (e.g., Duffy and Jonassen, 1996). Knowledge cannot be taught or imparted, only information can. Individuals have to expend mental effort to turn the information into their knowledge. Notice that Marie says, ''Get them to *do it themselves*'' as well as ''Get them to do it *for* themselves.'' Her mental model carried the belief in student ownership of their learning. It came as no surprise then, that our analysis of Marie's espoused and observable in-action mental models were now confirmed by Marie. She acted as the facilitator within a cognitive apprenticeship pedagogical framework. In this respect, there was no discrepancy between the in-action and reflective mental models.

We were curious to see if this was typical of other situations when students needed catalog help in the library. She explained what she did.

> Oh, well, I often wander over there at lunch time when there's a whole crowd around there. You'll see that someone's looking up a title and they've actually got the subject up on the screen. I'll say, ''What are you looking up?'' . . . I'll say, ''What is it?'' They'll tell me it's a title, and I'll say, ''Well, look on the screen; what is it that you have there?'' I wait. ''Do you know how to change it to title?'' ''No.'' So I say, ''Have a look for a clue at the bottom of

the screen," and so on, till they get what they want. It only takes two or three minutes. I wouldn't go beyond what they are looking up. I wouldn't go into a great big spiel about how you can look up this and you can do that.

She used questions to find out what students wanted to do and questions to guide them to the answer, without telling them what to do or doing it for them. She possessed a mental model that students wanted their mistake fixed and their query answered without having their time wasted. The students' mental model categorized any form of teaching for conceptual computer literacy in this "wasting my time" category (Rogers, 1992). Marie realized this. Although she asked some closed-answer questions, her pedagogy mental model guaranteed a technique that ensured the students were active in their own learning and not passive recipients.

Changing Mental Models

We were interested to see if Marie's critical self-evaluation of her teaching resulted in a change or a commitment to change any mental models she thought inadequate. We provide three examples. The first describes a mental model that did not change and the remaining two examples describe mental models that did change.

Marie did not have a positive mental model of her questioning techniques and mentioned this to us, particularly after Nathan's lesson. She revisited this mental model in the enhanced post-interview.

> I don't think I'm a good questioner, I never have actually. I know it's a teaching strategy I do use a lot and I try to get the kids to think and, you know, answer the questions and work it out for themselves. But I don't think I have a very good questioning technique because I think sometimes I take three or four questions to get what I want out of them. If I ask the right question, I might get it sooner. I don't know.

We previously mentioned that Marie had not improved her questioning to any noticeable extent in her lesson with Alana, although she had told us during the post-interview with Nathan she was consciously committed to scrutinizing her questioning skills in order to reword them in her head before voicing them. Her comments in this post-interview again indicate her long-term awareness of the problem and inability to do better during Alana's lesson. It was not unexpected then that her mental model could not be changed, even with this conscious awareness (Norman, 1983; also see chapter 2). Her first question remained a habituated reaction followed by a re-wording or a re-worded question. Her solution, "I think I need to get back and do a bit of teaching," would be inadequate by itself to change the ingrained mental model either.

As a result of the teaching session and the opportunities for retrospective and critical reflection, Marie changed her mental model of the CD *World Book* encyclopedia in a major way. Initially, she seemed to hold a mental model in which the technology with its visual and aural media would ipso facto result in learning.

> Because the encyclopedia comes with a universal language, like a camera icon means pictures, I mean everybody, even students who do not read well, sort of recognizes that. I think that there's a lot more discovery learning goes on using the [interactive multimedia] medium than it does with a book, you know. You have to be far more directive with kids with books, teaching them content pages and those sorts of things. But with the computer database, because it's such a visual medium, kids can do a lot more learning themselves without your direction all the time.

As we know, educational multimedia cannot, of themselves, make you clever. Learners have to make the effort to learn, no matter the medium. By her enhanced post-interview, Marie had reversed this mental model.

> I actually think that the *World Book*'s a better teaching tool than I thought it was beforehand. Without some sort of teacher direction, students fool around, although some do discover some of the things. I now think you really need to actually get in and teach some of the aspects of the encyclopedia. They [the students] can then transfer that over into other databases. You know, that's not something I consciously thought of before [this research project].

Marie had changed her mental model by overwriting the previous evaluation with strategies to capitalize on the features of the encyclopedia database to structure information research literacy activities.

Analogy Mental Model

We found consistency between a number of Marie's espoused, in-action, and reflective mental models. However, one noticeable discrepancy surfaced in the last enhanced post-interview. Marie told us that she used analogies as a favored teaching tool:

> Um, well I often talk about [the database] in the same terms as a book but with added features. [I point out the similarities and difference between what it does and the book does and doesn't do; things like that. I particularly use analogies or [I term them] little stories, particularly with the little kids. I start talking about the eight library computers, how they're really great big calculators. "Don't be scared of them" and "the mouse won't bite you," and things like that, why it's called a mouse with a tail. I say that "the computer

doesn't run you, you run the computer. Even though computers are supposed to be smart, they're not smarter than people." It's a good way to explain how a computer only identifies by matching and doing mathematics. It doesn't really read it the way we read it.

Not once did Marie use an analogy in the two lessons we videotaped. We called this a discrepancy, perhaps too harsh a conclusion given the nature of teaching and case studies.

It drew attention to a limitation of the research. Two lessons could not provide the repertoire of mental models held by a teacher-librarian. However, what the research has done is to highlight the consistencies and differences within and across the espoused mental models, the two in-action mental models, and the reflection mental models. We have utilized these slices of authentic practice to explore the impact of the types, role, and characteristics of mental models used, created, and evaluated by teacher-librarians.

Summary

Marie commented on how her critical self-reflection mental model changed aspects of other mental models. She observed that the research sessions had made her think about her teaching strategies and pedagogy mental models and had increased her desire to do more teaching. These were fairly significant changes to her espoused mental models. Initially, Marie's mental model of herself as a teacher held a belief that she had fortunately escaped from the classroom to running a school library. One reason was that her mental model held a view of herself as a poor teacher. Marie placed her teaching role mental model as a poor second to her administration mental model. The lesson with her second student indicated to her that she needed to be more proactive in reaching out to the classes that never came to the library. "Um, probably because I was teaching somebody who knew nothing, . . . it's given me the idea that I have to get on to that class and others, and talk to the teacher about getting them up [to the library computer lab] more." These teaching experiences seemed to unsettle her mental models in which her administrative thrust had dominated her teaching role.

WRAPPING UP MARIE'S CASE STUDY

After the pre-interview, we defined Marie's mental models as favoring library administration and public relations responsibilities over teaching large classes through a behaviorist lecture mode. She embedded a further mental model, co-planning with teachers to integrate computer technologies into the curriculum, as one of her established responsibilities in her teacher-librarian role mental model. Depicting herself as a leader in the school, another of her teacher-librarian role mental models, Marie fought for changes she thought were right.

In her mental model of herself as a learner, Marie described herself preferring hands on with computer technologies with guidance when necessary. An epistemological link in this "myself as a learner" mental model, was an evaluative self-perception that did not consider herself a learner for learning's sake. For instance, although enthusiastic about student use of electronic databases for information access, Marie carefully weighed the benefits of new technologies or software before she undertook the learning process.

Her mental models of herself as a learner and teacher were inextricably echoed in her mental models of how students learned best and how best to teach. She preferred to impart some information to students, let them explore the software by themselves, and give them guidance with problem solving when they had difficulty. Marie viewed her own errors in teaching computer technologies and software as an integral component of her students' learning. She preferred to use the mistakes as non-exemplars that could help students understand how the software worked. Most of the time, Marie enacted the more knowledgeable other role in her one-on-one teaching learning sessions with students but would trade roles when her students discovered something about the software that she did not know. One reason for this was her mental model in which she eschewed the teacher-librarian as knowledge expert. This was linked to another mental model that bestowed on her the flexibility to swap roles with the student occasionally and to adopt the learner's role to the student's teaching role. She used her prior experience with the software, including the problems she encountered, as an adequate foundation for her to say she could intuitively teach the use of computer technologies and software.

6

The Role of Stimulated Recall in Identifying the Effects of Mental Models on Teaching

I was thinking I didn't want him to leave having spent all this time and have no help on this research project. That's what I was thinking. At every instance I thought, "Surely this [technical and database problems] has got to stop!" And when I said, "Let's see if we can exit," I had no idea [pause] I was thinking, "I hope we really can [exit]." (Anne, stimulated recall interview)

Well, I just thought, "She doesn't know those two." So, I was thinking, "I'm going to have to use the questioning technique to get what she knows, but I'm going to have to impart some information to her as well." I thought, "I'll have to provide some information that I wouldn't have to tell a child who could honestly give me the right answer." (Marie, stimulated recall interview)

The power of stimulated recall to disclose unobservable events that had direct impact on the mental models and, hence, direction and outcomes of the teaching-learning lessons is the focus of this chapter. We utilize an across-case comparison in order to delineate the patterns emerging from both teacher-librarians' data (Ayres, Kavanaugh, and Knafl, 2003; Patton, 2002; Soy, 2003; Yin, 1994). The above quotes exemplify the themes that emerged from each teacher-librarian's stimulated recall thoughts: the product goal and technical problems were constants in Anne's lessons while, for Marie, her pedagogic strategy of using the student's answer to

181

her questions to guide the next step in the lesson was an endemic feature of her lessons. The across- or between-case study methodology provided a comparative lens to probe for substantiations, ambiguities, and revelations derived from the stimulated recall interviews of the two teacher-librarians' individual case studies that were explored in chapters 4 and 5, respectively.

Examination of the data collection instruments, in the sequence that they were administered (chapters 4 and 5), allowed insights into what resulted and arguably what was common and conflicting across all instruments. If we had elected to use a behaviorist process-product paradigm (see chapter 3), we would have observed the actual teaching-learning episode and coded the videotape transcript of the lesson's discourse and actions based on our assumptions about what Anne and Marie had been thinking during the lesson. In contrast, conducted with adherence to the strict protocols of the mediating processes paradigm (see chapter 3), our stimulated recall interviews maximized the reliability, credibility, and fallibilistic validity (see chapter 3) of the participants' recalled thoughts as well as the accuracy of our categorization of the stimulated recall in-action mental models.

It became clear that, because of the level of expertise and background experiences researchers bring to analysis, some categories of mental models identified from participants' thoughts using stimulated recall could have been replicated based just on a process-product examination of the videoed discourse. For instance, both the videoed and stimulated recall data identified a favored pedagogical mental model used by Marie; she confirmed her students' answers by reflecting them back to the student and extending the answers. However, anything we could have suggested as a reason for this pedagogy mental model—such as to extend the students' understanding or that this was her normal strategy—would still have remained conjecture on our part as products of using the process-product paradigm.

The worth of stimulated recall interviewing was continually demonstrated in the four lessons. There were significant occasions when stimulated recall presented unforeseen findings. The teacher-librarians' articulated thoughts during the stimulated recall interview often proved considerably different from the conclusions we drew through analysis of the pre-interview, our back-seat observation of the lesson, and videoed discourse (chapters 2, 4, and 5). Crucially, it was the stimulated recall interview data that allowed us to see the specificity of the way a teacher-librarian's mental models influenced her thinking and actions, and how various mental models, or fragments of them, locked together.

AN ACROSS-CASE COMPARISON

The use of stimulated recall methodology in the previous two case study chapters of two very different, dedicated teacher-librarians each teaching two students individually allowed us an insightful perspective for analyzing each participant's teaching. The intention of our research study was not to make a value judgment on teaching effectiveness but to use stimulated recall to facilitate an understanding of the complex basis for how and why teachers teach the way they do. This chapter's across-case comparison therefore differentiates the idiosyncrasies of, and commonalities between, the two teacher-librarians' mental models and the particular insights offered by their stimulated recall responses.

Table 6.1 is themed according to the more significant mental model categories grounded in the data and utilized in the individual case studies (chapters 4 and 5). A thicker black line distinguishes the groupings: role as teacher-librarian; self-concept characteristics; information technology literacy skills; and self as teacher coupled with pedagogy. The table spotlights the stimulated recall disclosures and therefore does not contain all the mental models identified in the two within-case study chapters (chapters 4 and 5). The table's synthesized findings summarize comparisons between the two teacher-librarians by contrasting their own and each other's stimulated recall mental models with espoused pre-interview mental models and in-action videoed lesson mental models. The amount of detail recorded in the table is purposely generous in order to enhance comprehensibility so that our conclusions concerning the worth of stimulated recall are observable. The focus on understanding how mental models illuminate teaching remains constant throughout the table.

Table 6.1 delineates various mental models in the across-case comparison. A crucial function of across-case comparison methodology is not just teasing out the consistencies and deviations in the data from different cases but also presenting the data in different ways. The latter promotes analysis from changing the perspective of the researcher because of how those data are restructured. Indeed, it was the tabulation in table 6.1 of the comparison of the two teacher-librarians' mental models, when teaching two lessons each, that accomplished this twist in our perceptions, thereby allowing us further insights. In table 6.1, we identified various espoused mental models and followed through with how these were enacted during the lesson and what thoughts about their lesson and espoused mental models were triggered, or not triggered, by the stimulated recall replay of the video coupled with the interviewers' prompts (see chapter 2). This generated the delineation of the following trends in the data.

Three major themes are exposed in table 6.1. One theme highlights the

Table 6.1. Stimulated Recall Revelations of an Across-Case Comparison of the Teacher-Librarians' Mental Models

Mental Model Data Category	Mental Model	Anne's Mental Model Examples	Marie's Mental Model Examples	Comparison of Anne's and Marie's Mental Models
Espoused (Pre-interview)	Major role as teacher-librarian	Teacher-librarian as information literacy expert.	Teacher-librarian as technology leader.	**Anne:** concerned about finding information resources for student and staff needs plus being co-curriculum planner with staff. **Marie:** concerned about automating library and providing technology tools for students and staff.
In-Action (Videoed Lesson)		Focused on students departing with a product (author, title, and/or call numbers).	Focused on students' information literacy needs.	**Anne:** students exited lesson with authors, titles, and call numbers. **Marie:** students exited with enhanced information literacy skills.
In-Action Stimulated Recall Revelation		Focused on finding product led to acknowledging she ignored chance for conceptual teaching to first student due to time constraints and lost focus of second student's understanding.	Focused on students' understanding the database tools in terms of what the tools did and how they worked.	**Anne:** focus on product goal of lessons maintained status and image as deliverer of resources within a limited time frame. **Marie:** focus was the students' procedural and conceptual understandings.
Espoused	Main service orientation as teacher-librarian	Finding last-minute on-demand information products for students and staff.	Helping students and teachers use technology, an enjoyable role.	**Anne:** oriented toward a product from a search. **Marie:** oriented toward people and technology

In-Action		Focused on finding a product for both students' assignments.	Used questions to find out what students understood and requested they demonstrate their understanding.	**Anne:** procedural focus. **Marie:** procedural and conceptual focus.
Stimulated Recall Revelation		Sense of responsibility for first student's inaction on assignment; reported she would find books in the school's library to give her; frustrated and stressed by setbacks to finding an immediately useful product in lessons, particularly second.	During students' next library visit, would check their procedural and conceptual understanding and work with them using same strategies.	**Anne:** product in the student's hands determined success. **Marie:** acceptance of incomplete results in current lesson as possible cost of building more complete conceptual future understandings.
Espoused	*Teacher-librarian as knowledge expert*	Teacher-librarian had status as knowledge expert.	Considered herself technologically knowledgeable with the computer and capable of teaching technology skills intuitively.	**Anne:** information literacy knowledge expert. **Marie:** learned how to use the technology and believed this would translate into effective teaching
In-Action		Had problems with dial-up procedures and finding a product that was useful and not already borrowed.	Obviously understood the technology programs and the quirks of the automated catalog; invited first student to share two short-cut tricks with her.	**Anne:** ensured students knew the technology dial-up problems had not occurred previously. **Marie:** demonstrably enjoyed learning from students.

(continued)

Table 6.1.   Continued

Mental Model Data Category	Mental Model	Anne's Mental Model Examples	Marie's Mental Model Examples	Comparison of Anne's and Marie's Mental Models
Stimulated Recall Revelation		Disappointed in her computer technology abilities, control of the lesson, and inability to find useful resources that were not currently borrowed.	No surprises; delighted with learning new skills from first student.	**Anne:** had practiced before lesson to maintain knowledge-expert status; was disappointed that it collapsed. **Marie:** willing to learn from students so sharing technology skills was reciprocal; assumed role as guide and life-long learner.
Espoused	Time management	Weakness with time management.	Not enough time in job to teach.	**Anne:** attended to emergent student requests as they arose. **Marie:** spent most of her time administratively but helped students "ad hoc" when struggling with electronic catalog.
In-Action		Mentioned need to find resources because time was running out.	Took cues for ending lessons from students' non-verbals.	**Anne:** time controlled session. **Marie:** students controlled session.
Stimulated Recall Revelation		Revealed she wanted to disband second lesson as stress levels were high because time was running out to obtain product; resulted in taking control of keyboard to increase speed of lesson.	First lesson extended to explore area entered by mistake and didn't want to confuse student. Second lesson significantly shorter because length of first lesson tired student.	**Anne:** time constraints pervasive in all her thoughts. **Marie:** relaxed and unfettered by time restraints; disappointed with not paying attention to time in first lesson because of effect on student.

Espoused	*Self-concept: characteristic trait*	Perseverance.	Patience.	**Both:** maintained they possessed relevant characteristics for teacher-librarians.
In-Action		Kept trying until got access and a product, e.g., call number.	Did not take over keyboard control with second student's slow typing; waited while first student read text.	**Anne:** showed some frustration often livened with humor. **Marie:** maintained interested calm non-verbals and posture.
Stimulated Recall Revelation		Thought seriously about quitting second lesson and rescheduling, which was her normal strategy, but did not, largely because of camera and research.	Admitted a little impatience in second lesson but turned it into a positive by teaching truncation.	**Anne:** perseverance had limits. **Marie:** patient, knowing learning would continue beyond session.
Espoused	*Information technology skills*	Novice level.	Leadership level for her school district.	**Anne:** novice. **Marie:** expert.
In-Action		Errors in remembering commands; told students she did not know why they were doing certain things; just following instructions given to her.	Exhibited considerable knowledge of databases; immediately solved the only technical problem.	**Anne:** grew frustrated with constant technical problems. **Marie:** computer technology skills not challenged in either session.
Stimulated Recall Revelation		Wanted to stretch herself; disappointing return to novice status in second lesson.	Pleased student could teach her new strategies.	**Anne:** frustrated, embarrassed, felt loss of knowledge-expert status. **Marie:** confident.

(continued)

Table 6.1. Continued

Mental Model Data Category	Mental Model	Anne's Mental Model Examples	Marie's Mental Model Examples	Comparison of Anne's and Marie's Mental Models
Espoused	*Technology literacy skills: Comfort level*	Fairly confident; had several successes working with teachers with Internet dial-up connection to public library.	Secure in ability to teach technology literacy skills intuitively.	**Anne:** critical to be knowledge expert in her teacher-librarian role. **Marie:** knew technology and was confident in her ability to teach its use.
In-Action		Some observable discomfort with errors because it had worked perfectly before; noted both she and second student had made typing errors; noticeably more comfortable once in familiar automated catalog.	Observable high comfort zone teaching information literacy skills to both students.	**Anne:** ensured students knew this lesson was not the norm and included second student in "blame" for "one error each"; comfort level increased when in familiar database. **Marie:** willing to learn from students.
Stimulated Recall Revelation		The more uncomfortable she became with lesson and database errors and inability to find relevant and obtainable resources, the lower she assessed second student's abilities; wanted to terminate second lesson.	No surprises; delighted with learning a new skill from student discovery. Wanted to share technology skills with students.	**Anne:** knowledge and experience vital to comfort level or lack thereof; tried to increase comfort level by including second student in "blame"; terminating the lesson was a solution she seriously considered. **Marie:** comfort level allowed her to relax with students and assume role as guide.

	Role of teaching for teacher-librarian		
Espoused	Teaching is a vital role.	Pushed teaching aside; favored administrative and technology role.	**Anne:** curriculum planning with teachers one of her successes. **Marie:** maybe get back to teaching once technology was well situated in school.
In-Action	Procedural teaching; directed students' involvement.	Socratic questions; requested students demonstrate skills.	**Anne:** student involvement minimal. **Marie:** students centrally involved.
Stimulated Recall Revelation	Parallel dominance of technical problems, time, and product MMs ensured direct instruction. Wondered why second student had not contributed.	Double-checked legitimacy of students' answer by inviting them to demonstrate understanding.	**Anne:** behaviorist teacher. Did not invite participation. **Marie:** constructivist teacher.
	Self-concept of ability as teacher		
Espoused	Successful teacher.	Escaped classroom teaching—"probably not a teacher."	**Anne:** strength was teaching information literacy one on one; small group **Marie:** escape from teaching was important.
In-Action	Taught procedures to find immediate products.	Taught how to use and understand respective electronic information resource tool for future use.	**Anne:** success of session depended on finding an information product. **Marie:** success of session depended on student involvement in their learning.

(continued)

Table 6.1. Continued

Mental Model Data Category	Mental Model	Anne's Mental Model Examples	Marie's Mental Model Examples	Comparison of Anne's and Marie's Mental Models
Stimulated Recall Revelation		Errors in command directives and inability to troubleshoot overwhelmed sense of self as successful teacher and knowledge expert; wanted to abandon second lesson.	Made some wrong choices with first student; lengthened lesson; disappointed that she reworded most of her questions in both lessons.	**Anne:** concerned about self as teacher dominated. **Marie:** concerned with strengthening her weaknesses as a teacher.
Espoused	*Pedagogy: Philosophy*	Facilitative, guide, disliked teaching large classes.	Facilitative, guide, disliked lecture-style with large classes.	**Both:** philosophically pro student-centered teaching strategies. **Both:** disliked teaching large classes.
Videoed In-Action		Hands-on and follow directives; took over keyboard in second session.	Hands-on; used questioning and probing strategies; on one occasion, probed until got "right" answer.	**Anne:** progression to product goal; instructivist. **Marie:** flexible road to information literacy goal; social constructivist.
Stimulated Recall Revelation		Intended show-and-tell-then-copy-me strategy; changed to hands-on and follow-my-directives strategy to get an information product within time limit.	Questioning important to ascertain students' abilities; required student to demonstrate knowledge rather than just accept student's response.	**Anne:** both strategies allowed procedural teaching; needed to control session. Both approaches ensured teacher was expert; sage on the stage. **Marie:** allowed questions, responses, and demonstration of understanding to control lesson, thereby scaffolding the learning; guide on the side.

Espoused	Pedagogy: Preparation	Found out about project but not IT skills from teachers.	Prior observation first student's information computer literacy skills and second student's non-use of automated catalog.	**Both:** no mention of lesson planning.
In-Action		Inquired what had done for project. Did not ask about database searching skills.	Asked questions to discover students' information and technology skills.	**Anne:** no focus on student computer technology literacy needs and understandings. **Marie:** ascertained students' prior understandings and went from there.
Stimulated Recall Revelation		Students' prior IT skills not her responsibility to ascertain; teacher-librarian meets emergent product needs; nevertheless, thought first student a novice and second student advanced in IT. Thought first student more IT knowledgeable than initially believed.	Students' answers and performance dictated strategies; surprised because assumed competent reading (first student) and keyboard (second student) levels; realized the lessons could have failed; used second student's weakness as a teaching moment.	**Anne:** students' prior knowledge not essential for teaching computer technology literacy because she met emergent needs and goal was always a product. Did not change lesson pedagogy when she thought first student was more able. **Marie:** realized she should never assume, even if assumption proved correct (first student); capitalized on second student's weaknesses by turning them into positive learning experiences.
Espoused	Pedagogy: Goal-product or IT as resource?	Concerned about finding information for student and staff needs.	Concerned about providing technology tools for students and staff.	**Anne:** concerned about products. **Marie:** concerned about using tools to find resources and products.

(continued)

Table 6.1. Continued

Mental Model Data Category	Mental Model	Anne's Mental Model Examples	Marie's Mental Model Examples	Comparison of Anne's and Marie's Mental Models
In-Action		Procedural teaching to obtain product; attempt at flexibility with second student by letting him choose a resource database from within a list.	Concerned about student understanding of the functions and characteristics of the IT tools.	**Anne:** taught procedures. **Marie:** asked students to predict what tools would do.
Stimulated Recall Revelation		Disappointed at overestimating second student's critical information literacy skills; not finding relevant resources led to taking back decision making; goal always to find useful product.	Concerned about students gaining procedural and conceptual understanding of the computer technology tools so they could be used more effectively.	**Anne:** vitally important that she retain her image and status as knowledge-expert who delivered the product. **Marie:** computer technology tools and skills used to promote conceptual understanding; the tool should service the student's needs.
	Pedagogy: Student responses	Responses vital to choice of teaching strategies.	Waited for students' verbal answers to determine teaching strategies.	**Both:** students' responses guided their teaching.
In-Action		Students' answers minimal because of the type of questions asked.	Probed both students for their information literacy understandings; in a couple of instances questioned until she got the "right" answer.	**Anne:** low-level questions **Marie:** mostly higher-order questions.

Stimulated Recall Revelation	Felt relief about first student's assignment because that meant it was easier to meet product goal within time limit; felt first student was following well and "was with her" and not jumping ahead.	Frustrated with continual repetition of re-wording her question; did not trust students' answers; verified that they knew; therefore asked them to demonstrate their understandings.	**Anne:** depended on low-level questions and assumptions about students and what was required of herself to accomplish goal. **Marie:** adjusted strategy and direction in response to students' answers; did not realize second student's answer demonstrated higher-level conceptualization than did the "right" answer she wanted; realized her questioning technique needed improvement—after both lessons!
Pedagogy: Student non-verbals			
Espoused	Non-verbals provided clues to teaching strategies and pacing.	Non-verbals guided her teaching strategies and pacing.	**Both:** students' non-verbals important to direction of teaching.
In-Action	Sat side on to students; looked at student for cues in first session; oblivious in second session due to problems.	Sat side on to students; looked for cues with both students.	**Both:** cues seemed vital.
Stimulated Recall Revelation	Disappointed that she had ceased to look for, or be aware of, second student's non-verbals; was more intent on achieving a product before the end of the lesson.	Reported also looking at eye movement and point of focus of second student to gauge keyboard skills, which had not been noticeable from video or observation.	**Anne:** governed by what she interpreted from the students, her goal for a product, and time constraints. **Marie:** adjusted as a response to her interpretation of students' non-verbals.

confirmatory trends between the espoused mental models and the in-action mental models, and then between both these mental models and the stimulated recall mental models of each teacher-librarian. A second involves the surprises divulged during stimulated recall. The third theme is that of linked mental models.

Confirmatory Trends

Although we point out the unexpected inconsistencies in the next section, there remained an acceptable degree of consistency among Anne's and Marie's pre-interview, in-action teaching comments and actions, and what they recalled thinking during their teaching (table 6.1).

One very obvious instance concerned Anne's two major roles as teacher-librarian (first two sections in table 6.1). Her mental model depicting herself as the school's information literacy expert dovetailed with her mental model depicting herself as provider of product resources. Her in-action teaching mental models and her stimulated recall mental models confirmed these as her goal and focus.

Table 6.1 progressively builds the case that Anne placed each learner secondary to finding an information product within a set time limit. For instance, although Anne executed her plan to provide an opportunity for decision making in her second lesson (see table 6.1; chapter 4), she withdrew this when the newspaper database did not appear to produce relevant information. If the focus had been to strengthen Andrew's conceptual understanding of the ways in which newspaper resources were useful to this and other school assignments, a teacher-librarian would have questioned him as to why he chose that database and what sorts of information he expected to find or, more in keeping with Anne's pedagogy, told him the answer to the latter question. Anne reported in the stimulated recall interview that, at this particular juncture, she blamed her assumption that Andrew had more critical information literacy skills than she now thought he had, and thus took back the keyboard to control the session in order to act out her mental model of finishing within the time limit. She focused more on finding a product than using this as a concept-building experience. This, of course, maintained compatibility among Anne's dominant mental models as revealed in her espoused views, her words and actions, and her thoughts while teaching.

An instance of the constancy of the teacher-librarians' in-action videoed and stimulated recall in-action mental models is that of their pedagogy in practice (table 6.1). Anne embraced a behaviorist teaching theory that was compatible with procedural teaching. Her hands-on-and-follow-my-directives strategy mental model supported, and was supported by, her various mental models that included: teacher-librarian as information literacy expert, service orientation as deliverer of product, time constraints, product goal, the dominance of low-level questioning, not inviting student-initiated involvement, and novice information communications online computer skills (table 6.1). Anne was the "sage on the stage" (see chapter 4). Marie embraced a social constructivist teaching theory that ensured procedural and conceptual teaching. Her cognitive apprenticeship mental model delivered scaffolded lessons that supported, and were supported by, her other mental models that included: service orientation to help students use computer tools effectively; focus on the student rather than the technology; utilization of questions to ascertain student understanding and demonstration of the students' knowledge claims; students actively involved and invited to teach the teacher; and expertise with technology and information computer literacy (table 6.1). Marie was the "guide on the side" (see chapter 5).

However, we cannot stress too strongly that it was the stimulated recall thoughts that allowed us to verify the teacher-librarians' consistency between many espoused and in-action videoed mental models with their inaction stimulated recall mental models virtually throughout the lessons. For instance, it was the stimulated recall interviews that revealed that both teacher-librarians had not created hard-copy lesson plans (table 6.1). Anne relied on her tacit knowledge to do this "on the fly" during the lesson itself (see chapter 4). We would not have realized that Marie deliberately used the students' answers and results of their demonstrations of their answers to guide the path of her lesson (table 6.1). Nor would we have realized that Marie took an incorrect path during her first lesson (table 6.1). When she was faced with the obvious tiredness of her first student revealed on the video, she recalled thinking that this was the negative effect of her decision to follow through with a meaningful exploration of a particular table in the dinosaur database, even though she recalled thinking that it was inappropriate for Grade 4–level students (table 6.1; chapter 5). Her decision was based on her judgment that it was more important not to confuse the student.

Another stimulated recall insight allowed a deeper understanding of how Anne associated her strategy, goal, and time mental models. The hands-on-and-follow-my-directives strategy saved time but only permitted procedural teaching and learning so that the lesson goal, a product to take away, was met. The demonstrate-and-then-copy mental model was embedded with a pedagogical approach that could allow a mixture of procedural and conceptual understanding while on the way to obtaining a product. However, this latter strategy would lengthen the lesson as, in effect, the same lesson would be repeated. The constancy throughout both lessons of Anne's time, product goal, and especially her self-concept need to be the expert mental models only became obvious through her recalled thoughts in the stimulated recall interview. The repetition of these mental models in many of the categories in table 6.1 was a powerful indicator of their fidelity.

Had we used only observation and interviews, we would have concluded that Marie moved between social constructivist methods and behaviorist methods depending on the student. When Marie's second student demonstrated that she had only seen others using the automated catalog and had weak keyboard skills, Marie seemed to be giving procedural steps for finding materials in the catalog. We would have missed the nuances of her conceptual explanations, which were tied to the level of her student's perceived understandings. We would not have known how strongly she used the student's reactions to decide on her next teaching strategy and how purposely she situated herself to identify those reactions (table 6.1, last section: Non-Verbals). The camera did not pick up on the way she watched the student's eyes, nor did our unobtrusive location for observing the teaching-learning episode allow us to watch the movement of Marie's eyes (see chapters 2 and 5). Stimulated recall allowed Marie to elucidate her actual thoughts during her teaching, thereby providing a virtual blow-by-blow window on how she was actually deciding what she would do next in the session.

Major Surprises Divulged during Stimulated Recall Interview

There remains a conviction that, though not perfect, there is a high degree of stable consistency among teachers' beliefs, goals, and actions. It was so with us—hence our surprise at the revelations stimulated by the recall interview techniques (see chapter 2).

There was a notable discrepancy in what Anne said in both the preinterview (espoused mental model) and lesson (videoed in-action mental model) and what she had intended as her pedagogic strategy (in-action stimulated recall mental model). When her lesson with Frances began, her original plan was to utilize a "demonstrate-then-copy-what-I-did" strategy that was rapidly changed to a "hands-on and follow-my-directives" teaching and learning strategy when she discovered that Frances had not started her assignment (table 6.1, Pedagogy: Philosophy). She twice emphasized to Frances why Frances should take control of the keyboard, perhaps because Anne was surprised at the switch in her mental model strategy. Her initial strategy sat within a comfortable mental model of how she learned and was taught to teach. Her hands-on directive strategy with Frances sat with her mental model of the teacher-librarian as deliverer of resources and her mental model of having to do this within the time allocated for the session. The hands-on and follow-my-directives strategy would take less time than the demonstrate-and-copy-me method to find a resource.

Another of Anne's stimulated recall revelations startled us on three counts. It occurred when the technical problems kept occurring, when her lack of prior exploration of the newspaper database in the public library affected her ability to direct her student, and when she was unable to find relevant resources in Andrew's session. This conjunction proved over-whelming.

First, through stimulated recall, we discovered that she gave serious thought to quitting the session. Anne's persistence mental model (table 6.1, Self-Concept: Characteristic Trait) was stronger than her frustration mental model and kept the session continuing. Because the lesson was videoed and part of a research project, her self-concept mental model that contained her concern for her image as a knowledge expert had to be re-asserted in order to present a satisfactory model of a successful teacher-librarian.

Second, what seemed particularly startling was her admission that her regular practice would have been to abandon the session. Yet, it is often what we all did as technology novices if the situation allowed it; for instance, in the classroom, we discarded the "non-compliant stupid" computer for chalk-and-talk when our inadequate skills did not allow us to work out a solution to fix the problem. Anne recalled—as a hindsight explanation—that after collapsing the lesson, she would have put a prod-uct in the students' hands, and later worked on solving her online prob-lems through practice. Then she would have initiated a new session that allowed the student, under her direction, to find another resource. In turn, part of the strength of these stimulated recall and hindsight thoughts (see chapter 2) and her tenacity mental model seemed to be in the product orientation that she held as an information specialist. Put a print resource or call numbers in the students' hands that relate to their topic and she had succeeded. Such was her mental model of a successful teacher-librarian. That number one priority and mental model carried her through both sessions.

Third, what had increased our surprise was that Anne's reaction to abandon the lesson was in contrast with her lesson with Frances. When her directives resulted in errors in Frances' session and when they could not find any resources that had not already been borrowed from the pub-lic library, Anne remained confident that she was in control. We surmised that it was perhaps because of her mental model of Frances' lack of strong computer knowledge compared with her mental model of Andrew as computer literate. Anne could admit her error to Frances and then use the incident as a learning experience. She also easily recovered by trying vari-ous steps within her procedural mental model and, as we discovered through her stimulated recall interview, she had already decided to search her school library and put the books into Frances's hands (table 6.1, Main Service Orientation as Teacher-Librarian).

Stimulated recall offered further unforeseen insights. Anne recalled thinking that she did not know if Frances had used either the school's or the public library's CD-ROM databases. Her mental models of starting a lesson, effective lesson strategies, and meeting emergent needs did not require her to ask her students about their information literacy or computer database skills at the beginning of the lessons. Furthermore, Anne also dismissed her lack of knowledge about the students' prior knowledge as not her responsibility to cover in this session because of her time limit and product goal mental models. This negation had parallels with Anne's stimulated recall thought that she had wondered why Andrew was not asking questions or providing comments (table 6.1, Role of Teaching). She did not report any retrospective or hindsight thoughts in the stimulated recall and enhanced post-interview (see chapter 2) about why she had not invited Andrew to contribute suggestions to help solve the problems or to ask questions. Frances had not been invited to be an active participant either; but when Frances asked questions, Anne responded positively. These examples strongly suggest that invitations for active participation were not part of her teaching strategies mental model and that her mental model of responsibility for student participation was devolved onto the student.

A major surprise was between both teacher-librarians' mental models of their pedagogy that they espoused in their pre-interview and the mental models demonstrated in their videoed words and actions and then confirmed in their simultaneous recalled thoughts about their lessons as they were teaching. Both had divulged that they did not like teaching large classes in their pre-interviews (chapters 4 and 5, respectively). Nevertheless, Anne espoused teaching as a crucial role of the teacher-librarian and a belief that she was a good teacher and a facilitator (table 6.1, Role of Teaching for Teacher-Librarian, Self-Concept of Ability as a Teacher, and Pedagogy: Philosophy). Marie professed herself to be an "escapee from the classroom," preferring to manage the library, creatively automate it, and assist staff and student use of library technology as opposed to teaching in which she deemed herself to be weak (table 6.1, Role of Teaching for Teacher-Librarian, Self-Concept of Ability as a Teacher, and Pedagogy: Philosophy).

Clearly demonstrated in the sections related to teaching and pedagogy in table 6.1 as well as in chapters 4 and 5, respectively, Anne's interpretation of a facilitator did not equate with the current pedagogic definition and Marie's belief that she was "not a teacher" proved incorrect. It is more common and acceptable in education to link facilitating with guiding students' learning through a constructivist or social constructivist pedagogy than with behaviorist, also interchangeably termed instructivist, pedagogy. Revealed in table 6.1 as well as in chapter 4, when Anne said "facilitator," she meant that she facilitated staff and student requests for resources by delivering those resources into their hands. In spite of the technical hiccups, Anne revealed herself as an accomplished behaviorist director, teaching for procedural understanding about how to use the databases. Anne directed students' actions and, except on one occasion, choices. Only when waiting for the modem to connect and when directly asked by her first student did Anne venture conceptual explanations. On other occasions she deliberately decided not to provide conceptual understandings, mainly because of her time constraint mental model, as revealed in her stimulated recall interview. We found out through stimulated recall that Anne ran her "checking for non-verbal cues" mental model with Frances in order to make assessments as to how much Frances understood about what they were doing. Perhaps Anne's confidence in her considerable use of non-verbal cues, a strategy that was strongly entrenched in her mental model, negated a need for questions that would probe Frances' understanding. Her questioning of Frances and Andrew was designed for procedural understanding.

In contrast, Marie was revealed in table 6.1 and chapter 5 as a more than competent teacher who invariably adopted a social constructivist pedagogy that aimed to facilitate her students' learning within their individual ZPD, not only about how to use their respective databases but also how these databases worked in the ways they did. She habitually waited for them to complete the task (table 6.1, Self-Concept: Characteristic Trait). Elucidating the wait-time strategy we saw on the video were her thoughts that exhibited patience and flexibility. However, without stimulated recall we would not have known that she had once mentally experienced a little impatience within her lesson with Alana (table 6.1, Self-Concept: Characteristic Trait). Indeed, without stimulated recall, we would not have realized that Marie exploited these mental models to take the "teaching moment" offered in order to provide Alana with a conceptual understanding of truncation (chapter 5). More importantly, stimulated recall furnished an opportunity to understand how a teacher overturned a negative, "we-are-wasting-time" mental model into a positive, and thereby decreased her frustration (chapter 5). In doing so, the impatience quickly dissipated and a worthwhile unintended outcome was accomplished. Marie maintained a scaffolded question-answer-demonstrate strategy throughout the lessons in order to facilitate both students' active cognitive and kinesthetic participation. Marie taught for student procedural and conceptual understanding.

Running Linked Mental Models

Without stimulated recall, we would not have understood the resulting entrenchment and overlapping effects of the teacher-librarians' linked mental models throughout each lesson. In the within-case studies (chapters 4 and 5) and in this across-case comparison, we have already provided ample evidence of the effects that running entrenched mental models afforded. The two following examples are adequate to highlight the strength of the links.

As shown in table 6.1, Marie's social constructivist pedagogic mental model governed all other mental models except that of the lesser role of teaching in her hierarchy of teacher-librarian roles and her self-perception as a failed teacher. She departed very little from her mental model as the cognitive guide.

The most spectacular example, underscored in table 6.1, was that of three of Anne's in-action mental models: the teacher-librarian as information literacy expert, the habitual need for a physical end product for her students, and the pervasive emphasis on time constraints in all parts of her job. These three mental models controlled much of what occurred in each lesson and what the outcomes had to be for Anne to be satisfied with that lesson. Her pre-interview mention of a weakness with time management, her description of her main service orientation toward helping students obtain last-minute information products, and her status as information literary expert ran together as mental models controlling her need to find a product. The clarity and habituated influence of these linked mental models on her teaching actions became obvious through her stimulated recall thoughts.

Summary

In review, the use of stimulated recall methodology allowed us the following categorized insights into the teacher-librarians' mental models as each lesson unfolded:

- how a mental model would run and thereby reveal its importance in their thoughts and actions, and influence the running of their other mental models
- how habituated their pedagogic philosophy and strategies were throughout both of their respective lessons
- how these pedagogic mental models effected other mental models; for example:
  - Anne created a generalized mental model of not overestimating a student's abilities from her prior knowledge of the student

- Marie maintained her questioning and invitation to students to demonstrate and predict their understandings, regardless of the students' capabilities
- how their mental models of responsibility for active participation resided for:
  - Anne, with herself as the expert who imparted her knowledge to the student without inviting student participation beyond answering questions or carrying out directives
  - Marie, with herself as facilitator
- how and why their mental models of their respective students changed
- how their respective degrees of computer and online access competence mental models affected their strategies and other mental models, including views of their own lesson's success or failure

When this study, under the auspices of a Spencer Foundation grant, took place, our teacher-librarian participants had varying degrees of experience with electronic databases, ranging from two weeks to several years, and from little understanding to complex understanding of how the tools were accessed and how they worked.

Anne was part of the tradition of many veteran teacher-librarians who are dedicated to helping students successfully find appropriate information products as their ultimate service and teaching goal. They consider assisting the student with the process of finding and accessing information more of a priority than teaching them to understand concepts underlying the way the access tool works. This philosophy stemmed from the teacher-librarian's ability to place a paper-formatted access tool in the student's hands and assume the student could analyze visually how the tool worked through procedural instruction. However, online access to electronic information tools carries none of the prior familiarity of paper tools. Marie's situation was the opposite of Anne's in that Marie was a respected user and manager of electronic and online databases and an experienced troubleshooter of technical problems. Thus, their cases offered us the chance to examine and report the thinking behind teaching actions that is so important in understanding the how and why of the teaching act.

Through stimulated recall interviews, we confirmed various consistencies and discrepancies among Anne's and Marie's individual and across-case comparison mental models. Anne ran mental models that necessitated controlling the session, retaining the knowledge-expert status as teacher-librarian, providing students with an information resource, and finishing within a set time limit. Her mental models also focused on her lack of technology problem-solving skills. Her initial guidance, when her second student practiced decision-making skills initially, did not include conceptual explanations of the database contents or how it operated. Her sessions were teacher-centered information searches that followed a behaviorist framework. Marie ran mental models that allowed her to give the students tasks that capitalized on their prior experience, then take them to new understandings that they could relate to their prior experiences to contextualize them. These meaningful activities led to transformational learning that would be classified as learner-centered. Marie acted as a facilitator within a cognitive apprenticeship framework in both lessons, which was, in fact, the way her mental models performed.

If we had used interviews and videoed observations to make our assumptions about the how and why of their teaching, we would have missed many crucial elements behind their actions. We could not have clearly seen or described (a) the levels of influence existing in the relationships among their mental models, (b) what motivated the formation or recall of their mental models, (c) the in-action mental models they had not articulated in the pre-interview, and (d) the places where their "that was then" (see chapter 2) stimulated recall thinking contrasted with their actions.

CONCLUDING THOUGHTS

Woven Threads Mental Model Analogy

It was the tabulation in table 6.1 and its analysis that provided considerable impact and caused us to rethink how we have conceptualized our usage of mental models in short-term memory. Exploration of the mental model literature in chapter 3 presented three major ways to conceptualize how mental models act in short-term memory. One of these described mental models as running in parallel while being utilized for specific tasks. A second used an analogy of hypermedia access and use of mental models. A third was the notion of running only fragments of mental models (see figure 4.1). The within-case studies used these descriptions when identifying the mental models utilized by Anne and Marie.

During our exploration of the across-case comparison in this chapter, these no longer seem adequate. Parallel means that the mental models do not converge; they remain equidistant from each other. Hypermedia means that we access whichever mental model or fragment of that mental model that appears to be relevant at the time, as well as navigating our way through them in a random or structured sequence. The hypermedia World Wide Web analogy also suggests that when a mental model is clicked on (retrieved), the new mental model either replaces the old mental model or it overlays (hides) the previous mental model.

We propose that the data as highlighted in table 6.1 demonstrate an analogy of woven threads. Depending on the pattern, each thread has the possibility of being uppermost or hidden by one or more other threads. Each can also be thicker or stronger than the other threads. They can be knotted so that their joint impact is significant. They can be cut from the design and replaced with other single or multiple threads.

Anne's three crucial mental models—product goal, teacher-librarian as expert, and time constraints—can be used to clarify this analogy. At one time or another each ran separately, such as the goal mental model when Anne asked Frances about the nature of the assignment. Her answer saw the immediate addition of the other two mental models into the weave, to make the decision that the product goal would be easily obtained before the lesson-ending bell. Taking advantage of a teaching moment (see chapter 4), another different weaker mental model thread (a conceptual explanation to Frances) was fleetingly woven into the pattern for a small splash of color. When the first technical problem occurred, her three dominant mental models plus her mental model of the patterned dial-up procedure to access the public library (see chapter 4) were now joined by her novice troubleshooting skills mental model. This put increasing pressure on all the threads squeezing them together. In effect, it meant that they represented one chunk in short-term memory (Miller, 1956; chapter 2). It should have left more "space" in working memory to predict and then try solutions to the technical problem. However, it proved an illogical chunk. The troubleshooting mental model could not "get unwoven"; it just seemed to go around and around trying combinations of the pattern rather than sequentially choosing (retrieving) another strategy to see if it could resolve the problem and then discarding it when it did not. Her self-concept mental model as expert kept pushing the troubleshooting mental model more and more into the background. Then the time constraints mental model had its turn, which we noticed particularly in Andrew's lesson.

The analogy also appears to hold up with Marie's utilization of her mental models. For instance, one thread—her pedagogic philosophy—remained strong and thick, providing the supporting structure for the other narrower threads, such as her non-verbal cues mental model and her patience mental model while waiting for Nathan to read or Rosanne to find the correct key on the keyboard. Certain sections of her pedagogic philosophy were teased out of the dominant multi-skein thread and woven on top, such as her questioning strategy, when relevant to the pattern.

Perhaps the analogy is being molded too deliberately. Even if this is so, what this analogy offers is the woven combination of mental models. Our data suggest that there is a definite meeting of mental models, a woven linkage, particularly between dominant mental models. Our data therefore imply that each mental model or fragment of a mental model can be fleetingly retrieved and woven with one mental model (thread) or more mental models that, together, form a separate chunk that works successfully or problematically in working memory. The data further imply that mental models can have threads of varying strengths and widths that dominate or buttress other mental models and, hence, the thoughts and actions when teaching.

Worth of Stimulated Recall

If one of the roles of stimulated recall methodology is to ascertain the degree of compatibility and divergence among the complexities of the teaching role in action, then this across-case comparison has certainly delivered. If the purpose of each of our case studies and the across-case comparison was to identify and analyze the teachers' mental models, their changes, and their influences on their teaching, then the use of stimulated recall in Marie's and Anne's cases, indeed in all our cases, would prove essential to the development of reliable understandings about teaching, rather than relying on observations and pre- and post-interviews to help us make assumptions as the process-product paradigm would have had us do.

One Story Left to Tell

What intrigued us was that the stimulated recall interviews revealed Marie's use of conceptual pedagogic theory in Alana's lesson as well as in Nathan's lesson. From our observations of the lessons, we debriefed only in terms of Marie's behaviorist strategies in Alana's session and social constructivist strategies in Nathan's lesson. How wrong we would have been if we had only used the observation and pre-interview method of analysis. Also, given the propensity to maintain one's mental models (see chapter 2), our process-product observation mental models could very well have slanted our coding and categorizing of the videotape transcripts. During the actual stimulated recall interviews, our mental models of Marie's strategies changed in some places and wavered in others. We began to see Marie's mental models of her teaching with Alana differently and labeled it social constructivist. Through the decoding and analysis of the stimulated recall transcripts, we confirmed our mental model changes concerning Marie's teaching paradigm in Alana's lesson. This enlightening episode exposed the power and usefulness of stimulated recall as both a research instrument and a researcher self-monitoring mental model tool.

The surprise discrepancies in the teacher-librarians' mental models indicate that researchers and teachers have to go beyond (videoed) observation, interviews, and reflection to obtain confidence in the trustworthiness and fallibilistic validity of their findings and analysis. Stimulated recall interviewing methods can illuminate the links among our thoughts, words, and actions during a teaching episode. In this way we gain understanding about what is happening in our teaching, which mental models we control, and which mental models control our actions. This is the topic of the next chapter.

7

Use of Mental Models to Analyze and Understand Teachers' Pedagogies

I think that I hesitated to take control as much as I should have, thinking that his decision-making abilities were a little more advanced than they were and that his assessment abilities were a little bit more advanced. And I didn't want to insult him by telling him some things. I'm still not, I'm not sure that exploring, [pause] I don't know [*sic*]. I hope he got something valuable out of it regardless. But I'm frustrated. I don't feel good about it. (Anne, enhanced post-interview)

I think I prompted her a lot more, because she's far more hesitant than Nathan was and obviously [pause] I was thinking in the lesson she was more uncomfortable. She seemed to be more uncomfortable, probably not as outgoing as he is and . . . I don't know whether she has a computer at home or not but that particular class has had no experience at all and when they do come to the library to borrow, very few of them use the catalog unless specifically asked to. . . . She was, I remember thinking, she was very hesitant and I could see that. A couple of times I was watching her face and I could see that she really didn't know what I was talking about and needed prompting when she was watching the screen. She didn't have a clue, unlike Nathan, he knew where to look for clues, but she, I could see her watching the top of the screen all the time where the Winnebago cat was and she wasn't even looking to go down to the bottom of the screen where the clues were, so I had to sort of prompt her to go down. (Marie, enhanced post-interview)

Pre- and post-interviews were utilized to discover espoused and reflective mental models along with videoed lesson transcripts and stimulated recall methodology to elucidate in-action mental models. This allowed us to compare and contrast the numerous mental models that influenced our teacher-librarians' ways of thinking and teaching. We chose teacher-librarians as our participants because of their traditionally under-recognized information literacy teaching role, and now technology literacy role. For this book emphasizing stimulated recall methodology, we analyzed the two most reflective teacher-librarians who had different pedagogical approaches to their teaching. In each case, the interplay of their in-action stimulated recall mental models during the teaching-learning sessions provided a unique way of understanding how they chose strategies to use during their teaching and why they taught the way they did based on their pedagogical mental model belief systems.

As identified in chapter 1, we had four major research objectives in our research. The first objective was to identify and categorize the teacher-librarians' espoused mental models (pre-lesson), videotaped in-action and stimulated recall in-action mental models, and reflective (post-lesson) mental models from their interviews and videoed lesson transcripts. The second objective was to investigate how these various categories and types of mental models were reflected in various phases of the lesson cycle (preparation, teaching, and reflecting) and how the mental models influenced the teacher-librarians' pedagogy and critical self-reflective mental models during and after each of two lessons. The findings and analysis of these aims are reported in chapters 4 and 5.

The major rationale for this book was the stimulated recall research methodology focus in the across-case comparison (chapter 6). The across-case comparison revealed the consistencies and discrepancies among the teacher-librarians' espoused and videoed lesson mental models with their in-action stimulated recall mental models. The comparison also teased out the effects of their mental models on their lesson verbalizations and actions.

Stimulated recall is also an essential player in this chapter (chapter 7), which more fully explores our third and fourth research objectives. The third objective was to identify and analyze if and how the teacher-librarians controlled and managed their mental models by changing and letting them evolve according to the needs of the lesson or if and how their mental models controlled the way the lesson proceeded. The fourth and final objective sought to examine when the teacher-librarians' voiced a commitment to change their teaching strategies based on their stimulated recall and critical self-reflection mental models and whether and how this occurred in their succeeding lesson.

In this chapter we also address how our research confirmed mental model theory and some of its variables and characteristics. In chapters 4 and 5, we explored the multitude of mental models and fragments of mental models that both teacher-librarians utilized during segments in their lessons in parallel, in hypermedia, or, more realistically, in woven mode (chapter 6). We now compare our two teacher-librarians' mental models, examining how their mental models influenced or affected their choice of teaching strategies. Also discussed is whether our teacher-librarians' mental models enabled the teacher-librarian to change focus and goals as the conditions of each lesson changed, or whether the mental models were so controlling that the teacher-librarians were unable to respond satisfactorily to the events and change their teaching practices. Finally, we present a tentative prediction model that associates specific mental models with specific teaching strategies and goals.

GROUNDED-DATA CONFIRMATION OF MENTAL MODEL THEORY

As we worked through the two individual within-case studies (chapters 4 and 5) and the across-case comparison (chapter 6), it became increasingly apparent that the mental models that we identified as grounded in our data confirmed the types, roles, functions, and characteristics of mental models described in the mental model research literature (chapter 3). Tables 7.1 through 7.3 provide comparisons that we explore in the answers to numbered questions following each table. Each table focuses on a major category that was also identified in the literature: novice and expert mental models; lesson preparation and goals; and pedagogy in-action. Figure 7.1 delineates the teacher-librarians' management and control of, or by, mental models. By comparing and contrasting the two teacher-librarians' mental models within the categories identified in the literature, we verified the power of mental model research to project the functions and relationships of our participants' mental models.

Novice and Expert Mental Models

Table 7.1 shows the comparison of our two teacher-librarians' mental models that corresponded to categories suggested by the research literature. We built the table to compare categories of mental model influence as described in mental model theory with the mental models we discovered in our data and how each teacher-librarian responded to them. Following the table, we describe each teacher-librarian's response to these mental models and link the descriptions numerically back to the table. Items 1–6 in table 7.1 are concerned with the notion of expert versus

Table 7.1.   Comparison of Anne's Novice Mental Models with Marie's Expert Mental Models

Item	Mental Model: Type, Function, and Characteristics	Anne's Examples	Marie's Examples
1	Expert or novice	Unable to understand why problems that were happening constricted her teaching strategy, which remained procedural; hung onto image of role as knowledge expert	Considered herself an innovator with computer technologies; was confident; treated "hiccups" as enjoyable, solvable problems
2	Possessed procedural, formulaic, or step-by-step novice mental models or expert mental models that were conceptual; used analogies	Novice mental models of online access; very dependent on patterned procedures; utilized analogies	Conceptual mental models of computer technology; knew how and where to find answers; did not use analogies
3	Utilized mechanistic and procedural problem solving or utilized heuristics	Mechanistic and procedural problem solving; had few past experiences with technology problems	Heuristic problem solving; knew how to strategize about problems; asked students questions that required them to think about and predict solutions
4	Confidence to find what they could not remember	Confident in the automated catalog—a familiar teacher-librarian tool—but not during process entering it	Self-assured with computer technologies; enjoyed students teaching her new shortcut "tricks"
5	Appropriate response to the unpredictable equates with status as expert	Unable to respond quickly or effectively to the unpredictable; became flustered; afraid status as knowledge expert was damaged	Competently solved the only technology problem; maintained social constructivist pedagogy in response to unpredicted student technology skills
6	Used analysis	Did not use analysis to solve technical problems but used it on at least one occasion with both students	Analyzed her students' abilities and understandings fairly accurately; was dissatisfied with wording of her questions

novice mental models. We examined our data to confirm and thereby illuminate mental models identified in the literature.

1. *Did the teacher-librarians demonstrate novice's mental models that restricted or constricted action in response to problems or did they demonstrate expert "innovator" mental models that allowed them to identify technical problems as solvable minor hiccups (Henderson and Bradey, 2004; Holyoak, 1991; Jacka and Henderson, in progress)?* Anne lagged behind Marie in skills and confidence. Each had motivated herself by necessity and recognition of the power of computer information tools. Anne had been using the access procedures for two weeks prior to her first lesson and three weeks prior to her second lesson. She noted in her pre-interview that the computer technician who had explained the procedure to her spoke so quickly and technically that she could only copy down the steps rather than obtain more than a procedural understanding. Even so, prior to her first lesson, she had a mental model of having successfully helped a teacher use the dial-up access as well as having spent time with the print tutorial, practicing the dial-up access, and using it herself. Prior to her second lesson, Anne practiced and taught some teachers how to use the online dial-up connection. However, because Anne had patterned her dial-up commands, she did not use notes in the second lesson, even after her login-command mistakes in the first lesson. Unfortunately Anne's novice stature translated into her inability to remember the pattern and enter the online database without error. Her perceptions of the repetition of the same errors as more than "minor hiccups" made her lessons painful for her in many ways. Her courage in entering into the research project demonstrated her mental model of recognizing her need to learn to use the electronic computer technologies as a developing major information access tool for teacher-librarians, teachers, and students.

Marie had an "innovator" mental model from her work with computer databases over the years. As she mentioned in her pre-interview, she provided expert troubleshooting support to her teacher-librarian colleagues in a fairly extensive geographical area. Holding a mental model of herself as a technology knowledge management innovator increased her responsiveness to hiccups as teachable moments and enjoyable problems to solve. When she went into the tables area in the database in her first lesson, Marie realized this area was problematic but solved it by internally treating this as a "hiccup." In this way, she maintained her guided approach to facilitate Nathan's understanding.

Both teacher-librarians had automated the school library but while Anne knew only the general commands for its use, Marie's mental models contained not just the how-it-works procedures but also the why-it-works conceptual understandings.

2. *Did they think in terms of a formulaic series of steps to take to solve prob-*

lems or in terms of concepts and analogies (Puerta-Melguizo and van der Veer, 2001; Rochelle and Greeno, 1987)? Anne's response to problems was to repeat a patterned series of steps to correct a technical problem. When the database did not respond to those steps or respond to certain commands that she thought would solve the problem, she did not have additional problem-solving strategies other than to start over. Although she referred to the database a couple of times with an analogy to the school's automated catalog, she did not articulate where the analogy example had secure linkages conceptually and where the analogy contained non-example links. She did not have strong past experiences with such linkages on which to rely. Her inexperience with electronic databases made her reluctant to experiment with new strategies or even to conceptualize a possible new approach to the problem.

Marie used concepts and did not appear to have any hard and fast series of steps she had to take to solve problems or continue the lessons. Marie actually waited until she found out more about the students and their answers to her ongoing questions as they proceeded with learning about their respective databases before she decided on each path or phase in the lesson. She was so familiar with the technologies to have confidence that she could guide the students to think through or predict solutions to any problems that might occur with the technology and databases.

These findings from our research confirm the findings presented by Dutke and Reimer (2000). Adult computer novices performed poorly when their mental models only held a list of action steps, like Anne's did. However, those, like Marie, who held mental models of how functions work were able to problem solve their way through new situations.

3. Did the teacher-librarians describe problem-solving tasks in mechanistic and procedural terms, or did they use strategies that utilized heuristics (Anzai and Simon, 1979; Bilby, 1992b; Newell and Simon, 1972; Newton, 1996)? Anne definitely responded in mechanistic and procedural ways. When her procedures did not work, she had no recourse to other types of strategies. She was not able to analyze the problem conceptually, admitting several times to her students that she did not know why the computer was acting the way it did and why it would not accept her commands. When Anne's one use, which required propositional "if—then" thinking (Meiser, Klauer, and Naumer, 2001) by Andrew to choose a relevant database from the list provided, did not work out, she took control of the decision making. As Driscoll (1994) pointed out, "What this means is that people bring to tasks imprecise, partial, and idiosyncratic understandings that evolve with experience" (p. 152), instruction, and guided discovery. Marie thought in conceptual terms, focusing on her students' learning rather than the tool per se, and preferred to have her students learn through discovery with her guidance through problem situations. Marie made use of heuristics in the form of exemplars and non-exemplars (see table 7.3, number 6 below) and propositional and predictive reasoning to facilitate acquisition of additional strategies for using their respective databases, thereby helping Nathan's and Alana's ability to build mental models capable of better problem solving.

4. *Did they have the confidence that they could find what they did not remember, that is, leave some of their "knowledge out in the world" (chapter 3), or did they have to remember everything (Jonassen and Henning, 1999; Mayes, Draper, McGregor, and Oatley, 1988; Norman, 1988; O'Malley and Draper, 1992; Payne, 1991)?* Three instances will suffice. First, Anne was aware, if not of the term itself, then certainly of what leaving knowledge out in the world meant. In her reflections during the enhanced post-interview, she mentioned that she recognized that Frances had obtained clues and feedback from the computer interface. The second instance is a non-exemplar. When logging into the database, Anne had to remember (or, which she did not use in the lessons, have notes on which to rely; stimulated recall interview). Her mental model of entry procedures was patterned in her mind. Anything that upset the pattern—for example, not having her hands on the keyboard, which was how she practiced the login and password patterns, or encountering possible stress over being videotaped— meant that she was unable to use any support from feedback from the computer screen. The third instance provides both an example and a non-example. It occurred when Anne did not know if they would be able to exit the newspaper database. She could not depend on her knowledge out in the world to sustain problem-solving efforts in a database where Anne had not been. In contrast, Anne was able to transfer elements from her experience with the school's automated catalog once they had entered the public library's online automated catalog because she had extensive experience with both databases. In these instances, she relied on leaving her knowledge out in the world.

Marie's confidence came from having generalizable mental models of how different categories of databases worked. Her expertise allowed her to utilize the interface of each database, rather than retrieve a mental model, to assist her response spontaneity. This left more room in working memory to assist if other problems arose in comparison with Anne's two situations which demonstrated poor use of what working memory was diminishingly available (see chapter 2; Miller, 1956).

5. *Could they claim expert mental models by making appropriate responses to situations that contained a degree of unpredictability (Cohen, Thompson Adelman, Bresnick, Lokendra, and Riedel, 2000; Henderson and Bradey, 2004; Jacka and Henderson, 2004; Sloboda, 1991)?* Anne's status and image as knowledge expert was critically important to her self-efficacy as an information literacy specialist. Pulling against that status was her novice status

with computer technologies, although her motivation to learn and use them as part of her repertoire of literacy tools was extremely high. However, she did not want to have that lack of expertise on display, particularly for her second student. When she felt that her mistakes damaged her image, she centered her thoughts, as recalled during the stimulated recall interview, on her discomfort and stressful feelings rather than on making the errors into teachable moments as she had espoused, and twice put into action in her first lesson. She thought that students expected her to know the answers and she had a hard time when she did not know them.

Compounding her technology mistakes was her inability to find relevant resources that had not been borrowed from the public library. This situation was totally unpredicted, even in the second lesson. Perhaps this was because both students had different topics. Her stimulated recall inaction thoughts revealed that Anne's responses to the unpredictable in both lessons differed. Anne resolved the situation in the first lesson by thinking that when the lesson had finished, she would find relevant books in the school library and put them in Frances's hands. With Andrew, the increasing number of technology mistakes and their inability to find relevant resources in the newspaper database or currently available at the public library combined with the knowledge that the bell would soon mark the end of the lesson had three outcomes: Anne took control of the keyboard; she directed Andrew to copy down the call numbers of resources that were unusable because they were in circulation, and she seriously considered abandoning the lesson (see chapters 4 and 6).

Marie presented a calm, technologically savvy role model to her students, particularly the second student when she quickly and efficiently solved the server problem. (This was the only technology problem Marie had to face during both lessons.) Although Marie blamed most unpredicted "responses" from the computer on her mistakes, she generally reacted by using them as teachable moments and continued to rephrase her questions until Nathan could analyze what happened or could suggest how they should correct the situation. The major unpredicted event occurred in her lesson with Alana. Even though Marie knew that Alana had not used the automated catalog, Marie did not foresee that Alana would not know where most of the keys were on the keyboard or how to find information. Marie maintained her social constructivist pedagogy and provided prompting hints, asked questions which required prediction of outcomes, and demonstrated patience as the ZPD guide to Alana's learning both procedural and conceptual strategies.

Anne thought that she could not make good responses to unpredictable situations. Instead, she admitted in her stimulated recall and post-interviews that she experienced much frustration and anxiety. Several times the gravity of the unpredictable unnerved her and emphasized her novice status. In contrast, because of Marie's knowledge of the databases she was teaching and her self-confidence in responding to the unpredictable that had been built upon over the years, Marie coped like the expert she was.

6. *Did either teacher-librarian use analysis as part of their mental models (Halford, 1993)?* Analysis is an important function of mental models (figure 2.2) and the ability to use analysis effectively and quickly as demanded in lessons demonstrates expertise or the novice status usually associated with beginning teacher-librarians.

Anne did not know how to analyze or troubleshoot the cause of telecommunication errors with the dial-up procedure. She tried to correct the errors using a return to the steps she remembered as part of her patterned learning. Her thoughts indicated that her panic shut down any possibilities for analyzing what had happened given her lack of conceptual understanding of why the dial-up software was reacting in ways that she had not experienced previously in the first lesson, and in ways that Anne thought she had rectified through her practice and teaching before the second lesson.

With her first student, Anne analyzed Frances's non-verbals and responses and recalled thinking in her stimulated recall interview that Frances was "with her and not trying to jump ahead." Anne decided, after analysis of her second student's choice of the newspaper database and its lack of relevant resources, that Andrew did not know as much about evaluating information resources as she had assumed. She used this analysis to change her teaching strategy to take control by not giving Andrew any further choices and by taking over the keyboard.

Anne was critically analytical of her own teaching during both the stimulated recall and enhanced post-interviews. Because of the tight conjunction of her diminishing self-concept as expert mental model, time constraints mental model, and increasing inability to find relevant resources which were not in circulation, her analysis was such in her second lesson that she wanted to disband it.

Marie demonstrated that her analysis of her students' abilities was fairly accurate. The only moment where she admitted she had momentarily panicked was when she had directed Nathan into an area in the dinosaur database that she then thought was beyond his grade level. Nevertheless, Marie analyzed her options: she could go ahead without acknowledging where the software had taken them and possibly lose him, return to where she wanted to go without acknowledging the change and perhaps confuse him, or address the software's response to their commands to teach new tools for procedural and conceptual understanding, and then return. She chose the latter so as not to confuse Nathan. The notable exception was her overestimation of her second student's keyboarding and reading the computer interface abilities. Her analysis then focused on her second student's eye movements, thus discovering that Alana was only looking at the top of the computer screen. The quote at the beginning of the chapter supports this with there-and-then and here-and-now reflective thoughts about the lesson. Marie constantly analyzed her students' responses to her questions and their demonstrations of their understandings. She then changed her teaching strategies according to what she found. She also intensely analyzed her questions for their clarity during her teaching as indicated by the many thoughts she expressed about how much she rephrased her questions until she felt the student could understand what she wanted. She also concluded that her constant rephrasing could be confusing to the student.

The ability to analyze problems provided Marie the opportunity to respond to her student's needs through her adjustments to her teaching strategies. Anne's lack of ability to identify, analyze, and cope with unpredictable technology problems, which came from her novice status with the technology she was using, so damaged her self-esteem as the teacher-librarian expert that she came very close to ending her second session without achieving her primary goal of finding an information product for her student.

The ability to leave knowledge out in the world and to analyze within a variety of known and unforeseen contexts thus influences the strength of a number of other mental models, such as problem-solving ability, emphasis on student understandings, and choice of teaching strategies. The lack of the same skills in known and unpredicted contextual situations reinforces procedural patterning and prevents the teacher-librarian from understanding and responding to the needs of the moment.

Pedagogy: Lesson Preparation and Introduction Phase
Mental Models

Table 7.2 deals with the teacher-librarians' mental models concerning the preparation and beginning phases of a lesson as well as the effects on teaching of their assumptions and consequent strategies on their teaching.

There were two major mental models identified in the literature that our data confirmed. These concerned the teacher-librarians' levels of comprehension of the students' tasks and the students' information literacy abilities.

1. Were their mental models dependent on the depth of understanding and familiarity they had with the assignment, student, and student's information literacy needs (Cohen et al., 1995)? Certainly Anne's mental models of each student influenced her responses to much of what happened in both ses-

Table 7.2.   Comparison between Anne's and Marie's Lesson Preparation and Introduction Phase Mental Models

Item	Mental Model: Purpose	Anne's Examples	Marie's Examples
1	Targeted finding out about students and their assignments before lessons	Talked with teachers about assignments and formed mental model of students' abilities before the lessons started; altered mental models of both students during sessions	Decided what she would teach based on prior observations: Nathan's class did not use features of database; Alana did not use the automated catalog; altered mental model of Alana during session
2	Targeted student's prior knowledge and status of project at beginning of lesson	Questioned students about what research they had already conducted but not about their self-concept mental models of their technology and information literacy skills	Questioned students at the beginning of sessions about technical information literacy skills with their respective database mental models; decided on teaching strategies based on their answers

sions. She did not know Frances very well, but assumed Frances was very much a beginner with computer technologies, which allowed Anne to relax more about her image as the expert. Her information specialist mental model became more powerful upon finding out that Frances had not started her assignment. Anne respected Andrew's intellectual and technology abilities and allowed this mental model to control her preparation of the lesson mental model. Anne consulted both teachers about the topic of the class project each had set as assessment. Based on this information about the student and their respective project, Anne chose the database she would utilize for the lessons.

Marie knew that Nathan had an authentic assignment and knew what she wanted to do with Nathan because of working with his class the week before on finding information in an electronic encyclopedia (see chapter 5). If, as she had observed of the rest of his class, he read the electronic text like the paper copy of the encyclopedia, her goal was to guide his usage and understanding of some of the electronic encyclopedia's searching tools to help him locate information more effectively and efficiently. Marie did not ask Alana's classroom teacher about a relevant assignment for Alana's lesson. Having observed Alana's many trips to the library to find her two favorite authors' books and knowing her older sisters, Marie felt that she knew Alana better than she did Nathan, who was fairly new to the school. She had never observed Alana using the automated catalog and assumed that Alana did not know how to use the catalog. She had always noticed Alana browsing the same shelves and deduced that Alana did not know what other interesting books could be found elsewhere in the library. Marie deemed that in both cases, teaching for both conceptual and procedural understanding would serve each student well.

2. *Did the teacher-librarians ascertain the students' mental models, their content and technology knowledge, and their self-concept with respect to the tasks in hand at the beginning of the lesson to ensure their planning had been appropriate (Newton, 1996; Vosnaidou, 1994)?* As discussed above, Anne commenced each lesson with strong assumptions about both students and their assignments. She queried both students at the beginning of the sessions as to the assignment and their past experiences, but not their self-concept mental models with computer information literacy tasks. Anne espoused a mental model of not knowing Frances as well as Andrew. In fact, she had occasionally experienced Frances's lack of self-control in the library. Prior to this session, Anne learned from Frances's teachers that Frances had made recent efforts to increase her workload. Only with stimulated recall "that-was-then" thoughts (chapter 3), did we learn that Anne worried about Frances's motivation to follow up on retrieving the information products that they would find and finish her assignment. Thus Anne's beginning mental model of Frances as a student was somewhat negative concerning Frances's potential interest in learning. Once in the session, Anne rapidly changed her negative mental model to a positive mental model of Frances based on Frances's interactions with her during the session (chapter 4).

Before the session, Anne assumed that Andrew possessed strong computer technology skills and could handle conceptual learning about evaluating resources. Then during the session, she changed this positive mental model to a negative one based on his selection of resources and several explorations that he wanted to do that she considered wasting their time. Once she decided she needed to direct the lesson and take over the keyboard from Andrew, she forgot to pay attention to his responses (chapters 4 and 6). Anne had no idea of what Andrew might have learned from the lesson or how he reacted to it. She needed to see him to find out his reactions to the lesson before she could more accurately change her own self-concept and teaching mental models and her mental model of Andrew.

The students' prior skills and prior knowledge that Marie discovered during her initial questioning at the beginning of the lessons governed her choice of teaching strategies. We learned from Marie's stimulated recall interview that her lesson preparation mental model contained this introductory questioning strategy. There was no mismatch between these mental models. She never wavered from a student-centered focus, but in directing the students' responses back to them, she would add more detailed information depending on the student's level of understanding. This she did with Alana and to a lesser extent with Nathan (chapters 5 and 6). As confirmed in her stimulated recall thoughts, Marie spent time at the beginning of, and during, each lesson, analyzing each student's continuing level of understanding mental models as demonstrated by her questioning, her requests that the students demonstrate their level of comprehension rather than assume that they knew because of their answer, and her subsequent action in the lesson. In effect, Marie's philosophical and pedagogical mental models held that effective learning would not occur unless the students' current and progressive understandings were not ascertained and monitored. According to Bransford, Brown, and Cocking (2000), this demonstrated the mental models of an expert or, in their terms, "highly competent virtuoso" (p. 38).

Both teacher-librarians changed their mental models of one or both of their students as a result of various pedagogic strategies that they used during the lessons. In three cases, the teacher-librarians changed their mental models: First, Anne changed to a more negative mental model with Andrew; second, Marie changed to a more realistic one with Alana. Both had assumed more skills or more knowledge by the students; and in the third case (Anne with Frances), where the teacher-librarian had a poor opinion of the student's attitudes, skills, and understandings prior to the lesson, Anne's mental model of the student rapidly became more positive based on the student's continuing expression of interest. Anne did not distinguish whether her student's responses indicated interest and understanding or just interest.

Pedagogy: Procedural or Conceptual Mental Models

Table 7.3 delineates examples revealing the pedagogy mental models that Anne and Marie held and put into action in terms of teaching for procedural or conceptual understanding. The first pedagogy, teaching for how-to-do-it procedures, denotes a behaviorist teaching and learning style while the latter, a how-it-works pedagogy, entails a constructivist or social constructivist teaching and learning philosophy.

The following seven questions that correspond to the seven itemized categories in table 7.3 pertain to the influence of our participants' mental models on their thinking and actions. Questions one through seven investigate whether the teacher-librarians had dominant mental models that promoted teaching procedural steps for using the technology, or whether they had dominant mental models that promoted conceptual understandings using a forced prediction strategy.

1. Were their initial instructions to their students procedural or did they

Table 7.3. Comparison between Anne's and Marie's Pedagogy In-Action Mental Models

Item	Mental Models Incorporated:	Anne's Examples	Marie's Examples
1	Procedural instructions or conceptual activities	Procedural instructions with both students; offered second student one opportunity to make conceptual information literacy choice	Conceptual questions and activities for first student; procedural and conceptual with second student; asked both to demonstrate their learning
2	"How-it-works"; that is, conceptual understandings	Only used as either a teaching moment with first student or as a deliberate choice for second student until problems arose, then reverted to all procedural	Adopted a conceptual emphasis with first student, worked on possible command results with second student
3	Discovery—work out for self	Preferred to learn by being shown how to operate computer technologies; gravitated toward doing the same with teaching	Believed that students should have some guidance, then be left to discover and learn by themselves
4	Notion that procedural meant fast, easy, how-to-do lesson expectation	Thought first lesson would be more difficult and second session quick and easy; assumed first student not experienced and second student computer knowledgeable	Appropriate understandings more important than time constraints; espoused philosophy that best teaching was the momentary guidance when students had problems
5	Forced prediction to demonstrate their conceptual understanding	Informed students; asked questions requiring a choice that sometimes involved prediction	Forced more predictions with first student; asked what would happen with specific moves
6	Non-exemplars	Had them because of mistakes with technology commands	Did not have them because she could problem solve and anticipate correct technology commands
7	Shared mental models	Shared her frustrations mental model when they had so many technology problems but didn't bring students into problem solving	Shared discoveries and shared mental models of effective search strategies; shared student discoveries with second student

engage the student in conceptual activities (Bilby, 1992b; Williams, 1996)? Did they present both procedural and conceptual understandings (Seel, 1995)? After admitting that she didn't know why the online dial-up process worked the way it did, Anne maintained a consistent procedural approach to what she was teaching in both lessons. Anne's emphasis was so strongly on producing an information product suitable for her students' assignments that she leaned almost exclusively on procedural understandings in relation to technology literacy skills rather than conceptual understandings. After the beginning technology fiasco with Andrew, Anne still tried to keep to her original mental model of facilitating a decision-making experience, requiring him to choose the appropriate information resource based on his assignment criteria. But she became frustrated when he chose a database that she did not know and did not think would produce a relevant immediate information resource. Thus, she abandoned her conceptual understandings goal, steered him away from his choice of a resource, and led him back into the automated catalog with which was familiar and which she thought would help them locate an adequate information resource product for his assignment. Her objectives as a teacher seemed to focus on imparting a how-to-do-it type of understanding rather than stretching Andrew's understanding about how to make more appropriate choices based on what he expected to find, and what his goal was for the lesson.

In comparison, Marie engaged her students in conceptual activities, as well as procedural, based on their prior knowledge. This meant that she did not use the questions listed on the dinosaur research activity handout from Nathan's teacher to direct the lesson so that Nathan could answer specific questions. Marie ensured that she built Alana's foundational procedural and conceptual knowledge to the point where Alana could answer questions about what the electronic catalog database would do with certain commands and how it would respond when she entered commands certain ways.

2. *Did the teacher-librarians concentrate on "how it works"; that is, conceptual-type teaching that required students to deduce and infer during task performance (Duff, 1989, 1992)?* Anne tried to figure out by herself how to solve her technology problems. Her lack of experience with the technology prevented her from having strategy options to share. Although she rarely required her students to deduce or infer during task performance, Anne thought she had tried to demonstrate this by talking out loud about her thinking and frustrations during the dial-up errors. However, these were not inferences or deductions that permitted analysis or predictive troubleshooting. They were simple comments like, "perhaps it was a typing error" or "this has not happened before."

Marie utilized "how it works" as one of her main strategy mental models for both students but Alana was at a much more elementary level, needing more information in order to deduce or infer. In the end, Marie felt that Alana still had too incomplete a mental model of the automated catalog to work it by herself successfully, particularly if there was a time lapse before she tried to use it again. Marie's pedagogical approach mental models for Nathan never wavered from teaching for conceptual and, in the process, procedural understanding.

Research (Ohtsuka, 1990, 1993a, 1993b) has suggested that students construct and utilize one-dimensional mental models when they are provided or, in Anne's lessons (chapter 4), directed through procedural (ordered) step-by-step instructions when accessing and searching online databases. In contrast, two-dimensional mental models appear to be constructed when students are provided with the global how-it-works conceptual information. An example of a two-dimensional mental model occurred when Marie required Nathan to predict what would happen when he typed in a search query. She was testing Nathan's conceptual understanding of the connections between his search query and the dinosaur section (like a sub-database) within the larger encyclopedia database. The research (Ohtsuka, 1990, 1993a, 1993b; Troy, 1994) further suggested that a two-dimensional interwoven threads mental model is effective for the creation of transitory and long-term mental models and retrieval from the latter.

3. *Were their students required to work something out for themselves that might be more taxing and time-consuming, not just for the student but for themselves as teachers (Duff, 1989, 1992; Rogers, 1992)?* Anne did not allow for this beyond a few procedural choices with Frances. With Andrew, she began the session thinking that he should make decisions about the materials he should examine. However this translated to a choice of which database to access within the public library's online database list of offerings. When that caused more problems for her quick-session agenda, Anne rescinded further options. It was the case with her second session of getting quite messy and time-consuming that she had not allowed for in her thinking. Directing or demonstrating to students how to do something in a step-by-step manner required less time; it was an easier and quicker option for the student and teacher-librarian, too (Rogers, 1992).

Carrying out a directive and waiting for the instruction to be carried out can be minimal in a one-on-one or small group situation and is a common teaching strategy of teacher-librarians. Taking over the keyboard, as Anne did, ensures an even speedier finish. Anne consistently demonstrated that her time constraints mental model was a constant throughout her lessons (chapter 6). Given this, she saw no option but quick focused lessons.

Marie provided an admirable example of a teacher-librarian who helped students work out what was needed in her session with Nathan. Her belief in using forced prediction to develop conceptual understandings proved one of her stronger mental models. Marie was not influenced by a time constraint mental model (chapters 5 and 6). Even in her shorter lesson with Alana, Marie maintained a combined procedural-conceptual pedagogy and waited patiently for Alana to predict, explain the results of an action, and demonstrate her understanding, even though Alana had weak, and therefore excruciatingly slow, keyboard skills. Marie later reflected that even in ad hoc one- to two-minute automated catalog sessions, she still put her questioning for prediction and inference strategy mental models into action (see chapter 5).

4. *Did the teacher-librarians expect the session to be fast and remain a how-to-do-it session that could hinder later transferability of the procedures to a novel situation (Bransford, Brown, and Cocking, 2000; Duff, 1989, 1992; Seely Brown, Collins, and Duguid, 1996)?* Anne assumed that her second session would be a quick, how-to-do-it session and was considerably upset when the session went awry, in her opinion. She expected she would need much more time with her first student who would not be as experienced with computers. Anne stressed time constraints with each lesson, ever mindful of getting her students back to class. She was used to operating with time constraints with all her teaching and found these two lessons no exception, especially when their errors consumed an unpredicted amount of time. Anne may have given Andrew a choice of which database he wished to explore but this was well within her procedural pedagogic philosophy (see chapters 5 and 6). On the plus side, research literature reported that how-to-do-it procedural information literacy instructions seemed to enable faster and more accurate performance during the session and usually resulted in short-term recall (Duff, 1989, 1992). On the negative side, the consequence of procedural teaching and learning was an inert mental model (Renkl, Mandl, and Gruber, 1996) because the mental model would be unable to transfer to complex, unpredictable, and novel situations. Therefore, students would demonstrate poor accuracy and inadequate strategies in new or troubleshooting situations (see chapter 2). Anne was an exemplar of her own how-to-do-it strategy in all these outcomes.

Marie preferred fast sessions, which she thought were more effective in bringing students and staff immediate results to their queries. Nevertheless, she did not utilize how-to-do-it strategies, even with the one- or two-minute ad hoc intervention (see chapter 5). Marie questioned, asked students to predict the outcome of their answer, and then required that they demonstrate their understanding. However, contrary to what she preferred, Marie did not rush the two lessons in our research and spent time analyzing and teaching to the students' needs at the level where they were.

5. *Did the teacher-librarians engage in a strategy of forced prediction that required the learner to articulate a mental model of a situation, rather than remain passive and cognitively inert (Craig, 1943; Friedler, Nachmias, and Linn, 1987; Newton, 1994)?* By using a procedural strategy, Anne did not actively engage her students in forced predictions that they then would have tested to see if their predictions were correct. Forced predictions would have required her learners to articulate a mental model of a situation, rather than remain passive and inert as learners. If she had used conceptual pedagogy, she would have required her students proactively to turn their new information into personal knowledge. Anne's students remained relatively passive throughout the sessions. Although her questions probed for factual answers or resource choices, she did not ask her students to predict what would happen if they entered a certain command or what the computer was doing after they entered a command. On the other hand, Marie used forced prediction throughout her lessons, but lowered the difficulty level with Alana because of Alana's novice status. Marie was the strongest user of this strategy of all our 10 participants.

Gagne and Glaser (1987) pointed out that predictive, analytic, and troubleshooting skills cannot be left to chance and advocated that mental models should be deliberately taught to facilitate these skills. The need to teach for transfer was reiterated by Price and Driscoll (1997). Duff (1992) and Seel (1995) argued that, in the long run, effective database usage requires both procedural how-to-do-it and conceptual how-it-works understandings in order to solve problems effectively at each stage of acquiring that skill and especially in novel situations. Marie's mental models appeared to contain an understanding of these points as she acknowledged in both her stimulated recall and enhanced post-interview thoughts that she was unsure how much Alana would remember and be able to put into practice and that she would need further conceptual understanding. However, she was less concerned that Nathan would be unable to utilize his new procedural and conceptual understanding even though she would deliberately but unobtrusively check on his actions when he next used the database.

6. *Were non-exemplars as well as exemplars provided, thereby making use of errors as learning opportunities to assist in building mental models that contain both what is false and what is valid (Borthwick and Jones, 2000; Hazzan, and Zazkis, 1997; Johnson-Laird, 2001)?* Helping students construct their own understandings of new concepts relies on using examples together with non-examples (McTighe, as cited in Rolheiser and Fullan, 2002), particularly in the online environment (Borthwick and Jones, 2000). Explanatory examples and, especially, counter-examples have pedagogic value as stu-

dents gain insight into why a prediction or hypothesis fails (Dahlberg and Housman, 1997).

Anne provided a commentary on the experiences she and Frances had during the lesson and, in this way, provided examples and non-examples (see chapter 4). We suggested in chapter 6 that this was because Anne thought that her student had fewer technology skills and felt more comfortable admitting her own mistakes. In contrast, Anne quickly moved past the technology errors in her lesson with Andrew, whom she thought was more computer literate, without trying to gain insight. She did not capitalize on the non-exemplar provided by the poor match of the newspaper database with Andrew's information needs. In Andrew's stimulated recall interview, he was disappointed by this because he had no idea why the newspaper database was not a good choice for finding what he required for his project. We provide this example to demonstrate how an inadequate mental model reveals the need for exploratory discussion of the non-exemplar to build a useful mental model for future situations.

Marie made use of her error in taking Nathan into an area that she thought was beyond his grade-level curriculum (see chapter 6) as a learning opportunity to understand more about the database tools. Her error was in misjudging his understandings; thus, it did not qualify as a non-exemplar of effective tool use. In other situations, Marie made use of exemplars and non-exemplars; for example, of the rule for using capital letters in searches of the school's automated catalog compared with using the rule with other databases. The school's automated catalog used both the capitalized and non-capitalized versions of spelling to produce possibilities that the user might find useful. Alana was asked to predict what might happen, test her proposition, and explain what happened to demonstrate her understanding to Marie. Alana was delighted with this new knowledge.

Troubleshooting mental models also require exemplars and non-exemplars if they are to be used effectively and efficiently. In these ways, users create the understandings necessary for expert mental models. Indeed, as Watson and Mason (2004) pointed out, it is not uncommon for teachers and students to identify concepts from one or two early examples that have been demonstrated, stated, or explored. The problem is that early examples are usually uncomplicated so that learners and novice information technology teachers can be left with a partial and limited mental model of the concept. Watson and Mason (2004) further warned that a few non-examples can also have minimal impact, particularly if they conflict with previous and erroneous mental models (Fischbein, 1987). Of the four students, Andrew was more than ready for in-depth example and non-example learning, as were Nathan and Frances. Alana was less so, given her beginner background. Nevertheless, Alana coped well and enjoyed doing so. Neither teacher-librarian used the terminology *example* and *non-example*, nor explained the importance of these learning tools. Perhaps they were unaware of the theoretical and practical importance of these concepts. However, as Maria reflected, she noted that she needed to double-check that both her students were using their new mental models and she wanted to provide Alana with more experiential guided practice (chapter 5).

   7. *Did the teacher-librarians engage in sharing mental models with their students in order for the outcome to reflect mental models that incorporated both the student's and the teacher-librarian's incorrect or correct solutions to problems (Cohen, 1995; Johnson-Laird, 1983; Langan-Fox, Wirth, Code, Langfield-Smith, and Wirth, 2001)?* Anne shared her mental models with her students during her commentary of what was happening during the online connection with the public library and their computer, such as an incomplete mental model of not understanding why the errors were occurring when they had not done so in previous sessions with teachers and during her own practice sessions. She demonstrated that she found a solution by repeating patterned steps or as a fluke. Anne shared a satisfying analogy of their computer connecting with others in cyberspace with Frances. She also shared with Andrew her incomplete mental model of the public library's newspaper database as she had not entered the newspaper database before their lesson and was not sure how to exit from it. However, her students were too passive to engage in offering their own in return; yet Anne had not invited their opinions and remained unaware of her non-action even during her reflections in the enhanced post-interviews (see chapter 6). Thus, Anne's mental models did not incorporate her students' mental models. Instead, her mental models incorporated her assumptions about her students' mental models as she had not asked them to put their mental models into action through demonstration, prediction, explanation, or clarification. Mental models were shared in one direction only.

   Several times Nathan was able to teach Marie a new trick about a tool that Marie told us she then incorporated in other teaching-learning sessions before her second lesson with us. She was quite enthusiastic about sharing Nathan's discoveries. Throughout her lesson, she shared her strategies for finding information mental models and her mental models of the ways in which the encyclopedia tool improved this process, which Nathan picked up, demonstrated, and therefore absorbed. Where he could contribute because of the predicting he was being asked to do, he would share his new mental model in return. Because of Alana's beginner status, she did not have the opportunity to share mental models with Marie in the way Nathan did. Alana nevertheless appropriately demonstrated the mental models Marie was sharing with her.

MANAGING MENTAL MODELS VERSUS
MENTAL MODELS IN CONTROL

This section examines the crux of the role of mental models. On the one hand, mental models can be managed by their users to effect necessary changes. On the other hand, mental models can manage or control their users, thereby resulting in less than satisfactory outcomes. The flowchart (figure 7.1) reveals a diagrammatic model delineating key decision-making points in the four lessons. This sequence of decision making is repetitive before, during, and after the lesson because of the number of mental models utilized (see chapters 4 and 5). Nevertheless, for ease of comprehension, we suggest the following route through the flow diagram (figure 7.1).

1st Begin at the top three, and the vertical mid-left side, dashed-line rectangles that distinguish the four over-arching types of mental models identified according to when and how the data were collected: espoused (pre-lesson), videoed in-action (during), stimulated recall in-action (retrospective introspection interview), and enhanced reflective mental models (post-lesson) (figure 7.1; see chapter 2).

2nd Now follow the arrowed lines from each of these mental models to the second level in the flowchart, represented as rectangles, concerning mental model discrepancies (figure 7.1). At this juncture, queries were raised concerning the teacher-librarians' recognition of any mismatch or compatibility among the four over-arching types of mental models.

3rd Depending on the answers, the teacher-librarians moved to different third-level (rectangles) and/or further choices.
  a. Answering "no" meant that the teacher-librarians either acknowledged that there were no discrepancies or did not realize there were any discrepancies between their own mental model beliefs, actions, and thoughts.
  b. Answering "yes" meant that there was recognition of mental model discrepancies (figure 7.1).

4th Further decisions were required. Did the teacher-librarians commit to changing the mental models and outcomes they deemed inadequate? (Fourth level, bold oval rectangles, figure 7.1)

5th Their answers were represented in the fifth and final level as bolded ovals:
  a. If they answered "no," then their mental models controlled their lessons.

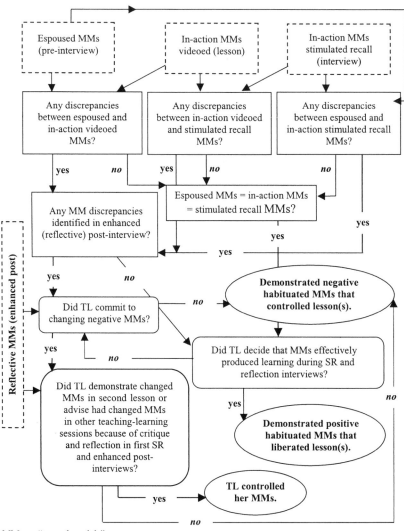

Figure 7.1.   Managing Mental Models Flow Diagram

b. If they answered "yes," then they controlled their mental models.

These outcomes, whether any teacher-librarian's mental models controlled them or they managed their mental models, are obviously not neutral for either teacher-librarian or student.

As researchers, we also asked and answered these questions and came to conclusions concerning mental model control and management.

An example relevant to the first category in the flowchart would be Anne's preparation mental model that espoused (top-left dotted rectangle, figure 7.1) a strategy in which she would control the computer and tell her first student the steps to use to access the local library for resources via the Internet (stimulated recall interview). Then, at the beginning of the lesson, Anne told us she changed her strategy to the student controlling the keyboard with her telling the student what to do (stimulated recall interview). This change corresponds to the second-level discrepancy between the espoused and in-action stimulated recall mental models, represented in figure 7.1 as a rectangle. There was no discrepancy between this in-action mental model and her reflective mental model (another second-level question in figure 7.1). During the enhanced post-interview, Anne decided that this change in mental models had been a successful strategy variation that allowed Frances to learn more effectively. The question to this answer is found in the third-level oval rectangle in the bottom middle of figure 7.1. This evaluation resulted in a positive demonstration of an ingrained mental model that was self-liberating in terms of Anne's habituated teacher-directed behaviorist mental model. This outcome is represented in the middle fourth-level oval (figure 7.1).

An example from Marie's lessons begins at the reflection mental model level (vertical dotted rectangle, figure 7.1). Marie evaluated her questioning mental model during the enhanced post-interview and pronounced the constant re-wording of her questions as abominable and therefore committed to changing this; that is, her mental model (see second bottom oval rectangle in figure 7.1). However, in her second lesson there was no evidence of any change; her wording questions mental model remained habituated and controlled her actions (top oval, figure 7.1).

The significance of examining this facet of the degree of control we or our mental models have cannot be overstressed (see, e.g., Barker et al., 1998; Norman, 1983; Szabo, 1998). As we wrote in chapter 2, our mental models powerfully affect how and why we teach in the ways we do. Previous chapters, including this one, have established that many mental models produce worthwhile outcomes. Others do not; they are inaccurate or stagnant and in need of critical reflection and change. Mental models provide the foundation for success and failure in teaching.

Two fundamental questions therefore remain to be answered.

1. Did the teacher-librarians manage their mental models for positive outcomes or did their mental models direct what happened during the lesson and thereby control them and the outcomes? (See figure 7.1.)
2. After critical reflection on their lessons, did either teacher-librarian voice, commit, or demonstrate (in the second lesson) the changes they evaluated as necessary for enhanced learning outcomes? (See figure 7.1.)

Providing answers to these questions has been structured as follows. First, table 7.4 delineates comparative mental models and how these were exemplified during their teaching and reflection. Second, a series of sub-questions and answers tease out particular strands of this managing characteristic of mental models. In this way, we also reveal how the teacher-librarians engaged with the stages indicated in figure 7.1.

The following questions, questions 1 through 5, correspond to the item categories in table 7.4. They relate to whether teacher-librarians changed their mental models based on the lesson's events or whether the teacher-librarians did not allow the lesson events or student to influence their espoused pre-lesson mental models. We especially looked for evidence in the second lesson that the teacher-librarians had changed the mental models that they had committed to changing during their first enhanced post-interview. It was then possible to ascertain if their mental models controlled them or visa versa.

1. Did they manage the negative or positive attributes of their mental models during the lesson, resulting in the way their mental models affected the lesson (Szabo, 1998)? Anne had more "negative mental models" and seemingly less control over the lessons' direction. Her mental model of her helplessness with the dial-up access technology in both sessions threatened to sabotage the second session where she had attributed more technology skills to her student than he demonstrated. This threatened to disrupt her teacher-librarian as expert mental model. (Anne is now at the second and third levels in figure 7.1). Her mental models of not knowing how or why she made mistakes in her dial-up access procedures or how to find "information out in the world" when using the newspaper database managed her consequent teaching strategies. This created an unacceptable situation according to her mental models, when the "database would not cooperate" (enhanced post-interview). These problem events focused her need to redeem herself in her student's eyes even more so, triggering self-per-

Table 7.4. Comparison between Teacher-Librarians Managing Their Mental Models or Their Mental Models Controlling Their Thoughts and Actions

Item	Mental Model: Type, Function, Characteristic	Anne's Examples	Marie's Examples
1	Type of mental models affected teacher-librarians' reaction to lessons.	Negative attributes usually equated with negative reactions, particularly in second lesson.	Positive attributes equated with positive reactions to computer technologies; knew intuitively how to teach their use and how they could help students.
2	Edited mental models depending on what was discovered during lesson phases.	Became more responsive, shared her mistakes and mental models with Frances; unable to replicate these strategies with second student because of failure of concept of self as teacher-librarian knowledge expert vis-à-vis concept of student as being technologically more competent.	Edited mental model of second student to lower keyboarding skills; edited mental model of database in first session when student discovered new strategy.
3	Mirrored the lesson plan, steered the lesson's progress, or facilitated modification of the lesson.	Changed from quick show-and-tell to a hands-on strategy to help student remember; still directed student; with second student reversed teaching strategy and reassumed direction.	Used initial questioning to settle on specific topics and sequence; maintained preferred strategy to guide, not direct.
4	MMs affected reactions to levels of satisfaction and control of lessons.	Product goal, time constraints, novice mental models produced low levels compared with positive change in mental model of Frances.	Procedural and conceptual goals; constructivist pedagogy; time-as-teaching-opportunity mental models were constant and controlled.
5	Ingrained, liberating, or stultifying mental models.	Ingrained and stultifying; mental models governed emotional reactions and prevented adaptation.	Liberating; mental models focused on conceptual understandings; believed in exploratory learning; guided rather than taught.
6	Used reflections to facilitate changes to her teaching strategies mental models.	Reflected but did not change most of her strategies; changed mental model of second student's abilities; abandoned decision-making practice.	Reflections revealed she felt questioning was weak but did not change way she questioned during second session; on the other hand, questioning results led to changes in her teaching strategies.

mission to find an information product mental model to dominate her other mental models. This dictated how she responded to all subsequent events, including taking back control of the keyboard and making the decisions as to where to go to find materials.

Marie held a store of positive mental models. For example, Marie held a productive mental model of the usefulness of electronic databases and of herself as an information literacy facilitator who, because of her well-founded expert computer information literacy skills mental model, felt that she could teach information literacy intuitively. Nothing fazed her; not Alana's very weak computer literacy skills; not the server glitch; not accidentally going into the tables section with Nathan; and not the length of time and patience involved in teaching for conceptual and procedural understanding (see table 7.1; table 7.3, item 3; chapter 5). These mental models were habituated but positive, resulting in beneficial outcomes for her and her students (middle oval in figure 7.1).

What we discovered with our participants and their mental models was that mental models used negatively tended to dominate and control other mental models by stifling what the teacher-librarians thought they could do or what their students could do. Mental models used positively tended to give the teacher-librarians confidence to facilitate the effective running of other mental models and changing them as needed during the lesson (chapter 5). More often, the positive mental models, which would rise and fall in importance as the lesson progressed, could be effectively managed, while the negative mental models, such as the damaging imposition of a negative time constraints mental model, tended to control decision-making (chapter 4).

2. Depending on what they found out as they were teaching, did the teacher-librarians edit their original espoused mental models during the lesson (Cohen et al., 1995)? The difference in Anne's ability to manage her self-concept mental model or be controlled by it came partially from the level of computer Internet skills she credited to the students juxtaposed with her own novice skills. First, Anne changed her mental model of Frances, who had poorer Internet skills than Anne, when she found out that Frances was more responsive than Anne had thought would be the case (second level, figure 7.1). Second, this first change allowed Anne to share her own understandings more completely with Frances than she did with Andrew. A third example of managing her self-concept mental model positively during the first lesson occurred when dial-up errors caused disruptions in Frances's session. She treated some disruptions as teaching moments and, crucially, was able to admit her errors. These examples demonstrate the liberating effects of controlling her self-concept mental model (see chapters 4 and 6; middle and bottom oval, figure 7.1). It was usually the other way around during her second lesson. When errors disrupted her session with Andrew, to whom she attributed a higher level of Internet computer literacy than herself, Anne was not flexible enough to work past them. Her own lack of conceptual understandings of the computer tools and her need for control and comfort through procedural teaching had a dominating influence. When these events occurred, she imagined her image and status as knowledge expert and information specialist crumbling in his mind (stimulated recall interview). Her mental model changed to one that considered disbanding the lesson (chapters 4 and 6). Her self-concept mental model was negatively controlling the lesson at this point (top oval, figure 7.1).

Marie's espoused mental model goal for both students was to increase their information literacy and, hence, troubleshooting skills with their respective databases. Marie adjusted her teaching strategies mental models according to what she found out about the students during her initial questioning, their answers to her questions, and demonstrations of their understandings. For example, she changed her mental model to emphasize both procedural and conceptual understandings for Alana when she realized Alana's weak keyboard and virtually non-existent "reading-the-computer-interface" skills (see table 7.1).

3. *Did their mental models mirror the lesson plan, steer the lesson's progress, or facilitate modification of the lesson; or did the opposite occur (Cohen et al., 1995)?* Anne's mental models of the teacher-librarian as knowledge expert, procedural teaching strategies, product as lesson goal, awareness of time running out, and her novice technology skills steered the lessons. She could not cope well with unpredictable technical and database situations that she had initially predicted would be straightforward. For example, Anne told us, with cynical wonderment at her naïveté during her enhanced post-interview, that she had been convinced that her lesson with Andrew would be quick and easy. Through her in-action stimulated recall thoughts, we discovered that Anne's mental model of the lesson for Andrew changed rapidly once she judged him incapable of making worthwhile decisions about what resources to choose; this was not what her espoused mental model had predicted (oval rectangle, discrepancies between stimulated recall and espoused mental models, figure 7.1). She was not prepared to digress from her procedural lesson plan to help him build conceptual understandings of how to evaluate the worth of databases according to his information need. Thus, she allowed her information product goal mental model—always the major goal of both lessons—and time constraint mental model to resurface more prominently, as well as her directive teaching strategies mental model rather than a facilitator mental model. These mental models controlled her, stultified the lesson, and diminished the learning outcomes (top oval, figure 7.1).

Marie espoused a mental model of preferring guided-discovery learning, having decided that all students were capable of discovering how software worked, given some preliminary guidance. This never wavered, even in Alana's lesson. The espoused and both in-action mental models stayed constant (figure 7.1; chapters 5 and 6). Thus, she was confident she could help Nathan and Alana develop an ability to predict what would happen within the database when they keyed in certain commands. In these ways, she hoped they would learn how to use the database more effectively and be able to teach others what they had learned. Marie's mental models of her students, their needs, and their demonstrated degree of understanding guided her pedagogic philosophy and strategies mental models that were always in control, remaining constructively constant throughout her lessons (bottom oval, figure 7.1; see chapter 6).

4. *Did their mental models affect the teacher-librarians' reaction to, control over, and satisfaction with their respective database teaching experiences (van der Henst, 1999)?* The initial dial-up disasters in Anne's two sessions cast a pall over the lessons. However, her lesson with Frances turned optimistic when Anne unexpectedly found that Frances was responding closely to her (Anne's) teaching in a way that pleased Anne. As she changed her mental model of Frances toward a more positive one, Anne developed a greater desire to continue working with Frances and help Frances succeed; that is, find materials that would satisfy Frances's assignment information needs. High on Anne's priority list was her need to establish a good working relationship with Frances so Frances would come back and enlist Anne's guidance in the future. Working toward positive teacher-librarian and student relationships became a verbalized mental model only through Anne's reflective analysis of what was happening with her relationship with Frances (enhanced post-interview).

When the dial-up procedures and the newspaper database turned disastrous in her second lesson, Anne negated a more student-centered espoused mental model goal to help Andrew practice evaluating resource appropriateness when she took back control of the keyboard and essentially directed the choice making during the rest of the lesson. In figure 7.1, this change in mental models occurred in a second-level decision. (As mentioned in the introduction to figure 7.1, Anne, or any teacher and teacher-librarian, would not necessarily be progressing through the levels depicted in the flowchart sequentially but would often revisit previous levels.) Anne ran these mental models as she felt she needed to take the leadership and guide Andrew to the proper sources so that they would be successful in finding him materials. The complexity of a student-centered session where the student could explore and start to piece together conceptual understandings tried her patience after the initial disaster and pushed her into abandoning the effort. Jonassen and Tessmer (1996) pointed out that teachers who use behaviorist teaching-learning environments have mental models that still expect teaching information communication technology skills to be intuitively easy. With the onset of problems that lowered her confidence and defied her skills to solve them, her mental models of needing to lead and be in control, along with her need to salvage her expert status, overwhelmed her desire to work on Andrew's conceptual understandings. Her espoused mental model allegiance to teaching conceptually as well as procedurally was uncomfortable enough during the lesson to encourage her to revert to teaching as she was taught, a mental model comfort zone that we all find when other factors do not go well.

An enlightening indication of mental models controlling their owner is highlighted by Anne's stimulated recall admission that, when these sorts of complications occurred, her under stress mental model strategy to disband the lesson exerted itself. However, Anne then demonstrated an instance of managing this "bail out" stimulated recall mental model by reversing it when she continued the lesson by taking over the keyboard and decisions. Anne's need to obtain a product as a symbol of a successful session within the time left exercised the most influence and control on her decision making and subsequent thinking and teaching. Anne led her student quickly into the public library catalog where she could confidently maneuver. That they might not find any non-borrowed information resources in the public library never entered her mind during her lesson planning and up to this point in the lesson. She did not tolerate well the unpredicted happenings. During and after the lesson, Anne's thoughts and critical reflections indicated how she let these mental models take control of the lesson, her emotional reactions, and her choice of teaching strategies (stimulated recall and enhanced post-interviews; top oval in figure 7.1).

In contrast, Marie's mental models never contained doubts about her abilities to facilitate computer information literacy or her knowledge of the *World Book* encyclopedia database and the automated catalog. Instead, she lamented the mistakes still apparent in the catalog database and was quick to condemn its inaccuracies. Because she also knew what the mistakes were, Marie could prepare her students to predict what they should do when they found one of the mistakes. With less on her mind concerning the tool, she concentrated more on the student and what the student needed. Unlike Anne's situation, having one student with an authentic assignment task that was not due immediately and one who had an information literacy need meant that Marie had time to scaffold conceptual understandings through a higher level of search tool use with Nathan and an initial conceptual understanding of the ways to find materials in the automated catalog for Alana.

Marie ascertained the extent of Alana's use and knowledge of the electronic catalog mental models at the beginning of the lesson but soon realized she had made an error in not finding out more about Alana's computer keyboard skills. Marie had no problems switching her teaching goal from a higher emphasis on conceptual understandings to both procedural and conceptual understandings for Alana. Because her goal was constant in both lessons, one with a computer literate and one with a computer beginner novice, we speculated that Marie would maintain this goal even if her students had need of an immediate information product. In her enhanced post-interview, we asked her to role play how she taught ad hoc one- to three-minute sessions. Marie immediately verbalized a demonstration typical of her strategy when she was helping students who made requests of her. She used questions to guide their procedural and conceptual understanding so that they could find what they needed instead of giving them the answer or just directing their procedural steps. Marie facilitated such students' solving their own information problems rather than doing it for them. Marie's espoused, in-action, and reflective mental models demonstrated consistency in a variety of situations and her control over them for positive learning outcomes (middle and bottom ovals, figure 7.1).

  5. Were their mental models deeply ingrained and either liberating or stultifying (Fischbein et al., 1990)? A number of Anne's mental models were ingrained and stultifying. Three examples will suffice to make the point.

  The first example is that of her mental models of student time constraints and her responsibility as teacher-librarian to deliver information resources within that tight time limit. These mental models were so ingrained that she took responsibility for her first student's failure to have worked on the assignment before the lesson. The fact that Anne had made the decision to get relevant books from the school library (stimulated recall interview and reiterated in her enhanced post-interview) did not lessen her drive to produce an online information product for the assignment. Thus, she focused predominantly on finding a product and minimally on the development of conceptual understandings.

  This links with her espoused mental models of her pedagogy as student-centered and herself as a facilitator. From her reflections, thinking, and other actions, we found that her definition of student-centered teaching skewed toward the traditional teacher-centered tradition when enacted. In fact, her in-action thinking demonstrated that she did not include conceptual understandings as part of her responsibility in her first lesson. By student-centered, she was referring to her high degree of service orientation of helping students find the information they needed. That is, she facilitated their finding resources by finding them herself and giving the resources to the students (as occurred with Frances) or providing specifically directed how-to-find procedural steps so that the students could locate suitable resources (as occurred with Andrew). Having such a mismatch between pedagogy and terminology in her mental models would not have surfaced as false and therefore would not have entered her mind to critique during the enhanced reflection post-interviews.

The second example was her fear of students wiping out the computers' hard drives, which she could not fix. Her one experience with this kept her from freely offering her students use of the public library online access without her direct supervision. Instead of stressing that the students would not break the computers, as Marie and many of our other teacher-librarians did, Anne worried that her students could damage the computers' hard drives. The effect of how this mental model was realized was stultifying for the students.

The third example of ingrained mental model negativity concerned Anne's mental model of print materials. She was adamant that print resources were as essential as electronic information resources and that staff and students should value print resources and not be readily swayed by the hoopla about computer and Internet databases. These mental models kept her enthusiasm for electronic tools at a lower and less critical level than some of our teacher-librarians.

Like Anne, Marie valued both print and electronic resources. However, Marie's mental model stressed the particular value that electronic databases had for all students and staff. This mental model, though ingrained, was liberating for her, the students, and most staff. Alana's class teacher never booked sessions for his students in the computer lab; nor did he require them to use the automated catalog. After her lesson with Alana, Marie changed her mental model of her teacher-librarian role, and committed to becoming more proactive in cases such as this (enhanced post-interview). Marie's mental model of her preferred strategy of questioning also liberated her teaching because she could control making changes to the lesson depending on her student's knowledge of the resource, as she did with Alana (see chapters 5 and 6). Another example of how Marie was in control of her mental models occurred when she modeled herself as a co-learner with her first student and took pleasure in sharing discoveries about the tool, especially when her student made the discoveries.

Marie's ingrained negative mental model of a "teacher" as a chalk-and-talk lecturer imparting information as the knowledge expert, and her consequent mental model of herself as probably not a natural teacher, counter-balanced her espoused mental model of being able to teach intuitively with electronic databases because of all her work with them. This espoused mental model was confirmed by an effective pedagogic guided discovery in-action mental model as facilitator rather than as teacher. In each of her stimulated recall and enhanced post-interviews, Marie interchangeably used "facilitate," "guide," "scaffold," "[help students] discover for themselves," and "teach" but only once interchanged facilitator and teacher. Thus, in-action, Marie's mental models of her pedagogic label and role liberated her teaching, as did her preferred, ingrained, questioning strategy mental model. Used in conjunction, both allowed Marie to control making changes depending on her students' demonstration of their current understanding of the resource at various points in the lesson (see chapters 5 and 6).

Marie's mental model of the poor wording of her questions, which resulted in her constant re-wording of her questions, was ingrained and, in her evaluation, certainly not liberating to either herself or her students (stimulated recall and enhanced post-interviews; top oval, figure 7.1).

6. Did the teacher-librarians examine their mental models and express satisfaction with them and leave them unchanged or reflect on how they would change them? After committing to change, did they change their mental models in the second lesson? (Calford, 1993; Mankelow and Over, 1992; Power and Wykes, 1996)? Both teacher-librarians were among the most reflective of our participants and critically judged the worth of their mental models in-action during their stimulated recall and enhanced post-interviews.

Examples of Anne's satisfaction and consequences are provided. After the first lesson, Anne stressed that developing a relationship with the student, as she felt she had done with Frances, was "almost more important than any skills and awareness" (enhanced post-interview). Thus, paying attention to the student's responses was a critical mental model. Anne exclaimed that

> Most of what I did was in reaction to Frances but I don't know exactly how [pause]. Most of the points at which I decided to do something a certain way was because of some cue Frances gave me. . . . There was some way I had picked up that she was getting information from the screen and that I didn't need to explain it to her. (enhanced post-interview)

Anne's mental model acknowledged the value of non-verbal cues when teaching. This was stressed again in her assessment of her second lesson. Anne reflected that she had no idea how Andrew had responded to her teaching and whether he had learned anything from the lesson. Because of the errors and evident miscues, Anne's mental models of time, her status as expert, and her information product goal clearly overwhelmed her entrenched mental model of the need to be responsive to students' non-verbals. Thus, she lost her ability to cue her strategies to his responses during her second lesson and believed she had lost the valued relationship she had built over the years with Andrew. Indeed, Anne stated that she would be unsettled until she obtained feedback about the lesson from Andrew (enhanced post-interview).

On critical reflection, Anne stated that her use of questions was an effective teaching strategy with Frances "because from some of the questions, like asking her what would you choose [from the list of books returned by Frances's author query], I got a better grasp of where she needed to go" (enhanced post-interview). Anne adopted the same mental model questioning strategy with Andrew (chapters 4 and 6). To a certain extent, Anne was correct in her reason for adopting this type of question. However, unlike Marie, Anne did not take other steps to check the validity of her assumption by using forced prediction questions about what content each student thought would be in the chosen item or requesting that they justify their choice (see table 7.2, item 5). These sorts of questions would have revealed the degree of comprehensiveness and accuracy in the students' information literacy mental models to Anne and whether Anne was on the best path to counteract weaknesses in Frances's, Andrew's, and her own mental models (cf. Gagne and Glaser, 1987).

Anne also reflected that changing her mental model to allow Frances "to do [i.e., have her hands on the keyboard] was another of her effective teaching strategies" (enhanced post-interview; second-level decisions, figure 7.1). Initially, Anne had been committed to adopting a mental model of how she was taught, a demonstrate-show-and-tell strategy. There was no contrary evidence from either her stimulated or enhanced post-interviews that Anne questioned the implementation of her hands on the keyboard mental model with Andrew. As we have seen, Anne reversed this teaching strategy mental model toward the end of the lesson and justified it in terms of her time constraints and product goal mental models.

A final example of satisfaction was articulated after the first lesson when Anne reflected on the positive results of changing her espoused plan to have modem access already connected at the start of Frances's session. She did not accomplish this task because of other disruptions that morning. Ironically, the online access procedures presented Anne with her most troublesome technical problems but also gave her much satisfaction with the lesson. She felt that having her first student become aware of the telecommunications procedures that allowed use of a modem to access a computer off-campus was the most valuable experience for her student during the session. Anne stated:

> But I'm really glad I didn't because I think if we had not gone through that dialing mode, the impact would not have been made that this wasn't something inside this box. So I think there was a benefit for her understanding that this was a type of telecommunication, that we were actually going out-

side, that this was different from using a CD-ROM or a word processor or anything else. (enhanced post-interview)

Considering the Internet computer skill level that Anne had assigned Andrew, we might have concluded that she would have the access connected before his lesson because he already knew how. Such a supposition was not confirmed by Anne's thinking reported during her stimulated recall interview. Counter-balancing the need for having the access already connected would have been the successful sessions she had had with her teachers during the intervening week that gave her confidence.

There were two major instances where Anne voiced dissatisfaction and committed to changing her mental model and whether she implemented that commitment in the second lesson (level three, second round-cornered rectangle, figure 7.1).

First, although she had reflected during her first post-interview session that, "one of the differences that I would do, and probably should have done, was to have found out how computer literate Frances was so far as keyboarding skills," Anne did not question Andrew about his computer technology skills, having assumed his computer literacy. Additionally, even though Anne realized that what she had thought Frances had to produce had been wrong (stimulated recall interview), Anne did not question Andrew about his assignment other than ask how much research he had accomplished. She again assumed she knew what his topic involved from her talk with his teacher. As we pointed out earlier, Anne appeared to hold a different mental model of "culture" than did Andrew, who viewed it as incorporating political and economic contexts and not merely ethnicity and the arts. In this instance, commitment to change her mental model by putting the changed mental model into practice was not successful.

Second, Anne also reflected, "I think another thing that I might do differently that would be a little bit dissimilar would be to find out how familiar the student was with the regional library program. I was assuming Frances wasn't." She used this change in her teaching strategy mental model with Andrew, questioning him about his experience with the public library, reporting her thinking during the stimulated recall session:

Okay, the reason I was trying to find out if he was familiar [with the public library catalog], I thought once we got there he would be able to rapidly go through accessing the information and that this would just be an experience of doing something with a modem that he was used to doing. So I envisioned at this point, this is going to be a very quick lesson. I mean I actually thought this will go quickly.

The reason for her question was not only to do with Andrew's familiarity with maneuvering around the public library catalog but also, running along with her mental model of his catalog skills, was her mental model that emphasized matching the resource to the needs of the student: "I do really try to question the students to be sure we're matching the right resource before we go in." This product goal mental model was ever present.

Ultimately, Anne did not act on her reflective mental model after the first lesson that she should find out the computer skill level of the student through questioning, even if only for the keyboard skills. Even though she stressed the relationship she had formed with her first student during the session as being vital, she ignored this mental model during her second session once the technical problems began, admitting later that she had no clue as to what or how much Andrew had learned from her. This aspect of her teaching in the second session flew against her espoused, in-action, stimulated recall and post-interview reflections that she used student responses as impetus for choosing her teaching strategies and making decisions about what the student needed from her.

One example is provided of Marie's positive evaluation of her lessons. Marie prided herself on teaching instinctively when she was working with students and computers. She also ran this mental model of her computer database teaching with her mental model of questioning to find out what the students knew at the start of their lesson, then verbally recapping their answer and building on it. She did this with both students and ended up changing her teaching strategies when she found out her second student had poorer skills and less catalog knowledge than she had assumed. She was able to move easily to more procedural teaching with some conceptual teaching with her second student. Marie reflected that she would teach the same way with other sessions, recapping what the student knew, and changing goals in mid-stream depending on the student's needs.

A teaching strategy mental model that she wanted to change for her second lesson was to find out more about the student in order to assess the student's needs. She had made assumptions about Nathan that could have proven a problem if they had been incorrect, such as his reading ability. Not knowing how to read strongly would cause problems when trying to understand computer database searching tools. She also did not check with him at the beginning of the session about whether he knew or did not know the specific encyclopedia tools she was going to get him to use. He might have sat there without mentioning that he already knew, as happened to some of our other teacher-librarians in our study (stimulated recall interviews). (From Nathan's interviews we found out he had not utilized the tools.) With Alana, her second student, Marie again assumed, but this time that Alana might know more than she actually did about the automated catalog. Marie probed with basic questions about her use of the catalog (which was nil) and what the catalog could do or not do. When Alana could not answer the latter questions, Marie changed her teaching strategy plans in mid-stream toward a combined procedural-conceptual lesson (see chapter 5). She also paid very close attention to Alana's responses through Alana's eye movements, while Alana attempted to read the screen (see table 7.1, item 6). This tactic gave Marie much non-verbalized information about Alana's skill level.

However, in the above examples, Marie's commitment to changing her mental models to ask for information beyond the basics was, perhaps, somewhat pointless given Marie's constructivist pedagogy. Marie demonstrated very clearly that, regardless of what she knew or did not know about her students, changing her mental models was manageable because of her dominant teaching strategies mental models. Using questions and demanding demonstrations by students to assess their levels of understanding allowed her to implement changes in order to adopt appropriate content and strategies. Commitment to such mental model strategies interwoven with a healthy mental model of her technology literacy negated any stultifying outcomes for her students.

Marie thought poorly of her questioning skills and the way she worded her questions. This is how she critiqued her questioning skills mental models during her first post-interview:

> I don't think I'm a good questioner. I never have actually. I know it's a teaching strategy I do use a lot and I try to get the kids to sort of think about, you know, answer the questions and work it out for themselves. But I don't really think, I don't think I have a very good questioning technique 'cause I think sometimes . . . I sometimes take three or four questions to get it right. (enhanced post-interview)

She criticized herself for having to re-ask questions a number of times. From the videoed transcripts and our observations (chapter 3), it was apparent that Marie had problems with the wording of her questions and would re-word them before the student had a chance to respond to the first question (see chapters 5 and 6). Nevertheless, it was obvious that on one occasion, Marie was looking for the one right answer because she asked a question, got a response, asked another question, got a response, and did so until she received the answer she deemed correct. Also obvious was that she did not realize that Nathan had provided a deeper conceptualization than the one she sought (see chapter 5). In her second enhanced reflection post-interview, Marie again bemoaned the constant re-wording of her questions in her lesson with Alana and again committed to working on her delivery of questions. Despite her misgivings about the wording of her question skills, Marie held to the use of questioning as a viable teaching strategy with computers. She commented that she had been a more traditional, stand-up-and-lecture teacher when in the classroom but evaluated the questioning strategy as much more effective with the kind of teaching she was doing at present (second enhanced post-interview).

Summary

So far in this chapter, we have validated various mental models derived from the literature and our data. Our exploration of the teaching experiences of our two teacher-librarians, particularly in the immediately previous section, suggests a hypothesis for further study: that less-than-satisfactory habituated mental models cannot be readily changed even when our teachers' reflections were critically relevant and accurate during their stimulated recall and post-interviews; even though they acknowledged that the outcomes of some of their mental models were ineffective and problematic for students; even though they voiced a strong commitment to changing such mental models for improved lessons and student outcomes; and even when they identified how they would accomplish their commitment for change. Therefore, the teacher education literature (e.g., Bleakley, 1999; Ecclestone, 1996; Johnson, 2002; Zeichner, 1994) that lauds critical reflection and reflexivity as a crucial factor in promoting change may not be adequate by itself. We confirmed through research that mental model theory is correct in proposing that some ingrained and dearly held mental models were too difficult to change, particularly within a week and especially if the change required significant mental effort to implement (see chapter 2).

What our research is now adding to the literature is that even after insightful, no-holds-barred critical reflection of the inadequacy of one's mental models as demonstrated in the within-case studies (chapters 4 and 5) and across-case comparisons (chapter 6 and this chapter), this critical reflection or commitment or even both together is not enough to change those mental models deemed important to change.

DO MENTAL MODELS HAVE
PREDICTIVE POWER?

One of the most important issues in teacher education is helping teachers develop strategies and tools for teaching conceptual and procedural understandings as well as recognizing their own strengths and weaknesses in doing both. Our education system has expanded to specialized categories of teachers: content teachers, grade-level teachers, special education teachers, special-area teachers (art, music, physical education, etc.), and teacher-librarians. Some states in the United States have not categorized teacher-librarians as teachers and do not consider their teaching responsibilities when defining their roles. However, with the advent of computer technologies influencing information creation, access, evaluation, and application, teacher-librarians have primary responsibility for developing students' information and technology literacy skills, which influence their success in content learning and problem solving. However, the profession has traditionally concentrated on procedural instruction for information access. As we become more aware of the impact of conceptual understandings in the higher-order thinking capabilities of our students, we recognize that teacher-librarians also have a critical role in teaching conceptual understandings of the burgeoning electronic information literacy tools, as well as effective analysis, evaluation, synthesis, and application of the information these resources contain. The teacher-librarians' role in their students' learning achievements cannot be ignored. Paying critical attention to helping teacher-librarians, as well as all teachers, recognize and analyze the effectiveness of their teaching is no longer an option.

How teacher-librarians teach and what role mental models play in their teaching success or failure motivated our Spencer Foundation–funded research project. After studying ways that mental models could affect teaching (chapter 2), we decided that, in order to assess their importance, we had to identify what they were and whether they carried the characteristics assigned to them in the mental model literature. If the mental models did, then we proposed that we could investigate their influence on an individual's teaching.

For this book, we proceeded to identify two teacher-librarian's espoused, videoed in-action, stimulated recall in-action, and enhanced mental models before, during, and after a teaching lesson, respectively, to explore how these mental models could facilitate understanding about how and why the teacher-librarians taught and responded to teaching problems the way they did (chapters 4, 5, and 6; this chapter). If we could identify groups of mental models that operated together or served as controlling mental models, we conjectured that we could build a series of "if . . . then" situations that would result in a diagrammatic illustration of mental model combinations that would indicate the usual corresponding teaching strategies that teachers used.

For these two teacher-librarians, the diagrammatic models that resulted from their different teaching-learning episodes would look like the following figures (figures 7.2 and 7.3). Further research is warranted to confirm its possible generalizability.

Before directly answering the question posed in the heading to this section, "Can mental models be predictive?" a brief walk through figures 7.2 and 7.3 sets the scene.

Figure 7.2 displays the mental model relationships that actively influenced Anne's approach to her teaching-learning sessions. The figure portrays the multiple mental models running at the same time as well as the dominance over the lessons of the product goal (bold rectangle), time constraints (dotted-line rectangle), self-concept (dashed-line rectangle), pedagogy (bolded rectangle), and, to a slightly lesser extent, her novice Internet dial-up skills (dot-dashed-line rectangle) mental models. It also shows the links between these mental models and other mental models (rectangles) and effects on students and teacher (italicized text). The interplay between and among the mental models in figure 7.2 illustrates the multiplicity of mental models or fragments of mental models running at the same time. One immediately notices that the mental models are not

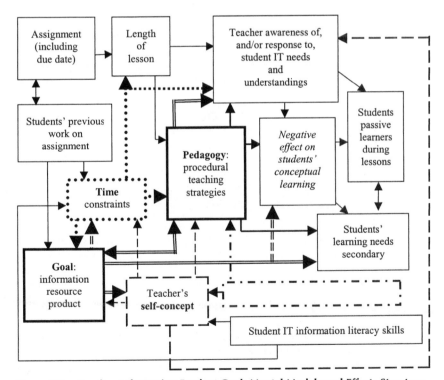

Figure 7.2.   Teacher Information Product Goal: Mental Models and Effects Structure

simplistically linked in a single linear sequence but rather associated in woven hypermedia mode (chapter 6) and, significantly, some mental models have two-way direction (see below). Unfortunately, we were unable to represent diagrammatically our contention that Anne's (and Marie's) key dominant mental models ran as interwoven threads (chapter 6) because the resulting graphic lacked clarity for ease of comprehension.

The doubled-lined arrows leading from the product goal emphasize that it is a—if not the—major dominant mental model during both lessons, with the other mental models influencing it or it subordinating most of the other mental models. That is, it wielded substantial control in the lesson as it was totally compatible with Anne's pedagogy mental model so that they ran in conjunction. Both were co-supported by Anne's other dominant mental models at different stages in each lesson (see figure 7.3).

Working through one of the interactive relationships between Anne's time constraint, product goal, and pedagogy mental models provides the following interpretation. To achieve her lesson goal, the time mental model was called on to regulate the length of time Anne planned to spend logging on, accessing the relevant database, and searching for and retrieving relevant resources in her teaching-learning episodes. Time-consuming technology problems worsened by her novice skills wove her procedural pedagogy mental model into a co-dominating position with her product goal and time mental models. Anne allowed them to push her from her initial plan to help her first student gain an elementary understanding about telecommunications and to help her second student practice his conceptual decision making about the applicability of particular information resources to his topic. Interestingly, Anne did not see that the dominance of these mental models had the effect of diminishing the relevance of any mental model associated with student learning beyond procedural steps to access resources. She did not associate the dominance of her mental models with the negative effects on students' conceptual learning. She acknowledged the influence of time and novice technology stressors within her reflective mental models during her post-interviews, particularly when she wanted to abort the second lesson (chapters 4 and 6). She commented that her students were particularly passive but did not associate this with her own strategies, goals, and time constraint mental models.

Marie's pedagogy was quite different. She began with a considerable conceptual understanding of the technology tool so that she was able to concentrate on sharing her conceptual tool literacy with each student. Figure 7.3 maps the flow of Marie's mental model influences running through her thinking while she was teaching. The same types of lines and rectangle borders are employed in figures 7.2 and 7.3: for example, the

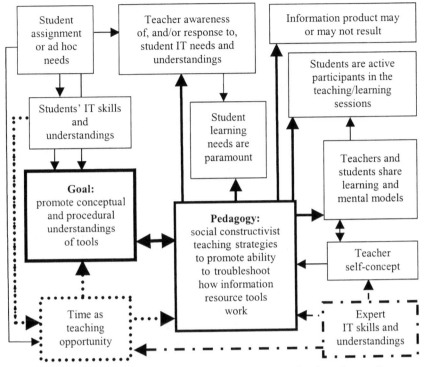

Figure 7.3. Teacher Goal for Student Conceptual and Procedural Understandings Mental Model

time mental model has dotted lines; the goal and the pedagogy mental model have bolded lines.

In comparison with figure 7.2, two things are immediately noticeable in figure 7.3: one, figure 7.3 is less cluttered and, two, there is a more direct or inter-woven linkage of one mental model to other mental models. For instance, figure 7.3 portrays graphically the confidence that Marie had in her technology background and skills as this mental model ran with and bolstered her positive self-concept mental model and then both of these linked to a social constructivist pedagogy mental model (middle of figure 7.3). Her expert information technology skills mental model also linked directly to her pedagogy and to her mental model of time (bottom dotted rectangle). Her goal mental model always promoted procedural and conceptual understanding of information communication tools (bold-lined rectangle, figure 7.3). As with Anne, Marie's goal and pedagogy were symbiotic and permanent, regardless of time, students' assignment or task, or a student's computer skills. In Anne's case, it should be "because" rather than "regardless" in the above description of "if . . . then" connectivity between the goal, time, task, and students' information literacy skills. As we see in figure 7.3, Marie's pedagogy mental models were linked proactively with her students' learning needs, resulting in interactive mental model sharing with her first student, which promoted his active involvement in his learning. Even at the lower level with her second student, Marie kept her pedagogical strategy of asking questions to get Alana involved in her learning within her ZPD.

Examination of figures 7.2 and 7.3 reveal insight into what is happening within each teacher-librarian's working memory. Figure 7.2 identifies a "busy" running of four key mental models (goal, pedagogy, time, and self-concept mental models) closely aligned with her novice skills and awareness or, in the case with Andrew, non-awareness of students' non-verbal mental models. This suggests that Anne's working memory has illogical chunking compounded by the on-and-off retrieval of the other mental models depicted in figure 7.2, which therefore resulted in little or no working memory space to strategize possible solutions to troubleshoot problems or teach for conceptual understanding. Figure 7.3 demonstrates a pared-back inter-woven running of key mental models. This inter-woven chunk (Miller, 1956) would allow more than adequate space in working memory to use taking-the-moment teaching opportunities to facilitate a student's guided discovery for conceptual understanding. The truncation example in Marie's lesson is an example of this (chapter 5).

Let us now work through some hypotheses that certain mental models interweave and run with particular mental models to ascertain if mental models can have predictability for those teacher-librarians or teachers who hold them.

- If we knew a teacher's *mental model of "time" in the context of their work*, would we be able to predict other mental models that the teacher would run in conjunction and what the outcomes would be for the students? In the cases of the two teacher-librarians, time meant different things. For Anne, time was always viewed as a constraint. Marie saw time as a teaching opportunity. Both perceived a difference between the preferred length of a "session" and that of a "lesson." A session represented the normal ad hoc calls by students (or staff) on their expertise whereas the lesson was planned for a specific purpose, such as for this research project or in response to requests from teachers. Caught up with a constrained time limit mental model, Anne's goal always required putting a product in the students' hands; her self-concept mental model as an effective teacher-librarian depended on her ability to do this. The outcome was the adoption of her customary direct instruction pedagogy. For Marie, her time as a teaching opportunity mental model resulted in a goal that was always to promote conceptual and procedural understandings that permitted troubleshooting skills. Hence, Marie adopted an habituated cognitive apprenticeship mental model. What becomes noteworthy is that Marie had planned a short lesson for Alana and thus spent less time with Alana than Anne did with either of her students. Obviously, time limits do not necessarily mean or require a behaviorist, step-by-step, how-to-do-it pedagogic approach as demonstrated in Anne's lessons. This signifies that a teacher's mental model of time has the power to dictate pedagogy. To put this hypothesis another way, knowing a teacher's mental model of time in the context of teaching should allow us to predict what goal and what pedagogy, behaviorist, or constructivist, would be utilized. Further research would allow us and other researchers to support or refute this hypothesis and possibly take our findings to a generalizable conclusion.

- Does having *novice information communication technology skills* automatically translate into adopting behaviorist direct instruction strategies? Education administrators, teachers, and researchers (e.g., Fluck, 2003; Mills, 1999; Pelgrum, 2001) have argued that a major reason that information communication technologies are woefully under-utilized in classrooms is that teachers have inadequate information technology skills and therefore require ongoing professional development. This seems logical and plausible because "novice" means that there would be inadequate conceptual understanding to troubleshoot when the (inevitable) technology hiccups occurred as happened with Anne, much to her chagrin. Our two case studies would appear to confirm this conclusion as the teacher-librarian with novice information communication skills implemented an instructivist do-what-I-tell-you procedural strategy and the teacher-librarian with expert information communication technology skills facilitated students' learning with a social constructivist approach (chapters 4, 5, 6, and this chapter).

However, this correlation is too simplistic. Another of our teacher-librarians, Sally, had less experience than did Anne with modem dial-up and online databases. When the inevitable occurred, Sally invited her student Margaret to help solve the dial-up logon problems. The student's only Internet experience was merely "looking over the shoulder" of another student using the Web (Margaret, enhanced post-interview). Both Sally and Margaret thought aloud and consulted. When the student solved the problem, Sally pinned a pretend "Bravo" button on Margaret's uniform, much to the fifteen-year-old student's delight (Andrew was the same age and Frances was one year younger at the time of the study). Through this sharing, both student and teacher-librarian enhanced their conceptual mental models of how it works for later troubleshooting experiences (see tables 7.1 and 7.3). One of Sally's teacher-librarian goals was to teach lifelong learning skills and she did just that by demonstrating that she, too, was still a learner and took delight in learning from students.

- Perhaps the key mental model in teaching for predicting other mental models and their effects is that of the *lesson goal*. From the above two explorations of time and information technology literacy skills, we can argue with conviction that the teacher-librarians' goals were consistent with, and therefore possessed capability for prediction of, their mental models of time, their respective technology skills, and self-concepts mental models as well as their mental model perceptions of their students' technology skills and the student's assignment. In figures 7.2 and 7.3, Anne's and Marie's goals demonstrated a marked importance during both lessons. If the goal is obtaining a resource, artifact, or call numbers, then the pedagogy is, ipso facto, focused on procedural teaching strategies to achieve this goal. Anne's lessons bear out this "if . . . then" contention. Anne adopted a hands-on-while-I-direct-you approach. Anne, and another five of our teacher-librarians who adopted the same pedagogic approach, provided a running commentary of what they were doing, rather than why they were taking particular steps (see chapter 4). Even though her espoused sub-goal with her second student was to enhance his decision-making strategies, Anne did not engage in conceptual "forced prediction" or "why this choice?" questions (see table 7.3, item 5) at the point where he chose the newspaper database; that is, before problems with this choice arose (chapters 4 and later).

- Supporting our argument that a *product goal* is tightly inter-woven with *entrenched behaviorist pedagogy* is the example when Anne's effective "using the teaching moment" occurred with her first student. Anne provided an analogy of the how computers are linked in the Internet, but asking what her student may have thought about what was happening during the dial-up procedure was not a relevant part of her pedagogy. Instructivist pedagogy ensures that a teacher's awareness of, and responses to, their students' information needs and understandings is always in terms of achieving the goal. The effect of this for Anne was a "students-as-passive-learners" mental model and the subjugation of the students' learning needs for conceptual understandings to enable troubleshooting the procedural steps to obtain the goal.

- From Anne's examples, it would seem that a lesson or session artifact or call number goal would predictably result in procedural behaviorist pedagogy. Marie's case substantiates this finding. Marie's goal, regardless of time, student help, or resource requirements, was to *facilitate students' conceptual and procedural information literacy. This goal was entwined with a cognitive apprenticeship pedagogy* mental model. If the goal is to "facilitate," and the teacher's definition of "facilitating" is to guide students to discover and understand how electronic databases work, then the pedagogy has to be, ipso facto, constructivist (either in terms of Piagetian or Vygotskian theory; see chapters 3, 4, and 5). From there, the inter-woven goal and pedagogy place student learning needs, not a product goal, paramount and thereby ensure mental models where the students are active participants in their learning (see figure 7.3).

- However, a resource product can be a legitimate outcome of constructivist pedagogy as long as the route implements constructivist philosophy and strategies. Sally's case study demonstrated this. For her, the product goal, a printout of one of the websites and returned hits, was provided as the motivational chocolate topping on an ice cream, so that each of Sally's students would be reminded that, because they had been involved in some troubleshooting activities, they could do it again, this time most likely by themselves. Marie's goal and pedagogy mental models could also predict use of two-way sharing mental models. Such prediction is appropriate as these are the characteristics of constructivist and social constructivist pedagogy and goals where the teacher or teacher-librarian is the guide rather than the expert (Collins, Brown, and Newman, 1989; Lave and Wenger, 1991; Newman, Griffin, and Cole, 1989; Wertsch, 1991).

- If we knew teachers' *mental models of "pedagogy"* and the definitions they held with this mental model, then could we predict the other mental models and outcomes for students? We argue that a product goal requires a behaviorist pedagogy whereas a conceptual teaching goal requires a constructivist or social constructivist pedagogy. We further contend that each of these pedagogies are linked to a de-emphasis and paramount emphasis, respectively, on students' procedural versus conceptual learning outcomes, on a one-way sharing of factual knowledge versus sharing distributed cognition (see Banks and Millward, 2000; chapter 5), and on passive versus active learners. We now argue that the reverse of both contentions is obvious and valid: knowing a teacher's pedagogy mental model would allow prediction of their other mental models. However, such validity should be recognized as fallibilistic validity (see chapter 3) because it is a more realistic concept since there always seems to be exceptions in such a subjective area as teaching.

While recognizing those exceptions, our research implies that engaging student teachers and experienced teachers in an examination of, and reflection about, their pedagogical standpoints through the use of stimulated recall methodology is valuable. In this way, the gamut of their numerous mental models—espoused, in-action, and reflective—and the effects on students' learning and their teaching would be exposed so that profound challenges to their mental models could follow.

CONCLUSION AND IMPLICATIONS

In this book, we have detailed the mental models of two teacher-librarians and how they relate to the way the teacher-librarians taught in one-to-one teaching-learning episodes using electronic databases as information resources. We did not do this for the purpose of evaluating either teacher-librarian's teaching capabilities, but rather to identify their mental models and analyze how their mental models contributed to the lessons. If we could do this successfully, then we propose that we have a powerful new tool for helping teachers learn how to teach through the analysis and awareness of the most powerful influences on their teaching, their mental models.

These two teacher-librarians both cared passionately about their students and their roles as teacher-librarians. They both were deeply self-reflective about their own abilities and skills as teachers and as believers in students' need for adequate information resource access. Both loved their jobs and both had been away from classroom teaching responsibilities for a number of years. Both knew the increasing importance of computer technologies in libraries, but our first teacher-librarian was less willing to give up print as the most critical information access tool, even as she started to realize and emphasize the potential of electronic technologies in her school's library. Our second teacher-librarian was a strong believer in the power of computer technologies to even the playing field for all students including the reluctant information seekers. Our first teacher-librarian was more behaviorist in her teaching belief systems, relying more on her past experiences as a learner to give her a comfortable method of teaching her students procedurally by imparting information through a mostly directive approach. The second teacher-librarian believed in constructivist teaching, acting as a guide when students developed problems in their information seeking. She used strong questioning strategies to help her students puzzle out their answers through their own thinking. She also realized that some students did not have enough foundation knowledge to learn using that strategy.

Both teacher-librarians considered themselves leaders and pioneers in their schools and school systems with computer technologies. Both were highly critical of their own teaching, particularly when they thought they had used their strategies ineffectively or made mistakes. Both were dedicated, highly respected, and concerned with their students' information needs and bringing their libraries into the computerized information era.

So far, we have discovered that the mental models that these two teacher-librarians held had powerful influences on their teaching. The teacher-librarian in these two case studies who was more behaviorist, procedurally oriented, and product focused and who held to the mental model of teacher-librarian as knowledge expert had more difficulty preventing her behaviorist mental models from controlling her teaching sessions and her attempts to guide student information literacy growth. Influenced by weak personal technology skill mental models, she exhibited less flexibility to change her focus or change her mental models as situations presented themselves that would benefit from change to her mental models. Our other teacher-librarian approached teaching in a facilitative role, considering herself more a guide through trouble spots than a teacher, who she defined as someone who stood before thirty students and lectured. She decided on her teaching strategies only after ascertaining what her students needed rather than go into her sessions with pre-ordained agendas. The difference between the two approaches was evident in the flexibility of the latter teacher-librarian to remain more student-centered. A variable in our comparison of the two teacher-librarians was the need for actual authentic information products for our product-oriented teacher-librarian. Even though one of the students had an authentic assignment but without a close due date and the other student did not, there was no need to provide a product for our constructivist teacher-librarian. However, the espoused mental models of the teacher-librarians, their in-action mental models, and their reflective mental models led us to believe that both individuals would have followed the same strategies if the student information needs had been reversed.

When information literacy tools were familiar and remained standard for decades, changing only in content rather than format, teacher-librarians, after initial procedural and conceptual instruction about the tool, could concentrate on helping students gain conceptual understandings about the information resources the tools offered, rather than how the tool worked. However, with electronic resources, these case studies reveal that conceptual understandings about the tool and how it works is of paramount importance before focus can productively switch to higher-order critical thinking about the appropriateness of the information accessed through the tool. The myriad of electronic tools available, each with differences from a slight amount to major differences, make it essential that the teacher-librarian help students build problem-solving strategies and conceptual understandings about the tools' structures if students are to progress beyond procedural knowledge that does not necessarily apply to more than one tool. We posit that these conceptual tool understandings will make it possible for the student to focus more successfully on the critical thinking strategies that make the content contained in, or retrieved by, the information technology tools useful and productive. Perhaps this is one of the major results of this research.

As we continue researching and teaching, we and other researchers (because of our detailed methodology trail) can use the way we have analyzed these case studies to bring mental models to the awareness of teachers and teacher-librarians as well as to that of our pre-service and postgraduate students to help them recognize the influence and control that their mental models have on their teaching. Our work highlighted the power of mental models to control actions and beliefs. It also underscored the inability of the teacher-librarians to change such mental models even when they voiced a strong valid commitment to such change. We surmised that a week was inadequate to reflect any change. Therefore, further research is warranted to explore the existence of any gap between the rhetoric and the reality of a verbalized commitment to changing stultifying and dominating mental models during the critical reflection phase of lessons and what actually occurs in subsequent lessons.

Stimulated recall methods and action research, in which introspection, reflection, commitment, and action are deliberately targeted and implemented, provide an appropriate within- and between-case study methodology to investigate whether and how teachers and teacher-librarians can or do change ingrained stultifying mental models over time. We encourage researchers to take on this challenge.

Our future work will add the students' mental models to the two cases discussed in this book to identify where our teacher-librarians showed effective awareness of their students' responses and where they did not. Knowing the circumstances surrounding such instances of compatibility and incompatibility between teachers' and students' mental models would help teachers develop strategies for increasing their ability to respond more accurately to their students' learning needs and, hopefully, change those mental models requiring change and applaud those that demonstrate quality learning outcomes.

Grainger (2003) eloquently pointed out that "a common sense interpretation of teaching is inadequate to expose the complexity of teachers' work and therefore inadequate to allow the professional artistry of teaching to be accessed and appreciated" (p. iii). Stimulated recall methodology allowed us to investigate that complexity.

References

Afflerbach, P., and Johnston, P. (1984). On the use of verbal reports in reading research. *Journal of Reading Behavior, 16*(4), 307–322.

Anderson, J. R. (1990). *Cognitive psychology and its implications* (3rd ed.). New York: Freeman.

Anderson, R. (1970). Control of student mediating processes during verbal learning and instruction. *Review of Educational Research, 40,* 349–369.

Anderson, T., Howe, C., and Tolmie, A. (1996). Interaction and mental models of physics phenomena: Evidence from dialogues between learners. In J. Oakhill and A. Garnham (Eds.), *Mental models in cognitive science* (pp. 247–273). Hillsdale, NJ: Lawrence Erlbaum Associates.

Anzai, Y., and Simon, H. (1979). The theory of learning by doing. *Psychological Review, 86,* 124–140.

Atkinson, R., and Shiffrin, R. (1968). Human memory: A proposed system and its control processes. In K. Spence and J. Spence (Eds.), *The psychology of learning and motivation. Advances in research and theory* (Vol. 2). New York: Academic Press.

Atwood, V., and Wilen, W. (1991). Wait time and effective social studies instruction: What can research in science education tell us? *Social Education, 55* (3), 179–181.

Ayersman, D. (1996). Effects of computer instruction, learning style, gender, and experience on computer anxiety. *Computers in the Schools, 12*(4), 15–30.

Ayres, L., Kavanaugh, K., and Knafl, K. A. (2003). Within- and across-case approaches to qualitative data analysis. *Qualitative Health Research, 13,* 871–883.

Bagley, T., and Payne, S. (2000). Long-term memory for spatial and temporal mental models includes construction processes and model structure. *The Quarterly Journal of Experimental Psychology, 53A*(2), 479–512.

Bainbridge, L. (1978). Forgotten alternatives in skill and workload. *Ergonomic, 21,* 169–183.

———. (1992). Mental models and cognitive skill: The example of industrial process operation. In Y. Rogers, A. Rutherford, and P. Bibby (Eds.), *Models in the mind: Theory, perspective and application* (pp. 119–144). London: Academic Press.

Banks, A., and Millward, L. (2000). Running shared mental models as a distributed cognitive process. *British Journal of Psychology, 91*(4), 513–531.

Barker, P., van Schaik, P., and Hudson, S. (1998). Mental models and life-long learning. *Innovations in Education and Training International, 35*(4), 310–318. Also retrieved November 28, 2004, from http://wheelie.tees.ac.uk/groups/isrg/papers/ieti98/ieti98.htm.

Barker, P., van Schaik, P., Hudson, S., and Meng Tan, C. (1998). Mental models and their role in teaching and learning. In T. Ottman and I. Tomek (Eds.), *Proceedings of ED-MEDIA/ED-TELECOM '98* (Vol. 1) (pp. 105–110). Charlottesville, VA: Association for the Advancement of Computing in Education.

Barrows, H. S. (2000). *Stimulated recall: Personalized assessment of clinical reasoning.* Springfield, IL: School of Medicine, Southern Illinois University.

Barrows, H. S., Norman, G. R., Neufield, V. R., and Feightner, J. W. (1982). The clinical reasoning of randomly selected physicians in general medical practice. *Clinical Investigative Medicine, 5*(1), 49–55.

Beaufort, A. (2000). Learning the trade: A social apprenticeship model for gaining writing expertise. *Written Communication, 1*(2), 185–223.

Bereiter, C., and Scardamalia, M. (1992). Cognition and curriculum. In P. Jackson (Ed.), *Handbook of research on curriculum* (pp. 517–542). New York: Macmillan.

Bibby, P. (1992a). Distributed knowledge: In the head, in the world or in the interaction? In Y. Rogers, A. Rutherford, and P. Bibby (Eds.), *Models in the mind: Theory, perspective and application* (pp. 94–99). London: Academic Press.

———. (1992b). Mental models, instructions and internalisation. In Y. Rogers, A. Rutherford, and P. Bibby (Eds.), *Models in the mind: Theory, perspective and application* (pp. 153–172). London: Academic Press.

Bleakley, A. (1999). From reflective practice to holistic reflexivity. *Studies in Higher Education, 24*(3), 315–331.

Bloom, B. (1954). The thought process of students in discussion. In S. J. French (Ed.), *Accent on teaching: Experiments in general education* (pp. 23–46). New York: Harper and Row.

Bolanos, P. (1996). Multiple intelligences as a mental model. *NASSP Bulletin, 80*(583), 24–28.

Borthwick, A., and Jones, R. (2000). The motivation for collaborative discovery learning online and its application in an information systems assurance course. *Issues in Accounting Education, 15*(2), 181–210.

Boudreau, G., Pigeau, R., and McCann, C. (2002). The effects of formal order and spatial content on reasoning in three dimensions. *International Journal of Psychology, 37*(4), 228–238.

Brand, E. (1998). The process of identifying children's mental model of their own learning as inferred from learning a song. *Bulletin of the Council for Research in Music Education, 138*, 47–61.

Brandt, D. (1999). Do you have an ear for searching? *Computers in Libraries, 19*(5), 42–44.

Bransford, J., Brown, A. and Cocking, R. (Eds.). (2000). *How people learn: Brain, mind, experience, and school*. Washington, DC: National Academy Press. Retrieved November 16, 2004, from http://books.nap.edu/catalog/6160.html.

Brewer, W. (1987). Schemas versus mental models in human memory. In P. Morris (Ed.), *Modeling cognition*. Chichester: Wiley.

Brookfield, S. (1995). Becoming a critically reflective teacher. San Francisco: Jossey-Bass.

Broughton, J. (1978). Development of concepts of self, mind, reality, and knowledge. In W. Damon (Ed.), *Social cognition* (pp. 75–100). San Francisco: Jossey-Bass.

Bruner, J., Goodnow, J., and Austin, G. (1956). *A study of thinking*. New York: John Wiley.

Byrne, R. (1992). The model theory of deduction. In Y. Rogers, A. Rutherford, and P. Bibby (Eds.), *Models in the mind: Theory, perspective and application* (pp. 11–28). London: Academic Press.

Cannon-Bowers, J., Salas, E., and Converse, S. (1991). Shared mental models in expert team decision making. In N. Castellan (Ed.), *Individual and group decision making* (pp. 221–246). Hillsdale, NJ: Lawrence Erlbaum Associates.

Carroll, J. (1971). Current issues in psycholinguistics and second language teaching. *TESOL Quarterly, 5*, 101–114.

———. (1989). "The Carroll model: A 25-year retrospective and prospective view." *Educational Researcher, 11*, 26–31.

———. *The Nurnberg funnel: Designing minimalist instruction for practical computer skills*. Cambridge, MA: MIT Press.

Cennamo, K. S. (1989, February 1–5). *Factors influencing mental effort: A theoretical overview and review of literature*. Paper presented at the annual meeting of the Association for Educational Communications and Technology, Dallas, TX. (ERIC Document Reproduction Service No. ED 379313).

———. (1993). Learning from video: Factors influencing learners' preconceptions and invested mental effort. *Educational Research and Development Journal, 41*(3), 33–45.

Center for Advancement of Learning. (1998). Attention and memory. *Learning strategies database*. Retrieved July 12, 2003, from http://www.muskingum.edu/percent7Ecal/database/Attback.html.

Chater, N., and Oaksford, M. (2001). Human rationality and the psychology of reasoning. Where do we go from here? *British Journal of Psychology, 92*, 193–216.

Chee, Y. S. (1996). "Mind Bridges": A distributed, multimedia learning environment for collaborative knowledge building. *International Journal of Educational Telecommunications, 2*(2/3), 137–153.

Chi, M., Feltovich, P., and Glaser, R. (1981). Categorization and representation of physics problems by experts and novices. *Cognitive Science, 5*, 121–152.

Chomsky, N. (1959). Review of 'Verbal Behavior' by B. F. Skinner. *Language, 35*, 26–58.

Clarke, A. (1995). Professional development in practicum settings: Reflective practice under scrutiny. *Teaching and Teacher Education, 11*(3), 243–261.

Claxton, C., and Jackson, K. (2002). In over our heads. *Community College Journal, 73*(1), 42–45.

Clement, J. (1985). *A method expert's use to evaluate the validity of models used as problem representations in science and mathematics.* Paper presented at the annual meeting of the American Educational Research Association (Chicago, April). (ERIC Document Reproduction Service No. ED286744).

Cohen, M., Thompson, B., Adelman, L., Bresnick, T., Tolcott, M., and Freeman, J. (1995). *Rapid capturing of battlefield mental models: Technical Report 95–3.* Arlington, VA/ Fort Leavenworth, KS: Cognitive Technologies/United States Army Research Institute.

Cohen, M., Thompson, B., Adelman, L., Bresnick, T., Lokendra, S., and Riedel, S. (2000). Training critical thinking for the battlefield: Modeling and simulation of battlefield critical thinking (Vol. 3). Arlington, VA: Cognitive Technologies.

Cole, C., and Leide, J. (2003). Using the user's mental model to guide the integration of information space into information need. *Journal of the American Society for Information Science and Technology, 54*(1), 39–46.

Cole, M., and Griffin, P. (1980). Cultural amplifiers reconsidered. In D. Olson, (Ed.), *The social foundations of language and thought.* New York: Norton.

Collins, A., Brown, J., and Holum, A. (1991). Cognitive apprenticeship: Making thinking visible. *American Educator, 15*(3), 6–11, 38–46.

Collins, A., Brown, J. S., and Newman, S. E. (1986; 1989). Cognitive apprenticeship: Teaching the crafts of reading, writing, and mathematics. In L. B. Resnick (Ed.), *Knowing, learning, and instruction: Essays in honor of Robert Glaser* (pp. 453–494). Hillsdale, NJ: Lawrence Erlbaum.

Craik, F., and Lockhart, R. (1972). Levels of processing: A framework for memory research. *Journal of Verbal Learning and Verbal Behavior, 11*, 671–684.

Craik, K. (1943). *The nature of explanation.* Cambridge: Cambridge University Press.

Dahlberg, R., and Housman, D. (1997). Facilitating learning events through example generation. *Educational Studies in Mathematics, 33*(3), 283–299.

deGroot, A. (1965; 1978). *Thought and choice in chess* (2nd ed.). New York: Mouton.

deKleer, J., and Brown, J. (1981). Mental models of physical mechanisms. In J. Anderson (Ed.), *Cognitive skills and their acquisition.* Hillsdale, NJ: Lawrence Erlbaum.

Dimitroff, A. (1992). Mental models theory and search outcome in a bibliographic retrieval system. *Library and Information Science Research, 14*(2), 141–156.

DiSessa, A. (1988). Knowledge in pieces. In G. Forman and P. Pufall (Eds.), *Constructivism in the computer age* (pp. 49–70). Hillsdale, NJ: Lawrence Erlbaum.

Doise, W., and Mugny, G. (1984). *The social development of the intellect.* Oxford: Pergamon.

Doolittle, P. (1999). Memory: Information processing theory. Retrieved September 10, 2003, from http://www.tandl.vt.edu/doolittle/isd/documents/memory .doc.

Doyle, W. (1975). Paradigms in teacher effectiveness research. Paper presented at annual meeting of the American Educational Research Association (AERA), April. [Also at ERIC ED103390]. Retrieved September 10, 2003, from http://www.education.ucsb.edu/~ed219b/Doyle.html.

Driscoll, M. (1994). *Psychology of learning for instruction.* Boston: Allyn and Bacon.

Duff, S. (1989). Reduction of action uncertainty in process control systems: The role of device knowledge. In E. Megaw (Ed.), *Contemporary Ergonomics* (pp. 213–219). London: Taylor and Francis.

———. (1992). Mental models as multi-record representations. In Y. Rogers, A. Rutherford, and P. Bibby (Eds.), *Models in the mind: Theory, perspective and application* (pp. 173–187). London: Academic Press.

Duffy, T., and Jonassen, D. (1992). *Constructivism and the technology of instruction: A conversation*. Hillsdale, NJ: Lawrence Erlbaum.

Dunkin, M. J., Welch, A., Merritt, A., Phillips, R., and Craven, R. (1998). Teachers' explanations of classroom events, knowledge and beliefs about teaching civics and citizenship. *Teaching and Teacher Education, 14*(2), 141–151.

Dutke, S., and Reimer, T. (2000). Evaluation of two types of online help for application software. *Journal of Computer Assisted Learning, 16*(4), 307–315.

Ebbinghaus, H. (1913; original 1885, translated H. Ruger and C. Byssenine). *Memory: A contribution to experimental psychology*. New York: Dover.

Ecclestone, K. (1996). The reflective practitioner: Mantra or a model for emancipation. *Studies in the Education of Adults, 28*, 148–160.

Ehrlich, K. (1996). Applied mental models in human-computer interaction. In J. Oakhill and A. Garnham (Eds.), *Mental models in cognitive science* (pp. 223–245). Hillsdale, NJ: Lawrence Erlbaum.

Ericsson, K., and Simon, H. (1980). Verbal reports as data. *Psychological Review, 87*(3), 215–251.

———. (1987). Verbal reports on thinking. In C. Ferch and G. Kasper (Eds.), *Introspection in second language research* (pp. 24–53). Clevedon, UK: Multilingual Matters.

———. (1998). How to study thinking in everyday life: Contrasting think-aloud protocols with descriptions and explanations of thinking. *Mind, Culture, and Activity, 5*(3), 178–186.

———. (1984; 1993; 1999). *Protocol analysis: Verbal reports as data* (2nd ed. 1993; 3rd ed. 1999). Cambridge, MA: MIT Press.

Ethell, R., and McMeniman, M. (2000). Unlocking the knowledge in action of an expert practitioner. *Journal of Teacher Education, 51*(2), 87–101.

Evans, J. (1996). Afterword. The model theory of reasoning: Current standing and future prospects. In J. Oakhill and A. Garnham (Eds.), *Mental models in cognitive science: Essays in honour of Phil Johnson-Laird*. London: Psychology Press.

Færch, C., and Kasper, G. (1987). From product to process: Introspective methods in second language learning research. In C. Færch and G. Kasper (Eds.), *Introspection in second language research* (pp. 5–23). Clevedon: Multilingual Matters.

Finney, M. (2002). The role of print and video in changing science misconceptions. *Electric Journal of Literacy through Science: Language Development and Science Education, 1*(2). Retrieved October 8, 2003, from http://sweeneyhall.sjsu.edu/ejlts/archives/language_development/finney.html.

Fischbein, E. (1987). *Intuition in science and mathematics*. Dordrecht, The Netherlands: Reidel.

Fischbein, E., Tirosh, D., Stavy, R., and Oster, A. (1990). The autonomy of mental models. *For the Learning of Mathematics, 10*(1): 23–30.

Fluck, A. (2003). Why isn't ICT as effective as it ought to be in school education? In A. McDougall, J. Murnane, C. Stacey, and C. Dowling (Eds.), *ICT and the teacher of the future: Selected papers from the International Federation for Information Processing Working Groups 3.1 and 3.3 Working Conference, 23*, 39–41.

Friedler, Y., Nachmias, R., and Linn, M. (1987). *Using micro-computer-based laboratory to foster scientific reasoning skills.* Berkley, CA: University of California.

Friedman, A. (1979). Framing pictures: The role of knowledge in automatized encoding and memory for gist. *Journal of Experimental Psychology: General, 108*, 316–355.

Forbus, K., Nielsen, P., and Faltings, B. (1991). Qualitative spatial reasoning: The CLOCK project. *Artificial Intelligence, 51*, 1–3.

Gardiner, J. M., and Parkin, A. J. (1990). Attention and recollective experience in recognition memory. *Memory and Cognition, 18*, 617–623.

Garner, R. (1988). Verbal-report data on cognitive and metacognitive strategies. In C. Weinstein, E. Goetz, and P. Alexander (Eds.), *Learning and study strategies: Issues in assessment, instruction and evaluation* (pp. 63–76). New York: Academic Press.

Garnham, A. (1987). *Mental models as representations of discourse and text.* Chichester: Ellis Horwood.

———. (1992). Minimalism versus constructionism: A false dichotomy in theories during reading. *Psycoloquy, 3*(63). Retrieved November 17, 2004, from http://psycprints.ecs.soton.ac.uk/archive/00000287/.

Gagne, R., and Glaser, R. (1987). Foundations in learning research. In R. Gagne (Ed.), *Instructional technology: Foundations* (pp. 49–83). Hillsdale, NJ: Lawrence Erlbaum.

Gass, S. M., and Mackey, A. (2000). *Stimulated recall methodology in second language research.* Mahwah, NJ: Lawrence Erlbaum.

Gentner, D. (1998). Analogy. In W. Bechtel and G. Graham (Eds.), *A companion to cognitive science* (pp. 107–113). Oxford: Blackwell.

Gentner, D., and Forbus, K. (1996). *Analogy, mental models and concept change.* Retrieved October 6, 2003, from Cognitive Science Division, Office of Naval Research website: http://www.qrg.ils.nwu.edu/projects/ONR-SM/analogy.htm.

Gentner, D., and Stevens, A. (Eds.). (1983). *Mental models.* Hillsdale, NJ: Lawrence Erlbaum.

Gilbert, W. D., Trudel, P., and Haughian, L. P. (1999). Interactive decision making factors considered by coaches of youth ice hockey during games. *Journal of Teaching in Physical Education, 18*(3), 290–311.

Gilroy, M. (1998). *Using technology to revitalize the lecture: A model for the future.* (ERIC Document Reproduction Service No. ED 437 123).

Ginsburg, H., and Opper, S. (1979). *Piaget's theory of intellectual development.* Upper Saddle River, NJ: Prentice-Hall.

Glaser, R. (1972). Individuals and learning: The new aptitudes. *Educational Researcher, 1*(6), 5–13.

Glenberg, A. (1997). What memory is for? *Behavioral and Brain Sciences, 20*(1), 1–55.

Goldstein, B. (1999). *Sensation and perception* (5th ed.) Pacific Grove: Brooks/Cole.

Grainger, S. (2003). *Accessing the professional artistry of teaching.* Unpublished EdD thesis, Griffith University, Queensland.

Green, T. (1990). The cognitive dimension of viscosity: A sticky problem for HCI. In D. Diaper, D. Gilmore, G. Cockton, and B. Shackel (Eds.), *Human-computer interaction. Interact 90.* Amsterdam: Elsevier.

Greenfield, P. M. (1984). A theory of the teacher in the learning activities of everyday life. In B. Rogoff and J. Lave (Eds.), *Everyday cognition: Its development in social context* (pp. 117–138). Cambridge, MA: Harvard University Press.

Greeno, J. G. (1983). Conceptual entities. In D. Gentner and A. Stevens (Eds.), *Mental models* (pp. 227–252). Hillsdale, NJ: Lawrence Erlbaum.

Greeno, J. G., and Simon, H. A. (1984). Problem solving and reasoning. In R. C. Atkinson, R. J. Herrnstein, G. Lindzey, and R. D. Luce (Eds.), *Stevens' handbook of experimental psychology* (589–672). New York: Wiley.

Gualtieri, J., Fowlkes, J., and Ricci, K. (1996). Measuring individual and team knowledge structures for use in training. *Training Research Journal, 2,* 117–141.

Halford, G. S. (1993). *Children's understanding: The development of mental models.* Hillsdale, NJ: Laurence Erlbaum.

Hambrick, D. Z., and Engle, R. W. (2002). Effects of domain knowledge, working memory capacity, and age on cognitive performance: An investigation of the knowledge-is-power hypothesis. *Cognitive Psychology, 44,* 339–387.

Hammond, N., Morton, J., MacLean, A., Barnard, P., and Long, J. (1992). *Knowledge fragments and users' models of systems.* IBM Human Factors Report No. HR071, IBM (UK) Laboratories, Hursley Park, Hampshire.

Hannigan, S., and Reinitz, M. (2001). A demonstration and comparison of two types of inference-based memory errors. *Journal of Experimental Psychology: Learning, Memory, and Cognition, 27*(4), 931–940.

Harris, J. C. (1993). Creating the reflective practitioner: Sources and causes of student teacher deviation from planned lessons. (ERIC Document Reproduction Service No. ED365715).

Hasselbring, T. (1994). Using media for developing mental models and anchoring instruction. *American Annals of the Deaf, 139* (special issue), 36–42.

Haycock, A., and Fowler, D. (1996). Mental models: Metacognitive structures. *SITE96.* Retrieved August 20, 2003, from http://www.coe.uh.edu/insite/elec_pub/html1996/18theory.htm.

Hayes, J. (1985). The problems in teaching general skills. In J. Segal, S. Chipman, and R. Glaser (Eds.), *Thinking and learning* (Vol. 2) (pp. 391–405). Hillsdale, NJ: Lawrence Erlbaum.

Hazzan, O., and Zazkis, R. (1997). Constructing knowledge by constructing examples for mathematical concepts. *Proceedings of the 21st International Conference for the Psychology of Mathematics Education, 4,* 299–306.

Henderson, L., and Bradey, S. (2004). Teachers as change agents in information technology diffusion. *World Conference on Educational Multimedia, Hypermedia and Telecommunications, 2004*(1) [Online]. Retrieved December 14, 2004, from *AACE Digital Library:* http://dl.aace.org/15690.

Henderson, L., Patching, W., and Putt, I. (1994, June 25–30). *Interactive multimedia, concept mapping, and cultural context.* Paper presented at the ED-MEDIA 94,

World Conference on Educational Multimedia and Hypermedia, Vancouver, Canada. [Online] *AACE Digital Library*: http://dl.aace.org.

Henderson, L., Putt, I., Ainge, D., and Coombs, G. (1997). Comparison of students' thinking processes when studying with WWW, IMM, and text-based materials. In F. Verdejo and G. Davies (Eds.), *Virtual campus: Trends for higher education and training* (pp. 162–124). London: Chapman and Hall.

Henderson, L., Putt, I., and Coombs, G. (2002). Mental models of teaching and learning with the WWW. In A. Williamson, C. Gunn, A. Young, and T. Clear (Eds.), *Winds of change in the sea of learning*. Proceedings of the 19th annual conference of the Australiasian Society for Computers in Learning in Tertiary Education (ASCILITE). (Vol.1) (pp. 271–278). Auckland, New Zealand: UNITEC Institute of Technology.

Henderson, M. (1996). *Multimedia interactivity: An investigation into learners' mediating processes during click-drag activities*. Unpublished BEd (Hons.) thesis , James Cook University of North Queensland, Townsville.

Herrman, D., Raybeck, D., and Gutman, D. (1993). *Improving student memory*. Seattle: Hogrefe and Huber.

Holyoak, K. (1991). Symbolic connectionism: Toward third-generation theories of expertise. In A. Ericsson and J. Smith (Eds.), *Toward a general theory of expertise: Prospects and limits* (pp. 301–355). Cambridge: Cambridge University Press.

Howe, C., Rodgers, C., and Tolmie, A. (1990). Physics in the primary school: Peer interaction and the understanding of floating and sinking. *European Journal of Psychology and Education*, 4, 459–475.

Howe, C., Tolmie, A., Anderson, A., and Mackenzie, M. (1992). Conceptual knowledge in physics: The role of group interaction in computer-supported teaching. *Learning and Instruction*, 2, 161–183.

Huitt, W. (2000). *The information processing approach*. Retrieved September 10, 2003, from http://chiron.valdosta.edu/whuitt/col/cogsys/introproc.html.

Jacka, L., and Henderson, L. (in progress). *Creating an iMovie: Education pre-service teachers' mental models*. Townsville: James Cook University.

Jane, B., and Perry, C. (1998). Reflections on stimulated recall as a technique for analyzing students' thinking in technology. In *Contemporary approaches to research in mathematics, science, health and environmental education 1997*. Deakin, Victoria: Deakin University.

Jenkins, J., and Tuten, J. (1998). On possible parallels between perceiving and remembering events. In R. Hoffman, M. Sherrick, and J. Warm (Eds.), *Viewing psychology as a whole* (pp. 291–314). Washington, DC: American Psychological Association.

Jih, H., and Reeves, T. (1992). Mental models: A research focus for interactive learning systems. *Educational Technology Research and Development*, 40, 39–53.

Johnson, G. (2002). Taking up a post-personal position in reflective practice: One teacher's accounts. *Reflective Practice*, 3(1), 21–38.

Johnson-Laird, P. (1983). *Mental models: Toward a cognitive science of language, influence, and consciousness*. Cambridge, MA: Harvard University Press.

———. (1987). Mental models. In A. Aitkenhead and J. Slack (Eds.), *Issues in cognitive modeling* (pp. 81–100). Hillsdale, NJ: Lawrence Erlbaum.

———. (2001). Mental models and deduction. *Trends in Cognitive Sciences, 4*(10), 434–442.

Johnson-Laird, P., and Byrne, R. (2000; updated September 29, 2003). *Mental Models Website*. Retrieved November 22, 2004, from http://www.tcd.ie/Psycholo gy/Ruth_Byrne/mental_models/researchers.html.

Jonassen, D., Campbell, J., and Davidson, M. (1994). Learning with media: Restructuring the debate. *Educational Technology Research and Development, 42*(2), 31–39.

Jonassen, D., and Henning, P. (1999). Mental models: Knowledge in the head and knowledge in the world. *Educational Technology, 39*(3), 37–42.

Jonassen, D., and Reeves, T. (1996). Learning with technology: Using computers as cognitive tools. In D. H. Jonassen (Ed.), *Handbook of research in educational communications and technology* (pp. 693–719). New York: Simon and Schuster Macmillan.

Jonassen, D., and Tessmer, M. (1996). An outcomes-based taxonomy for instructional systems design, evaluation and research. *Training Research Journal, 2,* 11–46.

Kane, R.G. (1993). *Knowledge in action: A longitudinal study of the propositional and procedural knowledge of the beginning teacher.* MEd thesis, Griffith University, Brisbane.

Karasti, H. (2000). Using video to join analysis of work practice and system design: A study of an experimental teleradiology system and its redesign. *IRIS 2000 Conference.* Retrieved September 12, 2005, from http://iris.informatik.gu .se/conference/iris20/31.htm.

Krieger, M. (1992). *Doing physics.* Bloomington: Indiana University Press.

Langan-Fox, J., Code, S., and Langfield-Smith, K. (2000). Team mental models: Techniques, methods, and analytic approaches. *Human Factors, 42*(2), 242–271.

Langan-Fox, J., Wirth, A., Code, S., Langfield-Smith, K., and Wirth, A. (2001). Analyzing shared and team mental models. *International Journal of Industrial Ergonomics, 28*(2), 99–112.

Langer, J. (1993). Approaches toward meaning in low- and high-rated readers. Report Series 2.2. Albany, NY: National Center on Literature Teaching and Learning. Retrieved July 22, 2003, from http://cela.albany.edu/meaning/in dex.html.

Lave, J., and Wenger, E. (1991). *Situated learning: Legitimate peripheral participation.* Cambridge: Cambridge University Press.

Lefebvre-Pinard, M. (1983). Understanding and auto-control of cognitive functions: Implications for the relationship between cognition and behavior. *International Journal of Behavioral Development, 6,* 15–35.

Lieberman, D. (1979). Behaviorism and the mind. A (limited) call for a return to introspection. *American Psychologist, 34*(4), 319–333.

Lunzer, E. (1979). The development of consciousness. In G. Underwood and R. Stevens (Eds.), *Aspects of consciousness: Vol. 1, Psychological Issues* (pp. 1–19). London: Academic Press.

Lyons, W. (1986). *The disappearance of introspection.* Cambridge, MA: MIT Press.

Mackey, A., Gass, S., and McDonough, K. (2000). Do learners recognize implicit negative feedback as feedback? *Studies in Second Language Acquisition, 22*(4), 471–497.

Mani, K., and Johnson-Laird, P. (1982). The mental representation of spatial descriptions. *Memory and Cognition, 10*, 181–187.

Manktelow, K., and Fairley, N. (2000). Superordinate principles in reasoning with causal and deontic conditionals. *Thinking and Reasoning, 6*(1), 41–65.

Manktelow, K., and Over, D. (1992). Obligation, permission and mental models. In Y. Rogers, A. Rutherford, and P. Bibby (Eds.), *Models in the mind: Theory, perspective and application* (pp. 249–266). London: Academic Press.

Marchionini, G., and Liebscher, P. (1991). Performance in electronic encyclopedias: Implications for adaptive systems. In J. Griffiths (Ed.), *ASIS '91, Systems understanding people. Proceedings of the 54th Annual Meeting of ASI,* (Vol. 28) (pp. 39–48). Washington, DC: Medford Learned Information.

Markovits, H., and Barrouillet, P. (2002). The development of conditional reasoning: A mental model account. *Developmental Review, 22*(1), 5–36.

Marland, P., Patching, W., and Putt, I. (1992). *Learning from text: Glimpses inside the minds of distance learners.* Townsville: James Cook University of North Queensland.

Mayer, R.(1989). Systematic thinking fostered by illustrations in scientific text. *Journal of Educational Psychology, 81*, 240–246.

Mayes, J., Draper, S., McGregor, A., and Oatley, K. (1988). Information flow in a user interface: The effect of experience and context on the recall of MacWrite screens. In D. Jones and R. Winder (Eds.), *People and computers IV* (pp. 275–289). Cambridge: Cambridge University Press.

McMeniman, M., Cumming, J., Wilson, J., Stevenson, J., and Sim, C. (2001). Teacher knowledge in action. In Department of Education, Science and Training (Ed.), *The impact of educational research* (pp. 376–549). Canberra: Australian Government Printing Service. Retrieved August 28, 2003, from http://www.detya .gov.au/highered/respubs/impact/splitpdf_default.htm.

Meade, P., and McMeniman, M. (1992). Stimulated recall: An effective methodology for examining successful teaching in science. *Australian Educational Researcher, 19*(3), 1–18.

———. (1994). Teacher knowledge in action: The theoretical base of effective teaching. Paper presented at Australian Association for Research in Education Conference. Retrieved December 10, 2004, from http://www.aare.edu.au/94 pap/meadp94404.txt.

Meiser, T., Klauer, K., and Naumer, B. (2001). Propositional reasoning and working memory: The role of prior training and pragmatic content. *ACTA Psychologica, 106*(3), 303–327.

Merriam, S. B., and Simpson, E. L. (1995). *A guide to research for educators and trainers of adults* (2nd ed.). Malabar, FL: Krieger.

Mezirow, J., and Associates. (1990). *Fostering critical reflection in adulthood.* San Francisco: Jossey-Bass.

Michell, G., and Dewdney, P. (1998). Mental models theory: Applications for library and information science. *Journal of Education for Library and Information Science, 39*(4), 275–281.

Middendorf, J., and Kalish, A. (1996). The "Change-Up" in lectures. *The National Teaching and Learning Journal, 15*(2), 1–7.

Miller, G. (1956). The magical number seven, plus or minus two: Some limits on our capacity for processing information. *Psychological Review, 63,* 81–97.

Mills, S. (1999). *Integrating computer technology in classrooms: Teacher concerns when implementing an integrated learning system.* SITE 99: Society for Information Technology and Teacher Education International Conference, San Antonio, Texas, February 28–March 4. (ERIC Document Reproduction Service No. ED432289).

Moray, N. (1998). Identifying mental models of complex human-machine systems. *International Journal of Industrial Ergonomics, 22*(4–5), 293–297.

Morra, S. (2001). On the information processing demands of spatial reasoning. *Thinking and Reasoning, 7*(4), 347–365.

Navarro-Prieto, R., and Canas, J. (2001). Are visual programming languages better? The role of imagery in program comprehension. *International Journal of Human-Computer Studies, 54*(6), 799–829.

Nelissen, J., and Tomic, W. (1996). *Representation and cognition.* Opinion/position paper, Open University, Heerlen, Netherlands. (ERIC Document Reproduction Service No. ED402 012).

Nespor, J. K. (1985). *The role of beliefs in the practice of teaching: Final report of the teacher beliefs study.* University of Texas, Austin: Research and Development Centre for Teacher Education.

Newell, A., and Simon, H. (1956). The logic theory machine: A complex information processing system. *I.R.E. Transactions on Information Theory, 2,* 61–79.

———. (1972). *Human problem solving.* Englewood Cliffs, NJ: Prentice Hall.

Newman, D., Griffin, P., and Cole, M. (1989). *The construction zone: Working for cognitive change in school.* Cambridge: Cambridge University Press.

Newton, D. (1994). Pictorial support for discourse comprehension. *British Journal of Educational Psychology, 64,* 221–229.

———. (1996). Causal situations in science: A model for supporting understanding. *Learning and Instruction, 6*(3), 201–217.

Nisbett, R., and Wilson, T. (1977). Telling more than we can know: Verbal reports on mental processes. *Psychological Review, 84,* 231–259.

Norman, D. (1983). Some observations on mental models. In D. Gentner and A. Stevens (Eds.), *Mental models* (pp. 7–14). Hillsdale, NJ: Lawrence Erlbaum.

———. (1988). *The psychology of everyday things.* New York: Basic Books.

Oakhill, J., and Garnham, A. (Eds.). (1996). *Mental models in cognitive science.* Mahwah, NJ: Lawrence Erlbaum.

Ohtsuka, K. (1994). *Where in the world am I? Mental models derived from text and spatial inference.* Paper presented at the annual meeting of the American Educational Research Association, New Orleans, April 4–8. (ERIC Document Reproduction Service No. ED371017).

O'Malley, C., and Draper, S. (1992). Representation and interaction: Are mental models all in the mind? In Y. Rogers, A. Rutherford, and P. Bibby (Eds.), *Models in the mind: Theory, perspective and application* (pp. 73–92). London: Academic Press.

O'Neill, A. (1996). *Promotion of nursing competence: Evaluation of the use of a curricu-*

lar innovation. Paper presented at Changing Assessment to Improve Learning 1st Northumbria Assessment Conference, University of Northumbria, United Kingdom, September 4–6.

Owens, K. (1994). *Visual imagery employed by young students in spatial problem solving*. Paper presented at the annual conference of the Australian Association for Research in Education (AARE), University of Newcastle, November 27–December 1.

Papert, S. (1993). *The children machine: Rethinking school in the age of the computer*. New York: Basic Books.

Parsons, J. M., Graham, N., and Honess, T. (1983). A teacher's implicit model of how children learn. *British Educational Research Journal, 9*(1), 91–101.

Patton, M. (2002). *Qualitative research and evaluation methods* (3rd ed.). Thousand Oaks, CA: Sage Publications.

Pausawasdi, N. (2001). *Students' engagement and disengagement when learning with IMM in mass lectures*. PhD thesis, James Cook University, Townsville.

Pausawasdi, N., and Henderson, L. (2000). Students' thinking processes when learning with computer-assisted mass lectures. In S. Shwu-ching Young, J. Greer, H. Maurer, Y. Chee (Eds.), *Proceedings learning societies in the new millennium: Creativity, caring and commitments. ICCE/ICCAI 2000 the 8th International Conference on Computers in Education/International Conference on Computer-Assisted Instruction 2000, Vol. 2* (pp. 1214–1221). Taipei: National Tsing Hua University.

Pavlinic, S., Buckley, P., and Wright, T. (1999). *Visualising molecules—Can computers help?* Paper presented at Australian Science Education Research Association (ASERA) 99, 30th annual conference, Rotorua, New Zealand, July 8–11.

Payne, S. (1990). Looking HCI in the "I." In D. Daiper, D, Gilmore, D. Cockton, and B. Shackel (Eds.), *Human-computer interactions. Interact '90* (pp. 185–191). Amsterdam: North-Holland.

———. (1991). Display-based action at the user interface. *International Journal of Man-Machine Studies, 33*, 275–289.

———. (1992). On mental models and cognitive artifacts. In Y. Rogers, A. Rutherford, and P. Bibby (Eds.), *Models in the mind: Theory, perspective and application* (pp. 103–118). London: Academic Press.

Pea, R. D. (1992). Distributed multimedia learning environments: Why and how? *Interactive Learning Environments, 2*(2), 73–109.

Pelgrum, W. (2001). Obstacles to the integration of ICT in education: Results from a worldwide educational assessment. *Computers and Education, 37*(1), 163–178.

Pitts, J. (1995). Mental models of information: The 1993–94 AASL/Highsmith Research Award Study. *School Library Media Quarterly, 23*, 177–184.

Poirier, L. (1994). *Conceptual and developmental analysis of mental models: An example with complex change problems*. Paper presented at the annual meeting of the American Educational Research Association, New Orleans, April 4–6. (ERIC Document Reproduction Service No. ED374975).

Posner, M. (1992). Attention as a cognitive and neural system. *Current Directions in Psychological Science, 1*, 11–14.

Power, M., and Wykes, T. (1996). The mental health of mental models and the mental models of mental health. In J. Oakhill and A. Garnham (Eds.), *Mental models in cognitive science. Essays in honour of Phil Johnson-Laird* (pp. 197–222). London: Psychology Press.

Pressley, M., and Afflerbach, P. (1995). *Verbal protocols of reading: The nature of constructively responsive reading.* Hillsdale, NJ: Lawrence Erlbaum.

Price, E., and Driscoll, M. (1997). An inquiry into the spontaneous transfer of problem-solving skill. *Contemporary Educational Psychology, 22,* 472–494.

Puerta-Melguizo, M., and van der Veer, G. (2001). Appendix C: Assessment of mental models for envisioning design. In M. Puerta-Melguizo, G. van der Veer, P. van der Vet, and H. van Oostendorp (Eds.), *Mental models of incidental human-machine interaction.* Project report May 1–December 31, 2000. Project-number: MMI99010. Retrieved December 2, 2004, from http://www.cs.vu.nl/~gerrit/mmi9910-report1.doc.

Putt, I., Henderson, L., and Patching, W. (1996). Teachers' thinking elicited from interactive multimedia professional development courseware. *Educational Technology Research and Development, 44*(4), 7–22.

Randell, M. (1993). Mental models as complex systems: The adaptive dynamics of cognition. Retrieved October 10, 2003, from http://babelfish.psy.uwa.edu.au/mar/research/93_Proposal.html.

Reder, L. (1982). Plausibility judgments versus fact retrieval: Alternative strategies for sentence verification. *Psychological Review, 89,* 250–280.

Redish, E. (1994). The implications of cognitive studies for teaching physics. *The American Journal of Physics, 62*(6), 796–803.

Renkl, A., Mandl, H., and Gruber, H. (1996). Inert knowledge: Analyses and remedies. *Educational Psychologist, 31*(2), 115–121.

Ritchie, S. (1999). The craft of intervention: A personal practical theory for a teacher's within-group interactions. *Science Education, 83*(2), 213–231.

Rogers, Y. (1992). Mental models and complex tasks. In Y. Rogers, A. Rutherford, and P. Bibby (Eds.), *Models in the mind: Theory, perspective and application* (pp. 145–150). London: Academic Press.

Rogers, Y., and Rutherford, A. (1992). Future directions in mental model research. In Y. Rogers, A. Rutherford, and P. Bibby (Eds.), *Models in the mind: Theory, perspective and application* (pp. 289–314). London: Academic Press.

Rogers, Y., Rutherford, A., and Bibby, P. (Eds.) (1992). *Models in the mind: Theory, perspective and application.* London: Academic Press.

Rohwer, W. (1972). Decisive research: A means for answering fundamental questions about instruction. *Educational Researcher, 1*(7), 5–11.

Rolheiser, C., and Fullan, M. (2002). Comparing the research on best practices. Retrieved October 18, 2004, from Centre for Development and Learning: http://www.cdl.org/resources/reading_room/compare_best.html.

Roschelle, J., and Greeno, J. (1987). Mental models in expert physics reasoning. (ERIC Document Reproduction Service No. ED285736).

Rothkopf, E. (1966). Learning from written instructive materials: An exploration of the control of inspection by test-like events. *American Educational Research Journal, 3,* 241–249.

———. (1970). The concept of mathemagenic activities. *Review of Educational Research, 40,* 325–336.

Rouse, W., and Morris, N. (1985). On looking into the Black Box: Prospects and limits in the search for mental models. *Psychological Bulletin, 100*, 349–363.

Rowe, A., and Cooke, N. (1995). Measuring mental models: Choosing the right tools for the job [and] invited reaction: Measuring mental models—thoughts on a research agenda. *Human Resource Development Quarterly, 6*(3), 243–262. Retrieved from ERIC Document Reproduction Service No. EJ511267.

Rowe, M. B. (1980). Pausing principles and their effect upon reasoning in science. In F. Brawer (Ed.), *Teaching the sciences* (pp. 27–34). San Francisco: Jossey-Bass.

Rudolph, F. (1996). The paperless classroom project. Retrieved August 20, 2003, from http://www.mindspring.com/-frudolph/3303/pc3303a.htm.

Rukavina, I., and Daneman, M. (1996). Integration and its effect on acquiring knowledge about competing scientific theories from text. *Journal of Educational Psychology, 88*(2), 272–287.

Rumelhart, D., and McClelland, J. (1986). *Parallel distributed processing: Explorations in the microstructure of cognition.* Cambridge, MA: MIT Press.

Russo, J., Johnson, E., and Stevens, D. (1989). The validity of verbal protocols. *Memory and Cognition, 17*, 759–769.

Salomon, G. (1983). The differential investment of mental effort in learning from different sources. *Educational Psychologist, 18*, 42–50.

Salomon, G. (1990). Cognitive effects with and of computer technology. *Communication Research, 17*(1), 26–44.

Santamaria, C., and Johnson-Laird, P. (2000). An antidote to illusory inferences. *Thinking and Reasoning, 6*(4), 313–333.

Scardamalia, M., and Bereiter, C. (1991). Higher levels of agency for children in knowledge building: A challenge for the design of new knowledge media. *The Journal of the Learning Sciences, 1*(1), 37–68.

Schank, R., and Cleary, C. (1995). What makes people smart? In R. Schank and C. Cleary, *Engines for education* (pp. 26–43). Hillsdale, NJ: Lawrence Erlbaum.

Schoenfeld, A. (1987). What's all the fuss about metacognition? In A. Schoenfeld (Ed.), *Cognitive science and mathematics education* (pp. 189–215). Hillsdale, NJ: Lawrence Erlbaum.

Schwamb, K. (1990). *Mental models: A survey.* Retrieved October 1, 2003, from Department of Information and Computer Science, University of California: http://www.isi.edu/soar/schwamb/pubs.html.

Schwandt, T. A. (1997). *Qualitative inquiry: A dictionary of terms.* Thousand Oaks, CA: Sage Publications.

Schwartz, D., and Glack, J. (1996). Analog imagery in mental model reasoning: Depictive models. *Cognitive Psychology, 30*, 154–219.

Seel, N. (1995). Mental models, knowledge transfer and teaching strategies. *Journal of Structural Learning, 12*(3), 197–213.

Seely Brown, J., Collins, A., and Duguid, P. (1996). Situated cognition and the culture of learning. In H. McLellen (Ed.), *Situated learning perspectives* (pp. 19–44). Englewood Cliffs, NJ: Educational Technology Publications.

Senge, P. (1990). *The fifth discipline: The art and practice of the learning organization.* New York: Doubleday/Currency.

———. (1992). Mental models: Putting strategic ideas into practice. *Planning*

Review, 20(2), 4–8. Retrieved September 4, 2005, from http://deming.eng.clem son.edu/pub/tqmbbs/tools-techs/menmodel.txt.

———. (1997). Through the eye of a needle. In R. Gibson (Ed.), *Rethinking the future* (pp. 122–146). London: Nicholas Brealey.

Shavelson, R., Webb, N., and Burstein, L. (1986). Measurement in teaching. In M. Wittrock (Ed.), *Handbook of research on teaching* (3rd ed.) (pp. 50–91). New York: MacMillan.

Shulman, H. (1997). The information-processing theoretic diagram of structures and processes in memory. Retrieved September 20, 2005, from http://www .cog.brown.edu/courses/63/memory_diagram.htm.

Shulman, L. (1986). Paradigms and research programs in the study of teaching: A contemporary perspective. In M. Wittrock (Ed.), *Handbook of research on teaching* (3rd ed.) (pp. 3–36). New York: MacMillan.

———. (1987). Knowledge and teaching: Foundations of the new reform. *Harvard Educational Review, 57*, 1–22.

———. (1996). Just in case: Reflections on learning from experience. In J. Colbert, K. Trimble, and P. Desberg (Eds.), *The case for education: Contemporary approaches for using case methods* (pp. 197–217). Boston: Allyn and Bacon.

Sloboda, J. (1996). The acquisition of musical performance expertise: Deconstructing the "talent" account of individual differences in musical expressivity. In K. Ericsson (Ed.), *The road to excellence: The acquisition of expert performance in the arts and sciences, sports and games* (pp. 107–126). Mahwah, NJ: Lawrence Erlbaum.

Slone, D. (2002). The influence of mental models and goals on search patterns during Web interaction. *Journal of the American Society for Information Science and Technology, 53*(13), 1152–1169.

Smagorinsky, P. (Ed.). (1994). *Speaking about writing: Reflections on research methodology.* Thousand Oaks, CA: Sage Publications.

Snow, R. (1974). Representative and quasi-representative designs for research on teaching. *Review of Educational Research, 44*(3), 265–291.

Soy, S. K. (2003) The case study as a research method. Retrieved December 12, 2004, from http://www.gslis.utexas.edu/ssoy/usesusers/l391d1b.htm.

Sperling, G. (1960). The information available in brief visual presentations. *Psychological Monographs, 74*, 1–29.

Stenning, K. (1992). Distinguishing conceptual and empirical issues about mental models. In Y. Rogers, A. Rutherford, and P. Bibby (Eds.), *Models in the mind: Theory, perspective and application* (pp. 29–48). London: Academic Press.

Sternberg, R. J., and Horvath, J. A. (1995). A prototype view of expert teaching. *Educational Researcher, 24*(6), 9–17.

Strauss, S. (1993). Teachers' pedagogical content knowledge about children's minds and learning: Implications for teacher education. *Educational Psychologist, 28*(3), 279–290.

Stripling, B. (1995). Learning-centered libraries: Implications from research. *School Library Media Quarterly, 23*(3), 163–170.

Suchman, L. (1995). Making work visible. *Communications of the ACM, 38*(9), 56–64.

Suchman, L., and Trigg, R. (1991). Understanding practice: Video as a medium for reflection and design. In J. Greenbaum and M. Kyng (Eds.), *Design at work: Cooperative design of computer systems* (pp. 65–89). Hillsdale, NJ: Lawrence Erlbaum.

Suzuki, H. (1998). *Ternary relation of analogy.* Paper presented at Workshop: Analogy Making. 5th International Summer School in Cognitive Science, New Bulgarian University, Sofia, Bulgaria, July 13–25.

Szabo, M. (1998). Updating our mental models to take advantage of modern communication technology to promote CMC. In Z. Berge and M. Collins (Eds.), *Wired together: The online classroom in K–12.* Cresskill, NJ: Hampton Press.

Szabo, M., and Fuchs, A. (1998). *Dealing with mental models: Module L3.* Retrieved October 29, 2003, from http://www.quasar.ualberta.ca/edmedia/TIES/L3 .html.

Taylor, H., and Tversky, B. (1992). Perspective in spatial descriptions. *Journal of Memory and Language, 35,* 371–391.

Thomson, D., and Tulving, E. (1970). Associative encoding and retrieval: Weak and strong cues. *Journal of Experimental Psychology, 86,* 255–262.

Timpka, T., and Arborelius, E. (1990). The primary-care nurse's dilemmas: A study of knowledge use and need during telephone consultations. *Journal of Advanced Nursing, 15,* 1457–1465.

Tobin, K. (1980). The effect of an extended teacher wait-time on science achievement. *Journal of Research in Science Teaching, 17,* 469–475.

Treisman, A. (1969). Strategies and models of selective attention. *Psychological Review, 76,* 282–299.

Troyer, S. (1994). *The effects of three instructional conditions in text structure on upper elementary students' reading comprehension and writing performance.* Paper presented at the annual meeting of the American Educational Research Association, New Orleans, April 4–8. (ERIC Document Reproduction Service No. ED373315).

Turner, J., and Belanger, F. (1996). Escaping from Babel: Improving the terminology of mental models in the literature of human-computer interaction. *Canadian Journal of Information and Library Science, 21*(3/4), 35–58.

Valli, L. (1992). *Reflective teacher education: Cases and critiques.* Albany: State University of New York Press.

van der Henst, J. (1999). The mental model of theory of spatial reasoning re-examined: The role of relevance in premise order. *British Journal of Psychology, 90*(1), 73–84.

———. (2000). Mental model theory and pragmatics. *Behavioral and Brain Sciences, 23*(2), 283–301.

———. (2002). Mental model theory versus the inference rule approach in relational reasoning. *Thinking and Reasoning, 8*(3), 193–203.

van der Veer, G., Kok, E., and Bajo, T. (1999). Conceptualising mental representations of mechanics: A method to investigate representational change. In D. Kayser and S. Vosniadou (Eds.), *Modelling changes in understanding: Case studies in physical reasoning* (pp. 44–60). Kiddlington, UK: Pergamon (Elsevier Science).

van der Veer, G., and Peurta-Melguizo, M. (2002). Mental models. In J. Jacko and

A. Sears (Eds.), *The human-computer interaction handbook: Fundamentals, evolving technologies and emerging applications* (pp. 52–80). Mahwah, NJ: Lawrence Erlbaum.

van Dijk, T., and Kintsch, W. (1983). *Strategies of discourse comprehension*. New York: Academic Press.

Vermersch, P. (1999). Introspection as practice. *Journal of Consciousness Studies, 6*(2–3), 17–42.

Vosniadou, S. (1994). Capturing and modelling the process of conceptual change. *Language and Instruction, 4*, 45–69.

Vygotsky, L. S. (1978). *Mind in society: The development of higher psychological processes*. Cambridge, MA: Harvard University Press.

Waldmann, M., Holyoak, K., and Fratianne, A. (1995). Causal models and the acquisition of category structure. *Journal of Experimental Psychology: General, 124*, 181–206.

Watson, A., and Mason, J. (2004). *Mathematics as a constructive activity: Learners generating examples*. Mahwah, NJ: Lawrence Erlbaum.

Watson, J. (1913). Psychology as the behaviorist views it. *Psychological Review, 20*, 158–177.

Wayment, H., and Cordova, A. (2003). Mental models of attachment, social strain, and general distress following a collective loss. A structural equation modeling analysis. *Current Research in Social Psychology, 9*, 18–31.

Wear, S. B., and Harris, J. C. (1994). Becoming a reflective teacher: The role of stimulated recall. *Action in Teacher Education, 16*(2), 45–51.

Wertsch, J. (Ed.). (1991). *Voices of the mind: A sociocultural approach to mediated action*. Cambridge, MA: Harvard University Press.

Wild, M. (1996). Mental models and computer modelling. *Journal of Computer Assisted Learning, 1*(1), 10–21.

Williams, D. (1996). Multimedia, mental models and complex tasks. *Proceedings of the CHI '96 conference companion on human factors in computing systems: Common ground*. Retrieved October 30, 2003, from http://www.acm.org/sigchi/chi96/Doctor-Consort/williams/dmw_dcon.htm.

Williamson, J. (1999). *Mental models of teaching: Case study of selected pre-service teachers enrolled in an introductory educational technology course*. Unpublished doctoral dissertation, University of Georgia, Athens.

Wilson, J., and Rutherford, A. (1989). Mental models: Theory and application in human factors. *Human Factors, 31*(6), 617–634.

Yin, R. (Ed.). (1994). *Case study research: Design and methods* (2nd ed.). Thousand Oaks, CA: Sage Publications.

Zeichner, K. (1994). Research on teacher thinking and different views of reflective practice in teaching and teacher education. In I. Carlgren, G. Handal, and S. Vaage (Eds.), *Teachers' minds and actions: Research on teachers' thinking and practice* (pp. 9–27). London: Falmer Press.

Zeichner, M., and Liston, P. (1996). *Reflective teaching: An introduction*. Mahwah, NJ: Lawrence Erlbaum.

Zwaan, R., Magliano, J., and Graesser, A. (1995). Dimensions of situation model construction in narrative comprehension. *Journal of Experimental Psychology: Learning, Memory, and Cognition, 21*, 386–397.

Subject Index

accuracy, 4, 13, 17, 31, 51, 63, 65, 88, 105, 182, 223, 239; recall, 65, 74–76, 78–79, 82–84, 86, 90

across-case comparison, 181, 183–84, 200, 202, 204, 208–9, 243

activity: retrospective, 63

analogic, 32, 34, 39, 44, 51

analogy, 15, 26, 28–30, 32–40, 39, 42, 44, 52, 178–79, 202–3, 212, 226, 250, 260, 269

analysis: discourse, 69, 70, 73, 78; interaction, 67–68, 91; interactive, 70; process, 87; protocol, 63, 259

artifact prompt, 58, 62, 65, 76–77

assumption, 17, 25, 37, 56, 81, 105, 117, 129, 143, 147, 150, 159, 182, 191, 193–94, 202, 204, 216, 218, 226, 239, 241

attention, 15, 20, 53, 57–60, 78, 82–83, 103, 107, 114, 123, 128, 134, 152–53, 158, 179, 186, 218, 238, 242, 244, 257, 260, 266, 270; involuntary, 57; selective, 57, 270; self-directed, 57

belief systems, 3, 18, 208, 252. *See also* mental models

behaviorism, 62, 165

behaviorist, 34, 61, 168, 179, 182, 189, 194, 196, 199, 202, 204, 219, 229, 235, 249–53, 270; behaviorist process-product methodology, 61

benefits of electronic databases to students, 138

cause-effect, 13, 72, 77; cause-effect relationship, 77

change, 4–5, 9–11, 13, 15, 21, 30, 32, 37, 48, 53, 69–70, 82, 161, 201, 204, 208, 227–28, 243, 253–54, 260–62, 264–66, 270; Anne, 99–100, 104, 106, 120, 122–23, 126, 129, 190–91, 215, 218–19, 229, 231–34, 240, 253; Marie, 135, 137–38, 160–61, 177–80, 196, 204, 215–16, 219, 229, 231, 233, 237–38, 241–43. *See also* commitment to change

coding, 11, 44, 57, 72, 74, 87–91, 135, 147, 152, 156, 204, 269; encoding, 40, 56, 58–60, 260, 269

cognition, 60, 75, 163, 251, 256–57, 260–61, 263, 265, 267–68, 271; metacognition, 26, 28, 32, 143, 156, 268

cognitive: apprenticeship, 65, 168–73, 176, 195, 202, 249, 251, 258; apprenticeship modeling tool, 65; mediating process, 6–7, 13–14, 56, 58, 60–61, 63, 72, 88, 156, 182, 255, 262; modeling, 262; performance, 261; process, 28, 47, 55–56, 60–62, 82, 108, 256; representation, 22–23, 26,

Name Index

About the Authors

Lyn Henderson, PhD, is a senior lecturer in the School of Education, James Cook University, Australia. Her undergraduate and post-graduate teaching, research, and publications target mental models and other thinking processes when learning and teaching with information communication technologies, including computer/video games. Henderson is building a research hub with national and international scholars and research students utilizing stimulated recall methodologies and mental models. She is a member of six international journal editorial boards and committees.

Julie Tallman, PhD, is a professor in the Department of Educational Psychology at the University of Georgia. She teaches and publishes in the area of school library media pre-service and in-service graduate education. A Fulbright scholar in Botswana, 1999–2000, Tallman has co-edited a volume in international education and has co-authored a book on the I-Search research/writing process.